D1433398

H50 130 948 7

4

TIM BELL

The Ultimate Spin Doctor

TIM BELL

The Ultimate Spin Doctor

Mark Hollingsworth

Hodder & Stoughton

British Library Cataloguing in Publication Data

Hollingsworth, Mark, 1959–
Tim Bell: his live and fast times
1. Bell, Tim 2. Advertisers – Great Britain – Biography
3. Political consultants – Great Britain – Biography
4. Electioneering – Great Britain
I. Title
324.9'41'0858'092

ISBN 0 340 61697 0

Typeset by Hewer Text Composition Services, Edinburgh
Printed and bound in Great Britain by
Mackays of Chatham PLC, Chatham, Kent.

Hodder and Stoughton
A division of Hodder Headline PLC
338 Euston Road
London NW1 3BH

'An ounce of image is worth a pound of performance'
Laurence J. Peter, (1919–90) Canadian writer and educationalist

Contents

List of Illustrations

Mark Thatcher's stag party in 1987 (*Solo Syndication*)
With Frank Lowe (*Alan Davidson*)
Greeting Joan Collins (*Alan Davidson*)
Bell receiving his knighthood at Buckingham Palace in 1991 (*Press Association*)
David Mellor poses with his family (*Solo Syndication*)
With Lord King in 1994 (*Keith McMillan*)
Bell reunited with Maurice Saatchi (*Keith McMillan*)

Preface

At 3.35 p.m. on Friday 24 June 1994, I received a telephone call from Sir Tim Bell. I was sitting in my office in Chesham Mews, Belgravia, just across the road from Lady Thatcher's headquarters in Chesham Place, with Paul Halloran, my co-author of *Thatcher's Gold*, a biography of Mark Thatcher. Lady Thatcher's media guru was abrupt and straight to the point. 'I understand you're interested in the flotation of Chime Communications [Bell's public relations holding company],' he said.

'Yes, I'd like to have a look at the documents available to the public', I replied. 'I understand Chime is now a listed company on the Stock Exchange.'

'Well, I'll consider any specific requests for information,' he remarked stiffly.

I then mentioned that I had been commissioned to write his biography and would like to talk to him about it. 'Yes, I know,' Sir Tim replied, clearly irritated, 'and I will do all in my power to ensure the book is never published.'

'Wouldn't it be sensible for us at least to talk about the project?' I asked.

'No,' he said firmly. 'I have no desire for this book to come out. I have my privacy and I want to keep it that way.'

'Well, I just think, in the interests of basic accuracy, it would make sense for me to come and see you.'

'The only person who knows the story of my life is myself and no one else can tell it, and so I will take any course of action that is available to me to defend my interests.'

'I'm sorry you feel that way,' I said, as we concluded our rather curt conversation.

For the next year I was unable to start work on this book as I was completing, with Paul Halloran, *Thatcher's Gold*. As soon as I embarked on the research in June 1995, it became clear that Sir Tim would remain true to his word. At first, most people were happy to talk to me but several changed their minds after consulting Bell, who asked them not to co-operate. Consequently, I have faced what can only be described as on-going obstruction in my attempt to present a balanced portrait. The following potential sources declined to see me, either after Sir Tim's intervention or after being told it was not an official authorised biography. Early Years: George Roberts, Linda Bell, Joan Smith, Bob Geers, Saatchi and Saatchi: Andrew Rutherford, Kenneth Gill, Richard Humphreys, Jeremy Sinclair, Chris Wilkins, Martin Sorrell, John Parkin, Mike Russell-Hills, David Dundas, Peter Bainbridge, Robin Wight. Lowe Howard-Spink: Frank Lowe, David Jones, Sean O'Connor, Marc Marcantonio, Geoff Culmer. Conservative Party Account: Sir Gordon Reece, Brendan Bruce, Lord Archer, Lord Parkinson, Kenneth Baker. Lowe Bell Communications: Sue Coupland, Michael Shea, Abel Haddon, Henrietta Hobart. Neither Maurice nor Charles Saatchi responded to my written requests for interviews.

Despite the obstacles and impediments, many people were fascinated by the project and realised that it was in Tim Bell's interests to talk to me. I would like to thank the following: Ralph Bofford, Mike Renvoize, Barbara Cowling (early years); Michele Field (Australia); Dick Raven (ABC TV); Frank Monkman, Mike Yershon, Roy Langridge, John French (Colman Prentis Varley); Paul Green, John Hegarty, Ron Leagas, Jennifer Laing, David Miln, Roger Neill, John Staten, John Perris, Tim Mellors, Paul Arden, Roy Warman, Terry Bannister, Paul Cowan, Alex Fynn, Malcolm Taylor, John Sharkey, Paul Bainsfair, Bill Muirhead, John Emerson, Carol Powell, Adrian Rowbotham, Margaret Bischoff, Peter Wallach, Keith Holloway, Alan Bishop, Ed Wax, Charles Scott, Bill Jones, Bernard Barnett, Christine Barker, Margaret Patrick, Trudi Pacter, Gail Amber, Philip Kleinmann, Alison Fendley, Emily Bell, Winston Fletcher, Martin Boase, David Bernstein (Saatchi and Saatchi); Stephen Woodward, Irving Samwell, Bruce Haines (Lowe Howard-Spink). Michael Dobbs, Lord Tebbit, David Boddy,

Baroness Young, Sir Christopher Lawson, Keith Britto, Sir Michael Spicer MP, Harvey Thomas, Sir Bernard Ingham, Shaun Woodward, Adrian Rowbotham, Paul Potts, Nick Jones, Bruce Matthews, Andrew Davidson, John Banks, Sylvia Jones, Bruce Anderson (Mrs Thatcher and Conservative account); Michael Eaton, Malcolm Edwards, Peter Heep, Mark Rogers (miners' strike); Ernest Saunders, Brian Basham, Rodney Dewe, Nick Kochan (Guinness and Hanson); Tony Good, Peter Bradley (Good Relations); David Mellor MP, Paul Halloran (Mellor); Martyn Gregory, Paul Davies, Peter Morgan (British Airways); Pamela Taylor, Brian Clifford, Ian Jack (BBC); Rod McGeoch, Gabrielle Melville (Sydney Olympics).

I was fortunate to receive the assistance of Tom O'Sullivan, associate editor of *Marketing Week* and former chief reporter of *PR Week*. Tom's knowledge, contacts and expertise in the advertising, public-relations and political lobbying world are unsurpassed. He made an invaluable contribution to this book in conducting background research and several interviews for me, particularly on Sir Tim's period at Colman Prentis Varley and Lowe Howard-Spink. His reporting is based on a refreshing scepticism which is not always a dominant characteristic of journalists covering the PR and advertising world.

I was also lucky to draw on Jamie Wilson and Mary Kalmus, both excellent researchers, for useful digging in libraries. As ever I am grateful to Olga Sheppard for her highly efficient transcribing of taped interviews. My luckiest break was to be assigned Hazel Orme as my editor. She did an excellent job in sharpening up the manuscript and it benefited greatly from her expert eye. I am equally indebted to my friend Andy Stewart for his investigative expertise.

I owe a special debt of gratitude to Mary Ann Nicholas for her excellent field research, her thoughtful editing of the manuscript and, above all, her support in countless ways. I also would like to express thanks to Pamela Grunninger Perkins who, along with other friends whom I cannot name here, relieved me of pressing personal responsibilities at a very difficult time so that this book might be written.

As for Sir Tim Bell, I wrote to him twice asking for an interview and for his full co-operation with this book. He did not reply to my letters. We eventually spoke on the telephone at 11.20 a.m. on 27 February 1996. He was calmer than he had been during our previous conversations but he remained opposed to this book being published.

'I don't want a book being written about me,' he told me. 'If I did, I would want somebody who knew me and not somebody who didn't. Not because I want somebody to write favourable things about me. I don't want a book written simply because I regard it as an act of grotesque vanity . . . I couldn't care less what the public thinks about me, but I have small children and I don't want them to read a book about their father which is written without my co-operation and approval . . . I do honestly believe it's the most extraordinary invasion of my privacy.'

I suggested that the privacy argument is difficult to sustain when he has been chairman of a prominent public-relations company for ten years, operates on a public agenda with a high media profile and has been a public figure for seventeen years as an adviser to the most powerful prime minister since the Second World War. 'It's a tiny little public company,' replied Sir Tim. 'It's hardly of any significance to anybody and the only reason I have a reputation is because I happen to have worked with people who really have made a contribution to society. It's a bit like writing the story of Margaret Thatcher's chauffeur frankly. When it first came to my ears that you were doing this, I was pissed off about it. I'm not pissed off now, I'm just irritated by it, because a lot of people who I haven't seen for years have been bothered about it and I don't want people to be bothered.'

Sir Tim then revived the issue of his offspring. 'I have small children,' he said. 'It is extremely likely that I won't be here when they reach their late teens and early twenties. My own father left home when I was four and I was left to discover about my father from gossip from other people, and I don't like that. I think that children should have their own private view of their parents and not have it presented to them in such a way that may not be accurate.'

'Then why not work with me and present a portrayal of you that you think is fair?' I asked.

But he was adamant that my research would not produce an accurate portrayal. 'However much you research this you won't get to know me,' he told me confidently.

Mark Hollingsworth
July 1996

Chapter One

Birth of a Salesman

'Tim always needed an audience'
Mike Renvoize

It was about 4.30 a.m. on Friday 4 May 1979, the night of perhaps the most dramatic and important general election since 1945. In a small top-floor office in Whitfield Street, central London, executives and copywriters of the advertising agency, Saatchi and Saatchi, were giving Lanson champagne a major boost as they prepared to celebrate the election of the UK's first woman prime minister. As dawn approached Alastair Burnet, the ITN anchorman, announced that the Conservative Party was virtually secure of an overall majority in the House of Commons. The festivities could now begin.

Saatchi's had good reason to rejoice. After all, it had been their innovative and controversial advertisements and broadcasts that had helped secure the Tories' victory. The successful campaign promised to produce untold commercial benefits for Britain's fastest-growing advertising agency.

Not everyone, however, was so happy. Tim Bell, Saatchi and Saatchi's 37-year-old managing director, was visibly upset, tears welling in his eyes. He had worked on the campaign day and night for several months and should have been overjoyed, but, as his colleagues toasted their good fortune, he could only mumble again and again: 'She doesn't want me. She has no use for me.'

'What's wrong, Tim?' he was asked by a colleague.

'She hasn't called,' he moaned. 'Why hasn't she called?'

She, of course, was Margaret Thatcher, and later that morning she did telephone Bell to thank him profusely for his contribution.

The agency chief's anxiety disappeared and as he hung up, Bell was ecstatic. A week later the new Prime Minister wrote to him, enclosing a photograph and expressing her deep gratitude. For weeks afterwards he carried the letter and photo with him in his inside jacket pocket, showing them proudly to reporters. During one reception, he produced it and, almost childlike, showed it to Philip Kleinman, the respected advertising journalist, as if it were a badge of honour. Later the signed photograph, with its handwritten message, 'From Margaret, with love', was framed and given pride of place in his office.

Timothy John Leigh Bell was a Thatcherite and proud of it. But it was more than just a political affiliation; he empathised with the new Prime Minister's attitude and approach to the Establishment because, like her, he was not a product of it. A grammar-school boy, with a solid middle-class background, he had little in common with the grandees who dominated the Tory Party until the mid-1970s. A self-made man, Bell rose to the top of his profession through instinctive talent, competitive guile, self-belief, raw ambition and hard work. 'I'm like her,' he said, many years later. 'It's not surprising that I passionately related to her, because she represented everything that I wanted to do . . . What happened in the Thatcher years was that a lot of people did things they would never have dreamt of even trying in previous decades. They did it, they were allowed to and people didn't criticise them because they weren't members of The Club [the Establishment].'[1]

By the end of the Thatcher decade, Bell was a leading member of the new ruling élite that John Lloyd, the *Financial Times* journalist, called the Disestablishment:

Britain is no longer run by an Establishment. In its place is a Disestablishment comprising men and women whose values, assumptions and habits are those of outsiders. Often they still perceive themselves as outsiders, radicals, anti-Establishment figures, but that is increasingly a pose. They have successfully dethroned much, though not all, of the old Establishment and in many crucial centres of power have taken its place.

The values transmitted by the Disestablishment are materialistic, efficient, demotic, hedonistic, internationalist and rule-breaking.

These contrast sharply with the ambient values of the old Establishment which was, if not anti-money, certainly not for it; amateurish, even sloppy in style; paternalistic; distrustful of pleasures taken beyond a 'decent point' . . . and jolly keen on the rules . . . The Disestablishment is not simply a reflection of 'Thatcherism' – since many of its members would violently disavow allegiance to the Prime Minister and her values. However, the changes which she has ushered in, or which are associated with her, are the largest single feature in its formation.[2]

Bell, whom Lloyd interviewed for his series of articles, personified those new values. He was dynamic, brash and flamboyant, contemptuous of old orthodoxies. As managing director of Saatchi and Saatchi, he sold advertising that ignored many of the old rules and conventions. At the same time he promoted the wisdom of advertising to people in the commercial and political world who otherwise would never have dreamed of using it. As an unofficial adviser to Mrs Thatcher, he was the most influential member – besides civil servants such as Sir Bernard Ingham and Sir Charles Powell – of her inner circle, providing secret counsel on the media and presentational aspects of her policies. At the same time he was a communications confidant to business tycoons and corporations. He became what James Pinkerton, a former aide to President Reagan, dubbed an ideological entrepreneur': a free agent, reporting to no central authority, power-broking between politics and commerce.[3] Bell was accountable only to his clients. His trade was networking and his commodity was information. By the early 1990s, he had expanded into public relations, crisis management and government lobbying.

Like the mythical hero in Woody Allen's film *Zelig*, Bell may seen relatively obscure to the general public, but he has been at the right hand of many of the most significant public figures of the past twenty years, while also being omnipresent during general election campaigns, strikes and takeover bids. If a company has an image problem, he will make a cameo appearance. If a friend has come under the media microscope, up pops Bell, ready to exert influence and cut deals. His career is testimony to the insecurities of the most powerful and wealthy, how even the most successful crave reassurance. Bell, with that soothing bedside manner, can provide it.

However, an outsider who is trying to break through the prejudices of the Establishment may experience enormous pressures. In their study of new business tycoons who flourished during the Thatcher years, Judi Bevan and John Jay, former City journalists on the *Sunday Telegraph*, analysed how outsider status affected their personality:

> It is the feeling of being different by race or social standing that so often inspires individuals to prove themselves – to prove that they are every bit as good, if not better, than the Establishment yardsticks against which they judged themselves. This insecurity shows itself early in an intense competitive drive, manifested most frequently in sport, less often in academic achievement. Later, life becomes a scoreboard where pound notes and accolades are the points. Capital – or 'fuck you money' in the words of Peter Beckwith [head of the property firm London and Edinburgh Trust] – spells, for the socially insecure, a control of life and power.

Despite his talent and self-confident swagger, Bell has indeed spent most of his life working desperately hard to demonstrate to his peers that he should be accepted as a Club member. He has always been fervently competitive and his school record bears out his preference for sporting rather than academic success. His time at Saatchi and Saatchi was dominated by his need to be accepted as the 'third brother' by Maurice and Charles. Possessing the most visible material signs of success also became important to him – owning the flashiest cars, wearing the smartest suits, eating in the most prestigious restaurants and earning a large amount of money. Later, he needed to ensure that people knew he was a close friend of the Prime Minister, captains of industry, the great and the good and other celebrities. This all culminated, of course, with the cherished knighthood in 1990 – the ultimate symbol that he had been accepted as a member of the new Establishment.

The journey from an unexceptional, north London childhood to an audience with the Queen in less than fifty years has been dominated by one other factor: speed. Everything in Tim Bell's life is done fast – driving, talking, socialising, working. 'Life is short' seems to have been his motto. He has always been a driven man, striving towards the next goal. Perhaps that is why he has never been fond of reflecting on his past.

* * *

Tim Bell has always been mysterious about his early life. 'He always gave me the impression that he worked his way up from the bottom of the heap,' recalled a former colleague. 'But he didn't like to talk about it, even though he would tell you virtually everything else about himself.' The rags-to-riches story is true in one sense: he started at the lowest step of the professional ladder in advertising. But he did have a prosperous middle-class upbringing.

From the early 1960s until the late 1980s, Bell often claimed to be Australian, and even gave the strong impression to Michele Field, an Australian journalist, that he was 'born in Balmain, Sydney, and left at the age of two'.[5] He supported Australia at cricket during Test matches against England. 'He used to tell everyone [that he was an Australian],' said his friend Bill Muirhead, a former Saatchi and Saatchi managing director from Sydney. 'I never really understood it, but I guess he wanted to be different.' Another former colleague and close friend, Roy Warman, told me: 'He did spread it around that he was Australian. I think he did it because in the early 1970s it was fashionable. You had the new successful tycoons like Murdoch, Kerry Packer and Robert Holmes à Court, and John Newcombe and Margaret Court were winning Wimbledon, so it was cool and trendy to be an Aussie then.'

As an 'Australian' he could transcend the British class system, which in the 1960s and early 1970s gave him a commercial advantage with clients: society was rapidly changing, and the public-school-educated gentlemen then running the advertising industry were on the way out. Anyone with a classless accent, a dynamic personality and deep Australian roots was well received.

In fact, Bell had been born in the rather less fashionable garden suburb of Southgate, north London, on 18 October 1941. It was his mother, Greta Findlay, who was an Australian, born in Balmain, Sydney, in March 1913. Greta was the daughter of Gilbert Findlay, a soft-goods salesman from Bishops Stortford, Hertfordshire, who had just arrived in Australia with his wife of three years, Ethel Schmidt, a 28-year-old from Stoke Newington, north London. Gilbert Findlay adapted well professionally to Balmain, which at the time was a tough working-class neighbourhood, largely devoted to ship-building, and set up a successful chain of agricultural equipment shops. But the Australian lifestyle did not suit the Findlays: in the mid-1920s they returned to London and moved into a house in Muswell Hill. Gilbert resumed his business career and became prominent in the City and Port Exchange.

Greta Findlay, Tim's mother, was slim with long light brown hair, engaging with a warm, open personality when in 1933, aged twenty, she met Arthur Bell. He was a strikingly handsome 27-year-old Irishman who lived in nearby Hornsey. Known as Paddy, he was a sweet-talking linen salesman with dark, carefully combed curly hair and a ruddy complexion and built like a rugby forward. He had just arrived from America. Born in Belfast, on St Valentine's Day 1906, Paddy Bell attended Queen's University in his home-town but his ambitions lay in entertainment. At nineteen, he moved to New York City and took up dancing, much against his father's wishes. 'It went so well that I hoofed my way right into selling linen,' Paddy said later, which pleased his father, William Bell, who was a linen manufacturer.[6]

Paddy Bell was perfectly suited to being a salesman: he loved to talk and meet people, and was always immaculately dressed. He had a magnetic personality. Greta was charmed, and in August 1934, she and Paddy were married at the Christ Parish Church in Hornsey. After moving into a comfortable mock-Tudor house on Friars Walk, in East Barnet, the couple settled down to have a family and Paddy became an export manager for an aviation company. Three years later Greta gave birth to their first child, Jennie, followed by another daughter, Linda. In 1941, Tim arrived and the family was complete.

Paddy had an active Second World War. He served with Bomber Command in the RAF and was wounded by flying flak when his plane was shot down. He also broke his neck and, by all accounts, displayed exemplary bravery.

After he was demobbed, Paddy returned to sales and worked as a representative for Crosse and Blackwell, the food manufacturers. But during the war he and Greta had drifted apart and eventually Paddy left his wife. In August 1948, after almost fourteen years together, they divorced.

Shortly afterwards Paddy had a bizarre encounter that changed the course of his life. Walking along a street in Manchester one day he passed a hunchbacked man and stopped to talk to him. 'Excuse me,' he said. 'Can I touch your hump?'

'That's most unusual,' replied the man. 'People don't normally comment on it.' The two fell into conversation and it turned out that the other man was a senior executive at Pan American World Airways. Paddy told him about his work in the aviation industry and his service in the RAF. 'Would you like a job?' he was asked.[7] Paddy was surprised at the impulsiveness of the offer, but accepted immediately.

He thrived at Pan Am, and after working for the company in several countries, he was promoted in June 1952 to managing director of Southern and East Africa, notably Kenya, Mozambique and South Africa. Based in Johannesburg, he prospered in his new home, which he described as 'this land of opportunity'.[8] He remarried, this time to a red-headed Irish girl, Betsy, and within a short time became chairman of the Public Relations Institute of South Africa, a council member of the country's Advertising Club and a director of the First National City Bank of New York (South Africa) Ltd (now Citibank).

Tim Bell's father, however, was best known as South Africa's most popular radio personality of the 1950s. Known as Uncle Paddy, he hosted a regular Sunday-night travel show on Springbok radio, interviewing celebrities and visitors from all over the world, and also a children's programme. On Tuesday night South Africans tuned into *Paddy Rings the Bell* to listen to his homespun philosophy and jokes, and he guested on popular features like *Just a Minute* and *Debate with a Difference*. But it was his weekly appearances on *Nice Work*, the South African version of *What's My Line*, that made him a national celebrity. The show took the country by storm and Paddy Bell was its star. A brilliant mimic and raconteur, he had audiences in stitches with his imitations of a Spitfire pilot and his different foreign accents. *Nice Work* even went on tour and thousands would turn out to see and hear Paddy tell his stories and jokes. 'I look on my radio work,' he said in 1954, 'just as if some genie had suddenly moved the broadcasting studio into the lounge of any home where the folks, enjoying a social evening, take over the programme as if I were a guest in that house.'[9]

He also became a sought-after, colourful figure on the Johannesburg social circuit. 'He had a wonderful personality,' recalled Ralph Bofford, his best friend during that period and the host of *Nice Work*. 'I would say he was a true professional Irishman in every respect. He had ineffable charm and was always telling funny stories at parties.'

Beneath the surface, though, Paddy was nervous and highly strung.

A heavy drinker, he would often start early in the morning. 'I remember going to see him at 10 a.m.,' Bofford said. 'He had a cup on his desk, so I asked him what was in it and he said coffee, but when I looked inside the cup it was gin! Drinking made him belligerent and aggressive, but he was certainly never a drunk. He was always a considerate man. He also strongly opposed the apartheid regime but he did so quietly so he didn't jeopardise Pan Am's interests in South Africa.' Tim was nine years old when Paddy moved to South Africa and so grew up with an absentee father. 'He flew over once a month to see me,' Tim said, many years later. 'He got free flights. But I didn't really know him as a father, he was just the man my mother divorced. I didn't like him much, because he tended to criticise my mother.'[10] His other recollections indicate an underlying bitterness: 'My father left my mother when I was about four years old, but that's another story', he said, during one interview[11], and perhaps more tellingly, 'My greatest heroes tend to be older, perhaps because I had no father.'[12]

Paddy's departure must have been hard for his son and, according to Mike Renvoize, one of Tim's closest friends over twenty-five years, he was acutely conscious of his father's life and achievements. 'There was an element of hero worship,' said Mike, 'and he was rather wistful about him.' Paddy spent the rest of his days working for Pan-Am in South Africa. His heavy drinking and smoking eventually caught up with him and he died of cancer in 1964, aged 58.

Sometime after Paddy's departure, Greta fell in love with the man who was to bring long-term stability into her son's life, Peter Pettit, the solicitor who had handled her divorce. A widower, five years older than Greta, he had been to University College, London, and became a successful lawyer. A more serious-minded man than Paddy, he was also a Conservative member of St Marylebone Council, and active on the housing and finance committees. 'It takes up a lot of time', he said, 'and so I have little time for other outside interests.'[13]

Greta and Peter married in July 1952, at Kensington Register Office, and moved with Tim and his two sisters into a spacious detached house on Totteridge Lane, in Barnet, close to the South Hertfordshire Golf Club. It was a fairly relaxed household: Greta was a responsible mother but she was not pedantically houseproud. She treated her teenage children more like young adults: quite often she would sit with Tim and his friends and join in their conversation.

'She had a lightness of touch and was a little bit saucy and familiar without it being misunderstood or misinterpreted', recalled Mike Renvoize. She had lost all trace of her Australian accent, and as a member of the Royal Horticultural Society and the Conservative Women's Institute, became integrated into the aspiring bourgeoisie of south Hertfordshire.

Tim's step-father was a kindly but detached man. The atmosphere was not quite as relaxed when he entered the lounge if the children were there. He would peer over his spectacles, mumble a pleasant greeting and return to his study to work. He and Tim shared a cordial if cool relationship. As Tim later pointed out, 'You can never replicate a father relationship.'[14]

Soon after his marriage to Greta, Peter Pettit became an alderman and in May 1961 he was elected Mayor of Marylebone. At the ceremony Pettit was described as 'a man with a sound legal and financial background' while Tim's mother was 'a charming lady who will be the greatest asset to her husband'.[15] Greta's life was filled with civic functions, openings and presentations, which all culminated in the Mayor's Ball in April 1962 at Seymour Hall where, as an elegant, well-groomed mayoress, she played host to 500 guests, including diplomats and politicians, who drank champagne and danced the twist.[16] It was a far cry from Balmain, Sydney.

Tim Bell was a bright, if not brilliant, schoolboy. After attending Osidge Primary School in Southgate, he passed the eleven-plus and in September 1953 enrolled at Queen Elizabeth Grammar School in Barnet. It was a traditional all-boys institution and was run like an English public school. Most boys were expected to go to university.

From 1930 until 1961 the headmaster was Ernest H. Jenkins, a former navy officer with a bluff, tough disposition, who set the tone for the school. Dedicated to the pursuit of academic excellence, he still believed Latin and Greek were the most important subjects and placed a strong emphasis on traditional sports. 'I have always found,' he wrote in his memoirs, 'that, unless a boy is utterly unsuitable, a classical training, even if he remains a weak classic, has more value than any other – except perhaps for Mathematics.'[17] During his annual address on Speech Day, Jenkins would often fulminate at the 'excessive time devoted to wireless and television – which has become something of a menace . . . or a film in which sex and gangsters were prominent features'.[18] In the early 1950s another favourite target was 'the poor training parents were giving to their feckless, untidy, self-centred little boys'.[19]

Discipline was rigid and corporal punishment was often used: pupils were caned for the most minor misdemeanour. Jenkins was fierce and despotic, and seemed to revel in his power. On one occasion, just before the Second World War, he beat the whole of the lower school because one boy did not own up to an offence. Most boys put up with this repressive regime but one of the few whose gestures made him stand out in a sea of uniformity was Tim Bell. By Queen Elizabeth Grammar School standards, he was a rebel. 'Tim was flamboyant and a bit of an exhibitionist,' recalled a former schoolfriend. 'He would push the dress and hair regulations as far as he possibly could. He would wear his cap backwards so that his hair had a quiff at the front. He would then comb his hair back in what was known at the time as the "Tony Curtis" look. He would also wear the tightest possible trousers he could find and wear a blazer without a badge.' This mild form of rebellion landed him in some trouble with the masters, but, according to Mike Renvoize, it was more about drawing attention to himself than resistance to authority.

Tim may have been flash, popular and mischievous, but he was not a serious trouble-maker. 'I can't remember him getting into any real trouble, but he wasn't prefect material either,' said Renvoize. 'We were wide boys without being delinquent.' Other former pupils remember Tim as a 'real chatterbox'. He would talk to anyone and, even then, was engaging and outgoing. Young Bell was more interested in sports and music than in passing examinations. Although he disliked rugby, in his final year he was still a regular member of the school's second XV. 'A promising back row forward with the knack of being at hand for the scoring chance,' reported the school magazine. 'Led the scrum well when required.'[20] He preferred cricket and was an effective middle-order batsman, making the second XI in his lower-sixth year. 'A very keen and fine fielder close to the wicket,' was his captain's verdict. 'Risky batsman, but had the merit of looking for runs and consistently made a few useful ones.' The following year Bell played a few games for the first XI but was less successful as a 'batsman on the look-out for runs, but bad in defence'.[21] He was also competitive.

'All I can remember is that he always wanted to win and be captain of the team,' recalls a fellow Old Elizabethan.

Outside school, Tim was passionately interested in jazz. He and Mike Renvoize would go to the Assembly Hall on Union Street, Barnet, where they listened to jazz every Tuesday night. Tim knew more about the scene than most of his friends, and particularly enjoyed Miles Davis and Chet Baker. He was also a capable pianist and trumpeter and even formed a band with Richard Williams – who later made the film *Who Killed Roger Rabbit?* – on guitar. They performed a few minor gigs in Totteridge Town Hall. 'Tim was very good,' said Renvoize, now a jazz musician. 'He had a decent understanding of the music and could play solos as well.'

Tim, then sixteen, was always able to blend into an older social scene, which gave him considerable self-assurance. 'He always needed an audience and to be at the centre of things,' said Renvoize. 'He always had to be noticed and be a cut above the rest. He was massively entertaining and that's mainly why he was a natural magnet for people.'

Tim was the first boy in his neighbourhood to own a flashy Italian suit. Bought by his parents, the jacket had four buttons and three-quarter-inch wide stripes each in a different colour. It was matched with pointed Italian shoes, or 'winklepickers'. As he had more pocket money than other boys, Tim, a heavy smoker, was also able to buy a Ronson lighter, which cost about forty-five shillings – a week's wages for some people in the mid-1950s.

Tim's sisters, Linda and Jenny, were also jazz fans and, in their early twenties, did not mind their younger brother hanging out with them. Jennie was an uninhibited attractive teenager: 'She was fairly wild', recalled Renvoize. 'I suppose she was the closest we had to a jazz groupie.' In 1957, aged nineteen, she emigrated to the United States. She now lives in a trailer park in Raton, New Mexico, and has not seen her younger brother since 1973. Linda is married with children and living in Brookmans Park, Hertfordshire. She would only talk to me if her brother gave permission. He didn't.

Academically Tim Bell 'got by', said Renvoize. His favourite subject was English literature and he was an avid reader of popular fiction. His favourite was *The Saint*, based on the smooth-talking personality of Simon Templar, written by Leslie Charteris and later portrayed on television by Roger Moore.[22] He passed four O levels and two A levels and left school in the summer of 1959. Tim looked back with some affection on the school. 'I was lucky,' he said, 'though the Prime Minister [Margaret Thatcher] always says the definition of luck is opportunity meeting readiness. I went to a very good grammar school, which was run like a public school with senior prefects and so on, and a sixth-form garden . . . I felt advantaged, not disadvantaged by going there. Because I hadn't been to a public school, I felt I was part of the *coming* thing, not the *going* thing.'[23]

After leaving school, Bell considered his career options. 'I really had three thoughts in my mind,' he said later. 'I could either be in the jazz world, which at that time was all about kicking over the traces, or be a school teacher and teach English, or just be financially successful. It was quite obvious to me at a very early age that although the pursuit of cash was not the greatest thing in the world, there are many things you can do with cash if you have it. I don't think I ever made a choice.'[24]

But his decision had been made for him: teaching was ruled out because he refused to go to university or any other further education. 'I didn't like the kind of people who went,' he remarked, looking back. 'They were always demonstrating about things they knew nothing about and whingeing.'[25] In another interview his distaste for students was more acerbic: 'They wasted time, wasted money and were stupid and facile.'[26] His contempt may have been raw and artless but it articulated his starkly meritocratic, materialistic view of the world: 'The universities sidelined themselves, with their totally archaic way of working. They spend a lot of time teaching useless subjects. They operate a ridiculous, old-fashioned élitest society, which still has that old British Empire thing of "It's better to get pissed than learn anything." It's all potty.'[27]

And for Bell, there was also a clear cultural schism: students wore duffel coats and sandals, he preferred Italian suits and pointed shoes. Students smoked pipes, while he puffed cigarettes. Worst of all, they listened to trad jazz in dingy basements when he liked modern jazz in clubs.

He began playing trumpet semi-professionally in the vague hope of performing and recording full-time. But he was uneasy about a musician's lack of financial security, and, besides, his mother made it clear he needed to find a job. In late 1959 he walked into the Stella Fisher employment agency in Fleet Street, accompanied by

Greta, and asked about his prospects. He mentioned that he had often thought of being an ITN reporter, but lack of a degree would prevent that ambition being realised. However, it was a time of full employment in Britain, so finding work was not difficult for a bright, personable young man. The agency offered three job interviews: one in publishing, one in insurance and another in television, with Associated British Picture Corporation. Bell chose the last. 'It was my generation who could, almost unconsciously, see the power of television and, by inference, the power of advertising in it,' he said later.[28] However, when he arrived for his interview, advertising was the last thing on his mind: 'I saw myself as a star in the making – an actor or a producer.'[29] He was soon brought down to earth when he landed the job of chart boy at ABC, which later became Thames Television, at the princely weekly salary of £7 10s.

The chart boy, or traffic boy, was right at the bottom of the advertising business. If a company was to advertise their product on television, it was Bell's job to reserve their space by writing 'Kelloggs', 'Flash' or 'Birdseye' on a little card and stick it in a slot on a chart thus reserving their airtime.

Bell was immediately fascinated by advertising and it was love at first sight. 'He enjoyed working,' recalled John Hume, a friend from that period. 'It was never a chore for him to go to the office. I think he knew straightaway that this was what he wanted to do. One of his closest colleagues at the time was Dick Raven, who started on the same day. 'He was a great character,' recalled Raven, now living in France. 'He talked a lot but was very intelligent. He wore those suits that were fashionable at the time and I always remember his pointed shoes which were curled up at the toe. He was also quite thoughtful and ambitious, even then.' Among his Barnet friends, the 20-year-old Bell always stood out. As they sat around, drinking and dreaming in the Orange Tree pub, Bell was always the smooth, focused one. 'I'm going to have the biggest advertising agency in the world,' he told Nigel Durrant, then a close friend, in 1961, 'and I'm going to be the most successful advertising man ever.' But he was also concerned that his schooling might hold him back professionally. 'You'll never get on,' he was told. 'You haven't been to a public school. Why didn't you go to a decent public school?' Bell resented this: 'I wasn't satisfied with it,' he later reflected. 'I lived in a middle-class society and I was entitled to a middle-class aspiration.[30]

Bell's talent as a communicator was noticeable even at this early age. Two of his closest friends, Dave Rattenbury and Nigel Durrant, had formed a second-hand car-dealing company called Durbury Motors. Based in a house next door to his parents on Links Drive in Totteridge, Bell advised his two mates as to the magazines in which they should place their classified advertisements. Durbury Motors were his first clients.

One of their first acquisitions was a Ford V8 Pilot, made in 1932, which they bought for £8. After cleaning it up and installing a radio, they sold it to the local vicar for £38 so that he could transport his six Boy Scouts around the village. But somehow Rattenbury and Durrant had forgotten to tell the proud new owner that the brakes did not work too well. A few days later the proud new owner went out for an inaugural drive down Totteridge Lane, where they failed and the vehicle crashed into the back of a bus. Furious, the vicar rushed round to Rattenbury's house to complain. Clearly briefed for such an occurrence, his mother told him: 'The boys have gone to Australia. You need to talk to Tim Bell down the road. I'm sure he can help you.'

He walked over to see Tim, and explained what had happened. 'Yes, I'm advising them,' he replied, and while extolling the virtues of Durbury Motors Bell considered what line to spin. 'You know, I'm also a Christian,' he said, 'and I've had the call of God. I will pray for the brakes to mend and I'm sure God will provide in the end.' Noticing that the vicar's irritation was receding, Bell added that the Ford V8 was a classic and a masterpiece, and he had it on good authority that it had belonged to Al Capone in Chicago. 'I'd hold on to it if I was you,' said Bell, 'and you'll be able to sell it for its variety value when you retire.' The vicar was placated and agreed not to pursue Durbury Motors for compensation.

Bell's next career move was partly fortuitous. He was playing rugby for an ITV seven-a-side when one of the team's opponents, the advertising agency Colman Prentis and Varley (CPV) whose top time-buyer for commercial TV was John French, needed a fly-half. 'Tim told me he was a good player and I offered him a job so he could turn out for us,' recalled French. 'Whether he was any good I'm not so sure but he certainly made up for it in the office.' Then, in 1961, CPV was one of the most prestigious agencies in Britain. Their clients included Ryvita, Sunblest, Knorr

Soups and Austin cars. During the 1959 general election campaign, they produced what were regarded as revolutionary advertisements. Voters were confronted with photographs of postmen, milkmen, miners and the slogan: 'I Am a Conservative.' Although Bell had no interest in politics, he was impressed and surprised by the audacity of the ads, for it was assumed then that working-class people voted Labour.

Bell arrived at CPV, barely twenty years old, on a salary of £20 per week, as one of the earliest recruits to television media-buying. At ABC he had received orders for ads, now he would be placing them. Media-, or time-buying, was uncharted territory: the independent television network was only six years old. 'The main role of the time buyer was to come up with value for money for the client,' said Frank Monkman, media director of CPV from 1959 until 1973. 'The television ratings were the only measure and it was the buyer's decision on which advertising slot to purchase. Everybody at that time was groping with the best way to deal with the new medium. The time-buyer had to ensure that shows like *Robin Hood* were delivering up the ratings to promote baked beans.'

Many admen, particularly those in newspapers, were sceptical that TV advertising would ever work. During pitches for new business, it was only occasionally on the agenda and then usually for ten minutes before everybody went to lunch. 'You have to remember,' said Mike Yershon, then a close colleague of Bell, 'that the media department at CPV was called the "Cinderella" department, because it was the first job for many people during a period when the last place any bright young man would go was be the media department of an advertising agency.'

But CPV understood the potential in TV advertising and hired hungry young salesmen. They were expanding and needed extra staff. His then boss, Frank Monkman, remembers Tim Bell well: 'He was good at his job. If he hadn't been any good I would have cut his legs off. I was not interested in whether he would become an agency chairman in the years to come – only that he could deliver value for money for our clients.'

The job involved hard bargaining in which bartering and tough negotiation were the keys to success. Later known as 'gorillas with calculators', the TV time-buyer's job was not glamorous, and privately Bell described it later as being 'like a bank clerk'. Publicly, he was more diplomatic. 'I started on what was considered the down-market side, media-buying, never on the creative side,' he said. 'Basically, I was a suit.'[31] However, it was excellent training for an aspiring young adman, as it required an eye for detail, negotiating skills and keeping clients happy. Alcohol consumption was a characteristic of the lifestyle. This was not just to keep clients happy. Media-buyers often had time on their hands. 'The press buyer tended to be the last one standing in the pub at the end of lunch-time because he would have already got the five-column spot on the front of the *Daily Telegraph* the next day,' said Mike Yershon. 'It was the same in TV – lunch at twelve, back at the office at three but when you arrived back you were not able to do much work. Tim Bell would have been obliged to consume alcohol. He was a TV buyer and there was little demand at the time – because there were relatively few advertisers and loads of availability – and so he would have spent a lot of time just negotiating free spots.'

Bell had a promising career at CPV, dealing with clients like Pepsi Cola, Sunblest bread and Penguin biscuits. 'People liked him,' said John French, 'and it soon got around that he was a quality buyer, but I wouldn't say he was particularly ambitious at that stage. Like most young men he was interested in girls, pubs, darts, drinking and sports.' Yershon, who replaced Bell after he left the agency, has a similar recollection: 'He was bright and personable – not exceptionally bright but you didn't have to be at that time. Very much one of the lads and down to earth. I always take people at face value and I would not have predicted the great things Tim has gone on to do.' Frank Monkman said: 'I was aware that he was not the type to just sit quietly and add up the numbers. But I didn't think he was screamingly ambitious. He was promising, very capable and I liked him very much. He had drive, initiative and was always confident about going into bat with the contractors to negotiate rates.'

By 1964 the 23-year-old Bell had developed enough of a reputation as a media-buyer to be poached by Hobson Bates, part of the American agency Ted Bates. Based in Gower Street, he was now earning £60 per week – a substantial salary at the time – but only with marginally more responsibility as a media-planner, responsible for recommending to a client in which area of the media – TV, magazines, newspapers – to place their ads. But it was essentially the same job, and Bell did not enjoy the rigid structures and stuffy atmosphere of the agency.

'It was not a good move for Tim,' said John French, who joined him there.

It was during his two-year stint at Hobson Bates that Tim Bell was married for the first time, on 12 June 1965, to Suzanne Melodie Winsor, an attractive blonde model, at St Andrews Church, Totteridge. The ceremony was attended by Tim's mother, Greta, but not Paddy, who had died a year earlier. After a reception at his mother and stepfather's home on Totteridge Lane, the newly-weds left for a honeymoon in Devon.[32]

The couple had first met in 1960 when Sue was a 16-year-old student at the Lucy Clayton School of Modelling and Tim was a jazz-obsessed 19-year-old in his first job at ABC TV. She was his first serious girlfriend and although Tim liked women he was never a womaniser. Sue's mother, Barbara Cowling, had been slightly apprehensive at her daughter being courted by this fashionably dressed young man but she was soon won over by his boyish charm. 'I was very impressed by him,' recalled Barbara, now living in retirement in Cornwall. 'He was very attentive and kind. I liked him a lot.' Sue's step-father Peter, also has fond memories: 'I come from an engineering background in the aviation industry and so I didn't see the need for advertising,' he said. 'I thought they were all parasites, so I had differences of opinion with Tim, but I always liked him and we got on well. I had a high regard for him, but I thought he was blessed with a fair amount of good fortune. He had a few scrapes with cars and his advertising career began just at the time that television was expanding.' Tim seemed to agree: 'I can fall in the sewer and come out smelling of roses' was then one of his favourite sayings.

The first Mrs Tim Bell was a self-contained, strong-willed character and mature beyond her years. She was popular and sociable with a generous nature, but no extrovert. 'She was always a good listener but she tended to keep her feelings to herself,' recalled her mother. 'I think I only saw her cry twice in her whole life.' A former close friend agrees: 'She was a quiet woman and could have moody moments when she wanted to be on her own. But then when she was on her own, she became miserable. She could be great fun, but she was difficult to get close to. She was often reluctant to talk about her feelings and emotions.'

After moving into a new house near Elstree studios in Borehamwood,

Hertfordshire, the couple settled down for what Sue believed would be a conventional middle-class marriage in suburbia. But she had not reckoned with her husband's ambition. He was a young man in a hurry. 'I remember Tim telling me that by the time he was twenty-one he would be earning a thousand per year,' said his then mother-in-law. 'He always had a tremendous drive to get on and make a lot of money. That was his goal.'

A year after marrying, in 1966, Bell, then twenty-five, joined Geers Gross, a small but dynamic and thrusting outfit, based in Soho Square. Founded by two Jewish New Yorkers, the firm was unconventional and highly successful with clients like Homepride Flour, part of Cadbury's and *Town* magazine (owned by Michael Heseltine's publishing empire). Appointed by John French, who had been best man at his wedding, Bell became deputy media director as the hottest young time-buyer in town. He was also the highest paid, at what was then regarded as the enormous salary of £11,000 a year. 'I took the view that if you paid people double the money you would get twice as much out of them,' said French.

And according to French and other former colleagues like Roy Warman, he was worth it. Tim's job was to buy advertising space for his clients, like Spillers, at the most favourable rates and the key to success was to negotiate not only the best price but also the most commercially advantageous slot on the ITV network. This meant that the precise time at which the advertisement was to be shown was of crucial importance – before, during or after certain programmes. By the late 1960s time-buying had become almost like commodity trading, with lots of wheeling and dealing, and Tim Bell established a reputation as a slick, competitive operator but one who was also difficult to deal with. One of his methods, according to Roy Warman, was to get into the office before 9 a.m to check out the TV rating books before his rival buyers. Then he would be first on the telephone, demanding discounts and concessions for his clients.

Bell's career at Geers Gross also marked the beginning of a life-long love affair with the telephone. He used it as if it was an instrument of seduction: 'I think one reason he got such great deals for his clients was that he charmed the pants off the female sales girls in the ITV companies,' said a former colleague. 'I suppose you could say he gave great phone.' He was also quick-witted without being flippant, self-assured yet not arrogant, and charming but not obsequious. In the small incestuous world of media-buying, Tim Bell was building a formidable reputation.

However, despite his success he was frustrated. His ultimate boss, the late Bob Gross, was a megalomaniac from Brooklyn and Bell did not trust him – largely because he dangled money and promotion in front of him without delivering either. 'I'll put you on the board', he once promised, without the slightest intention of keeping his word. It was a classic strategy for trying to keep a talented but restless employee satisfied but in Bell's case it failed. Soon he was looking elsewhere for new career challenges and adventures. 'If I haven't made it by the time I'm forty, I will have failed,' he told his friend John Hume at the time. That moment came sooner than he thought.

Chapter Two

Selling Saatchi

'One day we will be bigger than J. Walter Thompson and they won't laugh at us as two little Jewish boys any more'

Charles Saatchi

Despite his growing disillusionment with Geers Gross, as 1970 dawned life for the 29-year-old Tim Bell was prosperous and full of potential. In less than a decade he had gone from being a £7 10s per week chart boy to one of the highest-paid advertising salesmen in the country. His salary at Geers Gross had enabled him to buy a large semi-detached house on Wood Street in Barnet for £8,500 – a substantial investment in the late 1960s. He had traded in his blue Fiat 127 and purchased a second-hand Rolls-Royce in which he took Sue to France on expensive holidays. On one occasion they stayed at the legendary George V hotel in Paris, outside which Bell was seen proudly polishing his cherished new vehicle. Life was comfortable, but he was looking for a change of gear in his career.

While Tim Bell contemplated his future, two brothers of obscure origins were planning a radical new advertising agency. Like Tim, Charles and Maurice Saatchi were outsiders and even when they became successful, people were unsure about their background. Some thought they were Italian, others American. In 1985 Michael Wahl, owner of a large US sales-promotion company, was asked whether he would consider being taken over by Saatchi and Saatchi: 'No,' he replied. 'I don't want to sell out to the Japanese.'[1]

In fact, Charles and Maurice Saatchi – the name means 'watchmaker' in colloquial Arabic – were the sons of an Iraqi-Jewish couple. Their father, Nathan, was a successful textile merchant who imported cotton and wool products from Europe. Charles was born in Baghdad in 1943, and Maurice arrived three years later. Shortly after Maurice's birth Nathan decided to take his family abroad. After the war, Iraqi Jews had suffered a campaign of political, educational and economic discrimination, based on a national resistance to the creation of a Jewish state in Palestine. Nathan was smart enough to realise that the anti-Semitism would get worse and in 1947 he brought his family to England and bought a couple of cotton and wool mills. They settled in a large, comfortable house on Ossulton Way, on the edge of Hampstead Golf Club.

The young Saatchi brothers initially found it difficult to adapt to the cold, unfamiliar climate – both socially and meteorologically.[2] But they soon discovered that Jews in post-war Britain were thriving, in commerce, politics and the arts, and they found it relatively easy to integrate. Their parents had instilled in them self-confidence, drive and ambition, and it was just a question of how and where they would channel it.

Charles, a troublesome teenager with a restless spirit, was sent to Christ's College, an eclectic all-boys grammar school in Finchley, north London, where he showed no inclination towards or aptitude for academic or sporting achievement. He had no interest in any subjects except English, and failed at virtually everything else. He hated the rules and restrictions of school, and was often sent to detention for mischievous conduct.

Instead, like Tim Bell, he focused his energies on more hedonistic pursuits. 'Charles had a magnetic personality,' recalled Alex Fynn, who went to school with him and later worked at Saatchi's. 'He was always in the vanguard of any new movement or fashion. He virtually introduced rock 'n' roll to the school in 1956 by being the first to have Little Richard records. He was the first of us to discover women and he just seemed to be ahead of all of us in whatever he did, whether it was rock music, clothes, girls or cars.'

In 1960, aged seventeen, Charles Saatchi left school and developed a passion for fast cars and fast living. He spent a year working in the USA, then drifted into advertising largely because he was an avid TV watcher. In 1965 he joined Benton and Bowles, an American-owned agency based in Knightsbridge. There he discovered an outlet for his pent-up energy, quick brain and short attention-span – copywriting. Also, he met Ross Cramer, a senior art director who was witty, engaging and diplomatic – a perfect foil for him. The two worked well together but eventually felt frustrated at Benton and Bowles. In 1966 they moved to Collett Dickensen and Pearce, which was then a haven for new creative talent. There Charles developed a reputation as one of the most innovative copywriters of his generation. He could combine the American approach of directness and candour with the British sense of irony and lateral thinking. But patience and tact were not among his virtues. 'Charlie was the brooding kind of manic copywriter,' recalled a colleague. 'He would literally tell the clients to go screw themselves and would storm out of meetings if they didn't buy his work. He had mad long hair, really eccentric suits and crazy cars.'[3]

Although he increased his salary substantially – principally to fuel his near-obsession with classic cars – Charles Saatchi's priority was to succeed in advertising on his own terms. In 1968, he and Ross Cramer formed their own consultancy to provide creative work for agencies and some clients. It was an apposite time to launch a new advertising venture: Britain was in the midst of a cultural revolution in politics, fashion, music, media and the arts, and advertising encompassed all those elements. The prevailing mood, with which Charles identified, was one of irreverence and contempt for established institutions and conventions.

One of Cramer Saatchi's few but most notable clients was the Health Education Council for whom they devised a memorable anti-smoking campaign. One advertisement featured a hand holding a glass saucer into which a liquid stream of tar was being poured. The caption ran: 'No wonder smokers cough.'[4] Below that was the line: 'The tar and discharge that collects in the lungs of the average smoker.' It was ironic that, a mere two years earlier, Charles, a smoker, had produced some of his best creative work for Benson and Hedges. The anti-smoking ads received massive press coverage and boosted his growing reputation, which prompted a rare public comment from Charles that set out the Saatchi philosophy. 'Of course they're shocking,' he said. 'But the truth is shocking. What we did was dig out as many facts as possible about what smoking can do to you, and then present them baldly, ruthlessly and clinically.'[5]

Perhaps even more memorable was a poster for a campaign to promote contraception among the young. Jeremy Sinclair, one of Charles's most talented copywriters, came up with the idea of a 'pregnant' *man* appealing for help. His catchline was: 'Would you be more careful if it was you that got pregnant?' Within weeks the poster – displayed in doctors' waiting rooms and clinics – hit the headlines, although it wasn't until 1974 that it actually became an advertisement.

By the spring of 1970 Charles was keen to set up his own agency. He felt that most creative advertising was uninspiring and predictable and that he could do better. He asked Ross Cramer to join him but his friend declined as he wanted to direct films and commercials. Charles was bitterly disappointed and turned to his younger brother Maurice.

As in many successful partnerships, Maurice Saatchi was markedly different from his elder brother: he was academically more successful, disciplined and possessed a much quieter disposition. In 1964, aged eighteen, he secured a place at the London School of Economics to read sociology. His three-year stint there coincided with an intense period of militant demonstrations against the apartheid regime in South Africa and the war in Vietnam. Maurice remained aloof from the campus turmoil, although he was interested in politics. A cerebral, serious young man with a cool rational mind, he was awarded a first-class degree in sociology, and was keen to enter the business world. He chose Haymarket Publishing, which owned several trade magazines and was controlled by Michael Heseltine, then an ambitious Conservative MP, and his business partner, Lindsay Masters.

It was fortuitous timing. Haymarket was planning to launch *Campaign*, the advertising trade magazine – which would play a major role in the Saatchis' success – and Maurice was involved in its conception. Both Masters and Heseltine remember him as intelligent and far-sighted with an instinct for business. 'Some people learn by staggering around and falling over all the time, and then pick themselves up,' said Masters. 'Maurice doesn't fall over much. He seemed to be born with it . . . He was our one-man research and development department.'[6]

Charles had been impressed by his brother's perceptive comments on his new business venture and when Cramer declined his offer he persuaded Maurice to take his place. Saatchi and Saatchi was born. 'It's a bloody good name for a new advertising agency,' said Charles. 'Saatchi and Saatchi – it's so bizarre, no one will forget it in a hurry.'[7]

The early recruits to the agency were surprised at the 24-year-old Maurice's inclusion as partner. John Hegarty, the highly respected art director, asked Charles what his brother could contribute: 'Are you sure this is correct?' he asked.

'Well, it might not be correct,' replied the agency's founder, 'but I tell you something, John. Whatever happens, I know I can trust Maurice. And he won't put a knife in anybody's back. That's worth a dozen of another type of business person that might screw it up for us.'[8]

However, just months before the official launch, they had only one client – the Health Education Council – and Charles, an astute publicist, fully exploited that link. But they desperately needed more accounts.

The prospect of a second client occurred through a Jewish connection. The Citrus Marketing Board of Israel, which sold its oranges and lemons around the world under the Jaffa brand, were planning a major advertising campaign in Britain to take advantage of the growing boycott of South African oranges. The board's marketing director was persuaded to try out Saatchi's by his son Danny Levine, a young copywriter who was a friend of Charles.

Saatchi's spent days in preparation until finally the big moment arrived, when Charles and Maurice were visited by five executives from the Citrus Marketing Board at their Kings Court office in Goodge Street. It was a difficult meeting as Levene was a stuffy, former army officer. 'He was a sort of Colonel Blimp character, who thought it was an affront that he had to deal with us upstarts,' recalled Paul Green, then working with the Saatchis. But the Board was keen to advertise Jaffa on television.

Even by Saatchi standards it was a dramatic presentation. Using story-boards, Charles described the commercial: 'OK, visualise a big black screen and a massive great orange appears. Then you hear the sound of the clap of thunder and the voice of God announces: "Let there be Oranges. Full of Pureness and Health." The ad ends with "Jaffa: The Chosen Fruit".' The board's marketing director was unconvinced but the other executives, most of whom were Israelis, thought it brilliant to use God in the promotion and Saatchi's won the account. Unfortunately, though, the Independent Television Commission, which regulates all TV advertising, rejected the commercial because it was 'anti-Jewish'. It was unmoved by

protests from the brothers that 'We are Jews and we like it –
and the Israelis like it too.'

The aftermath of the meeting reflected the tension of those early
days and offered a glimpse into the psyche of Charles Saatchi and
his stormy relationship with his brother. During the presentation,
Maurice had said something that niggled with Charles. After the
Israelis left the office he launched himself across the table, grabbed
Maurice and screamed: 'If you ever question the creative work
again, I'll fucking kill you!' Charles's penchant for assaulting his
younger brother frequently asserted itself, and chair-throwing was
a favourite habit.

Soon afterwards Saatchi's secured Granada TV rentals as their
third major client and were ready to launch. First, though, they
needed the right personnel, and Charles already had his media
director in Paul Green. To Charles, media director was one of
the most important positions and he had wanted a hard-hitting
and imaginative bargainer, particularly with the ITV companies.
Green had worked with him at the Cramer Saatchi consultancy and
was one of the star media time-buyers of his generation – assertive,
hard-drinking, street-wise, cheeky and a tough negotiator – he would
tear up rate cards in front of clients to show his mettle. Green had just
set up his own outfit, Media Buying Services Ltd, the first independent
media advertising company but Charles respected his ability enough to
offer him the job at Saatchi's plus a 5 per cent shareholding. Green was
tempted but Saatchi's was an untried, untested agency and he already
owned 40 per cent of Media Buying Services, so he turned it down.
'Who do you recommend then?' asked Charles.

Green suggested three hot media-buyers: Alan Rich, from Davison,
Pearce, Baring and Spottiswoode, Mike Townsend from Young and
Rubicam and Tim Bell from Geers Gross. Unknown to the brothers,
Bell had been thinking about the Saatchis. 'Charlie Saatchi was my
god,' he said later. 'I thought he was a genius. As far as I was concerned,
he was the man who had written the "pregnant man" ad, the best ad
I had ever seen. Only later did I discover that was untrue. At the
time I saw him as the new Bill Bernbach [the American advertising
guru]. The advertising world in those days was terribly boring and
stultifying. Charles to me represented excitement and creativity.'[9]

One Sunday evening in the summer of 1970, he was having dinner
with Mike Renvoize and a group of friends. As they sat round the

table Mike asked everyone: 'If you could have a wish come true, what would it be?'

When it was Tim's turn to answer, he paused. 'Well, there's this new guy Charlie Saatchi and he's setting up his own agency, so I'd really like to be their media director.'

'Who is Charlie Saatchi?' asked Mike.

'He's the guy who wrote the pregnant man,' said Tim.

'Have you ever met him?'

'No.'

The next morning at nine fifteen Bell was in his office at Geers Gross when his secretary put through a call. 'It's Charles Saatchi on the line', she said. He refused to take the call, convinced it was Mike or one of his friends winding him up. But Charles kept ringing. Eventually Bell picked up his phone and said: 'Ho, ho, ho. Very funny. What a witty thing to do . . .' only to discover that it was indeed Charles Saatchi: 'I want to talk to you about setting up a new agency.'

Bell and two other candidates were interviewed in a tiny Soho restaurant over lunch where they were told: 'We intend to build the biggest agency in the UK.' Bell was ingenuous: 'It's very funny this should happen, because just the other day I was . . .' and went on to describe the dinner conversation at Renvoize's house. The Brothers were smitten.

Maurice telephoned Green and delivered the verdict: 'We can't have Rich because he's too short [Charles had read somewhere that advertising executives should be tall!] and too Jewish. Townsend is no good because he doesn't read *Campaign* but this guy Bell is fantastic so we're going with him.'

Alan Rich, who now runs The Media Business, said, 'Charles told me that I looked too young. He said they had to deal with government bodies and needed someone who was older.' Mike Townsend, now at Mediacom, was not given a reason why he was rejected: 'The main thing I remember about the interview was that it was more of a monologue than a dialogue with Maurice describing how terrific their agency was going to be.'

The Brothers saw their agency as innovative, ground-breaking and genuinely creative. During the mid sixties the industry had been dominated by American companies, who produced grey, predictable advertising. Charles wanted to tear up traditional copy and feed it through the shredding machine. Equally important, he wanted to be seen to be doing it. He did not mind being criticised: like Tim Bell, what he cared about was being noticed.

The vehicle for Saatchi and Saatchi's launch was characteristically bold. On 13 September 1970, the day before the agency opened for business, a full-page advertisement appeared in the *Sunday Times* with the headline 'Why I Think It's Time for a New Kind of Advertising' by Jeremy Sinclair. At a cost of £6,000 (25 per cent of the Saatchis' capital), it was a risky move but, as a clever piece of self-promotion, it had the desired affect. Adland talked about Saatchi and Saatchi.

The *Sunday Times* declaration made ambitious promises. The new agency would not employ account executives, who were responsible for liaising between the copywriter and the advertiser; instead, the writers would deal directly with the client. (This was broken within a few weeks when some account handlers were hired; a year later the agency employed six.) Also, every account would be shadowed by a special group of executives, who would objectively appraise the quality of a campaign – the 'Ghost Squad' – another idea that never took off.

In the early years the agency's progress was generated largely by hype. 'It was *Carry On* advertising in those early days,' said Alex Fynn, who joined in January 1973 as an account handler. 'Clients loved to pick up on what was fashionable and Charles's great talent was to exploit that. He was also a consummate PR operator and sold the agency through the pages of *Campaign*.' Charles was obsessed with seeing prominent headlines about his agency in the trade bible: 'He used to go round every Monday before press day on *Campaign*,' said Chris Martin, then a Saatchi's copywriter, 'and he'd say, "Give me a story for *Campaign*. Get out there and get in the pubs, any titbit you heard this week, give it to me and it will be passed on. If you don't know one, make it up!" '[10] Saatchi's received regular coverage, but only Charles talked to the press. He understood that information was a commodity and that he could ensure the agency's prominence in the press by trading it with journalists. It helped, of course, that *Campaign*'s joint owner, Lindsay Masters, who had become a close friend of Maurice, was also a secret investor in Saatchi and Saatchi.[11]

A favourite Saatchi device was to call the trade press under a fictitious name with a bogus story. Roy Warman, a former managing director, recalls being 'Jack Robinson', or whatever other name they conjured up, and making calls from a public phone booth, posing as an anonymous source: 'If Saatchi's and two rival agencies pitched for a new account and we wanted to put pressure on the client to get a decision out of them, we would tell the trade press – via Jack Robinson – that we had got the business. This was done because quite often clients took anything from a week to several months to make up their minds. It was a way of getting them to do so and for us to get some feedback.'

'Jack Robinson' would also be used if Saatchi's wanted to cause problems for other firms: 'If the client said he wanted to keep the names of the prospective agencies secret,' said Warman, 'we would get "Jack Robinson" to tell the trade press that another agency had secured the business. If the client accused us of leaking it, we could reply, "Why on earth would we announce that a rival agency had beaten us to it?" When the story was published this presented Saatchi's in a favourable light because it appeared they were the only ones to honour and preserve confidentiality. The whole exercise was designed to undermine our competitors.'

Twenty years later Tim Bell confirmed that this had, indeed, occurred. 'We [Charles Saatchi and himself] realised we could build our reputation way over and above its true potential by spreading lies,' he told a Marketing Society lunch. 'If you are going to lie, do it well.'[12] He told his rather stunned audience that, like Roy Warman, he used to phone *Campaign* from a call box, claiming to be 'John Richardson', and say that an ad account was moving with a budget of £500,000. It would appear, Bell claimed, as a brief news piece. The next week he would call again to say that the story was wrong, that he had seen a 'confidential memo' and the budget was really £5 million. Bell claimed that one year the false leads about billings amounted to a total of £427 million across the industry. Bill Jones, a senior *Campaign* journalist from 1971 to 1977, was dismissive of Bell's account: 'It's pure fiction. *Campaign* dealt in rumour and speculation but that claim is a figment of a fertile imagination . . . We had a sophisticated network of ad-agency contacts who twigged that Charles Saatchi played the game very well. Tim Bell learnt at his knee.'

The size of his agency was also important to Charles Saatchi: 'He was constantly telling *Campaign* we were bigger than we really were,' said Fynn. John Hegarty, a founding member who also had a 2 per cent shareholding, told me, 'Charles wanted to be the biggest agency first, the best second and most profitable third. I wanted to be the best first and then the biggest and that's why I left.' But Charles remained preoccupied with making the agency larger – or at least the appearance of it. As there were only nine employees, a favourite stunt was to drag people in off the street and hand them a fiver to sit at a desk to make it appear that the company was busy and thriving. 'Pretend you're talking on the phone,' they would be told. Perhaps the most telling incident occurred in the early seventies when Trudi Pacter, then a *Campaign* journalist and now a novelist, stood outside Saatchi's office with Charles. Suddenly he pointed up at the agency's sign. 'One day,' he said, with some passion and intensity, 'we will be bigger than J. Walter Thompson and they won't laugh at us as two little Jewish boys any more.'

CHARM OFFENSIVE

When Tim Bell joined Saatchi and Saatchi as media director, the atmosphere in the elegant open-plan offices at 6 Golden Square, in the heart of Soho, was egalitarian, irreverent and informal. Charles had a deep admiration for quality work, a contempt for convention, job titles and awards, and he encouraged others in the office to think in the same way. A product of their time and counter-culture, the Brothers were dismissive about traditional office hierarchies, while fostering a harsh, competitive edge between their employees. It was an intensely 'political' atmosphere, in which individuals were set against each other. Yet they also encouraged initiative and lateral thinking, and placed no restrictions on creative work. They never missed an opportunity to denigrate their rival agencies. Their office mottos were 'Success breeds success' and 'Nothing is impossible'. On business strategy, Maurice Saatchi set the tone: 'It's not enough for us to succeed, others must fail', and 'Saatchi is more than a company, it's an attitude.' He pioneered the tactic of trying to poach other agencies' clients by cold-calling companies and asking if they would like Saatchi's to take over their advertising. Saatchi and Saatchi saw themselves as the advertising underdogs – David against the Goliaths – and unless it was illegal, they would try anything in their quest for success.

At first Bell was taken aback by this approach. Until then, he had worked in agencies with conventional corporate structures where senior executives were respected. One day he was walking through the Saatchi's office when Jeremy Sinclair, a talented but then junior copywriter, leaned casually against a partition and said, 'Let's hear it from media, then.' Bell was surprised at the jibe. But he was sympathetic to their egalitarian approach and rapidly adapted to the atmosphere in which he found himself.

Early recruits found the pace of Saatchi's hard to take. 'Let's do it, let's get on with it,' Charles would say impatiently, cajoling everyone to greater efforts. Bell, a quick thinker and talker, thrived in such an environment and found it exhilarating. He could also cut through jargon, translating complex ideas into simple, accessible language and, after a few months, he became, in effect, marketing director, filling a gap that the brothers had been unable to bridge. At the time Maurice knew virtually nothing about advertising, having come straight out of the LSE, and Charles hated meeting clients and conducting presentations. Bell became the front man and managed the accounts, while Charles handled the creative side and Maurice controlled the finances.

The three emerged as a perfectly balanced team. Charles was the creative driving force, Maurice was the strategic thinker and Bell the instigator, who implemented the Brothers' ideas. But he was much more than that: he was alert, customer-friendly and knew how to give clients what they wanted. He understood their business pressures, how they needed to meet shareholders' expectations and their wider marketing priorities, and often advised them on broader aspects of their business. He was equally adept at dealing with Saatchi's copy-writers and creative executives. 'He's the greatest facilitator I've ever had contact with,' said Tim Mellors, a former Saatchi's creative director. 'He made the impossible possible. Nothing was too difficult or too much trouble . . . He always had his door open, you could walk in and have a chat. This wasn't just some myth perpetuated and it was that common touch that was part of his success.'[13]

*   *   *

In August 1973, Bell's contribution was recognised when he was appointed joint managing director with Maurice. Still only thirty-one, his career hit the fast lane. He began to work incredibly long hours – late nights and weekends, often sleeping at the office. In the evenings, business often blended with pleasure as clients liked to be taken to restaurants and on to nightclubs. However, despite Bell's seemingly unquenchable zest and energy, the extra pressures and responsibilities took a heavy toll on his marriage. Sue was neither materialistic nor ambitious and simply wanted a comfortable, quiet family life at home in Barnet. By early 1974 Bell was racing ahead and could not provide that kind of marriage. He tried hard to accommodate his wife, but his commitment to Saatchi's was too strong. 'It reached a point when she could not believe a word he said, especially about what time he would be home,' said Mike Renvoize.

The issue of children was the main reason that the marriage failed. Tim has always been keen on the idea of having kids, and was ecstatic when Sue became pregnant and told everyone at the office. Sadly, she miscarried and he was devastated, particularly when she told him that she was reluctant to try again.

The marriage finally came adrift early in 1974. The couple separated but Tim did not want a divorce, which Sue found somewhat puzzling. Years later, when he met Virginia Hornbrook, who eventually became his second wife, Sue asked him: 'Surely you want a divorce now so you can marry Ginny?' But he remained evasive and still could not bring himself to divorce her. According to Carol Powell, Bell's former secretary at Saatchis in the late seventies, Bell found it difficult to confront problems in his private life and could not bear personal disharmony and rows. And, of course, there was the spectre of his own parents' divorce. It was not until October 1985, eleven years after the separation, that the decree absolute finally went through.

Interestingly, Bell has always neglected to mention his first marriage in *Who's Who*. When asked why by Hunter Davies of the *Independent*, he replied: 'I don't know.' Davies pressed him: 'Oh, come on, there must be a reason.' Bell then gave a partly inaccurate response: 'I married my first wife when I was twenty-three,' he said. 'After five years [in fact it was nine] we realised it hadn't worked out and we parted, but we remained friends. She died later of cancer. We had no children.'[14]

Despite the separation Tim and Sue remained friends and met up occasionally for a meal. She made a precarious living as a buyer of bridal wear and never remarried. In 1989 she developed breast cancer, and, after a prolonged, painful and distressing illness, died in June 1993, three months short of her fiftieth birthday.

A NEW FAMILY

After the collapse of his marriage Bell devoted himself entirely to his other family, Saatchi and Saatchi. He accepted and respected Maurice as a superior intellect in the business sphere and a vital, driving force, but he idolised Charles, the father of the agency, and wanted desperately to please him. 'He had a clear need to demonstrate how close he was to Charles,' said Paul Bainsfair, a former Saatchi's account executive. 'He would always tell you what Charles had said or done. The subtext was how valuable he was to him.' Even though Tim was two years older than his mentor, he saw the agency's founder almost as a surrogate father: 'I looked up to Charles as a father figure,' he reflected in 1995. 'Charles always knew what was best for me.' Even in later years, when he had fallen out with the Brothers, he would say: 'Charlie Saatchi is one of my great heroes still.'[15]

Charles, in turn, admired Bell, because he liked people who could accomplish feats that he could not – or did not wish – to accomplish himself. As Bell excelled in acquiring and cultivating clients, which Charles hated, they developed a close relationship. Yet it was a frustrating and challenging one for Bell. Charles was the most creative but also the most demanding boss. 'The whole company wanted to please Charlie,' he said later. 'All you wanted was for him to tell you you'd done it. But you were always left feeling you could do more.'[16] Charles would fly into hysterical rages, and forget them twenty minutes later. Ads were either 'terrific' or 'shit'. Creatives would be told: 'Who do you think you are – Michael Fucking Angelo?'[17] Bill Muirhead, an account director, once witnessed a tirade: 'Tim walked backwards in the face of all this abuse from Charlie until he was almost up against the wall, up against a work of art which had various bits of broken glass sticking out from it. Charles suddenly stopped screaming and ran over to Tim, telling him not to move. I'm not sure if he was more concerned about the picture or about Tim at the time.'[18]

As Tim was always anxious to please or, at least, pacify Charles, it created perpetual tension for him. He was an account handler and a media man, and his focus was on keeping clients happy and giving them what they wanted. Usually he succeeded, but Charles was rarely satisfied, and if he was, certainly would not show it. Muirhead described one stupendous Bell presentation as 'the work of a genius', but 'Charles completely put him down. He said he was a little worm and how he dragged him up from the gutter – it was all done with a smile on his face.'[19]

Charles Saatchi became Tim Bell's most difficult client. But it was an impossible pitch, an account he could never win – no one could. Nevertheless, as Bell was a man who constantly sought accolades and approval, he was driven on and motivated by the hope of receiving them from his mentor and hero. When reassurance never came from that quarter, he focused his attention on those who provided it: Saatchi's clients and staff.

Tim Bell's greatest contribution to the success of Saatchi and Saatchi was in pitching for new business and ensuring that accounts remained with the agency. Quite simply, he was one of the best presenters in the history of British advertising. Bell realised that accounts were usually won by brilliant creative work but lost by lousy account handling, so, to him, no detail was too small, no task too trivial. He would make sure that clients were not kept waiting at reception and often greeted them himself. He made them feel special, as if they were the most precious and valuable clients of the agency.

Bell always took on the role of lead presenter in a pitch, and was at his best with a handful of client executives in an informal setting. He was less effective in front of a large, structured meeting – if more than ten people were present, he tended to ramble. The more intimate the atmosphere, the better he performed. He was the ultimate salesman. 'He could sell his way out of a lead box', said Ron Leagas, a former Saatchi's managing director.

Unknown to his colleagues, though, Bell had been polishing his powers of persuasion for several years socially with his friends.

According to Mike Renvoize, 'There would be a group of us and we would spend evening after evening having arbitrary arguments, taking it as far as we could over dinner or a bottle of whisky. It didn't matter which side we were on. We had an opinion about everything and anything and would argue it to the death. It was not preconceived but someone would provoke an argument. It was very competitive but never personal. Tim was very good at it and could argue for as long as anyone could listen.' Another old friend, John Hume, had similar long talks with Bell. 'I didn't think much of advertising and didn't see the point in it,' he recalled, 'but Tim would spend hours trying to persuade me about its merits. The gist of what he was saying was that if you heard an advert enough times it will have an effect on the consumer.'

Bell's success as a presenter was based on instinct, intuition, improvisation and an astonishing memory. He rarely used slides or charts, believing they cluttered his style. Instead, he preferred to take a cursory look at a complex brief and, like a barrister, walk in and deliver a mesmerizing sales pitch. He never rehearsed and only needed to be told the highlights and headlines shortly before the meeting. Paul Cowan, a former Saatchi's account executive, recalls spending weeks slaving over a long, detailed paper for a pitch for Wolford's, the hosiery manufacturer. On the big day, Bell skimmed the document, read the main points and never looked at it again. 'It was all in his head and he produced a flawless performance and we won the account. It was astonishing,' said Cowan.

This nonchalant attitude towards preparation often exasperated Charles, who was obsessively anxious not to lose business. In late 1973 Saatchi's made a pitch for Cavenham Foods, owned by James Goldsmith. It was a major operation with fifteen people involved – an unusually large number – and the meeting was scheduled for 2.30 p.m. At twelve Bell suddenly went out and could not be found for two hours. Charles lost his rag. 'Where is that fucker?' he screamed Desks were slammed and chairs were thrown. Then, at two fifteen, Bell strode in and produced a virtuoso presentation, which won the account. 'He got away with it only because he pulled off winning the account,' recalled a former Saatchi's account executive. 'Charles was irritated by him but appreciated how he could make a silk purse out of a sow's ear.'

By 1974 it was acknowledged that Bell's skill as a presenter was much enhanced by what he himself later agreed was his most noted quality: his irresistible charm.[20] That year Roger Neill, a Saatchi's colleague, was asked by an advertising journalist, 'What is the secret of Bell's success?' He replied, 'Well, he's so charming that dogs would cross the street to nuzzle up to him.' The phrase has entered Saatchi folklore, but Neill now says, 'Actually it was unfair to him, because the charm was based on honesty. He would always tell you what was on his own mind and was completely open on a personal level and on the issues. There was always substance behind the slickness.'

However, other former colleagues have a different take on the legendary charm. Malcolm Taylor, a former copywriter, pointed out to me that Bell wasn't above using sophistry: 'Tim could get away with almost anything. Even when he was late for important meetings, he would be forgiven, mainly because we loved to hear the entertaining excuses for why he was late. He would conjure up all kinds of tales.' These, and other Bell anecdotes, became known in the office as 'TimBellishments'. He was always performing. If he wasn't selling an ad, he was selling himself and a little economy with the truth often helped.

Alex Fynn worked closely with him on several accounts: 'Tim is one of those people whose motto might be "Why tell the truth when a good lie will do?" simply because it's more interesting to busk it. There was nothing malicious about it. What happened was that clients came in and were prepared to be conned into what was fashionable. Tim believed they wanted showbusiness and glitz and so he would embellish a simple truth, and he got away with it because he was a great storyteller. For example, we won the Cunard *QE2* business purely on his charm and presentation. There was no creative work and we didn't even have to show them any ads. But there was also no research. It was just a one-man show with Tim spell-binding Bernard Crisp, Cunard's marketing director. I had written the document with him but the flair was all Tim. He just mesmerized Crisp with his delivery. We claimed that we had researched this and researched that but the only people we talked to were our own colleagues in the office in Charlotte Street, and we kept Cunard for several years.'

Bell's tendency to hyperbole was confirmed by Mike Renvoize. 'There was always a germ of truth in whatever he said,' reflected Mike, 'but he exaggerated all the time, because he wanted everything he said to be entertaining and exciting – so you would never really believe what he said. He was always very good at telling people what they wanted to hear and make it seem like the truth, which I suppose is the definition of advertising, really.'

Bell relished knowing what difficult, resistant clients wanted to hear. He loved going into a meeting with arrogant, stubborn businessmen and turning them round – or, at least, persuading them to consider other options. He would edit himself as he delivered the pitch, feeling out the client and noting how they were reacting. He was like a Method actor, constantly improvising and trying different techniques. During a pitch for *TV Times*, a relatively small account, Bell knew that Bob Phillis, its managing director, was antagonistic to Saatchi's so he focused on him and concluded: 'I want to tell you that everything I've said to you today is true, but I would also like to say – off-the-record – that I personally believe it to be true'. Or, in other works, 'In this case, even I actually believe what I'm saying.' It was an ingenious if risky strategy, but Phillis was won over by the sheer audacity of it.

RUNNING THE AGENCY

In 1974, despite promising financial results in the first three years of operation, Saatchi and Saatchi were hit hard, like everyone else, by a major recession in the advertising industry. It was not a temporary blip. The agency survived the storm but Maurice, in particular, realised that only corporate expansion could protect them from the bitter chill of future recessional gales. By the summer of 1975, they had cast their gaze on Garland-Compton UK, the eleventh biggest agency in Britain with billings of £17.44 million. Its most attractive feature was its substantial client list, notably Proctor and Gamble, United Biscuits and Rowntrees. But it was a badly managed, tired, complacent agency, led by capable but pedantic and uninspired executives. By contrast, Saatchi's had no real client base, apart from British Leyland – after a superb pitch by Bell – and the Health Education Council, their financial position was bleak and their accounts and financial records chaotic. They possessed, though, one priceless asset: a competent staff with creative, innovative and dynamic copywriters and account handlers.

Maurice Saatchi knew that the two agencies complemented each other perfectly, and persuaded Ken Gill, Compton's chairman, that a merger would make sense. Gill agreed and, in September 1975, the deal was signed. It was billed as a marriage made in heaven with Compton's the bread-winner and senior partner. But the front page of that week's *Campaign* told a different story. 'Saatchi Swallows Up the Compton Group', screamed the headline. Gill was appalled. The Brothers were ecstatic. In their minds, they *were* taking over Compton's. They just hadn't told them yet.

The person who perhaps benefited most from the 'merger' was Tim Bell. After Saatchi and Saatchi moved into their new offices in Charlotte Street, the Brothers were happy to move back into the shadows and Bell was made sole managing director. At the first meeting of the merged agency, he galvanized the new combined staff with a typically pioneering speech, full of bravado and gusto. He told them they were going to be the most famous and greatest agency in the world without jeopardising their creative standards. They would win major new accounts and it would be his job to co-ordinate everything.[21] Saatchi and Saatchi was now the fifth biggest agency in the country and Bell, who had just celebrated his thirty-fourth birthday, was running it.

Based in a new ground-floor office close to the reception area, Bell was at the peak of his powers: he was the focal point of the agency, in charge of 150 employees. He was involved in everything – pitching for new clients, retaining existing ones, liaising with the creative department, helping colleagues with personal problems and, crucially, acting as the bridge between the Brothers and the staff. He could absorb endless waves of pressure. If there was a crisis with a client, Bell would be there to sweet-talk the agency back into line.

His office was like a cross between a railway station and a film set. There was a bank of telephones across his desk, which was built very high like a reception table so he nearly always stood up. A typical scenario would consist of Bell holding a meeting with the phone ringing constantly. He would always take the call and would often hold two conversations at the same time while his secretary ran in and out with message and papers for him to sign.

People would often wander in for a chat, particularly at the end of the day. Obscure jazz would be playing in the background and there was always a bottle of whisky and glasses. It was open house and Tim was at the centre of everything – always accessible, hyped up, showing off, holding court, regaling his audience with the latest gossip, always rushing and always late. The staff loved it. 'The atmosphere was wonderful,' recalled Paul Bainsfair. 'He had the ability to make you feel he was looking after your interests while also doing his own job. He was very unconventional and an obsessive gossip so you also felt you were getting the inside track.'

Everyone liked Tim Bell. He would walk around the office in his socks with a friendly word for everyone. He was renowned for knowing everyone's name – from the most senior to the junior staff – but on the rare occasions that he forgot who someone was, he compensated: 'Thanks, Prince,' he would say, giving a junior employee a glow after talking to the managing director. 'Someone once described him as a "foulweather friend" and that was a fair description,' recalled one former creative director. 'The quote "God Sees the Fall of Every Sparrow" comes to mind when I think of Tim,' said Paul Bainsfair. 'He was the kindest and most generous of men,' agreed Alex Fynn. 'I have a handicapped daughter. Tim tried hard to help by finding medical support for me.' Known as Father Christmas in the office, Bell helped colleagues with their mortgages, ensured they received decent pay rises and bonuses, organised and sometimes paid for their holidays. The Saatchi attitude was to keep employees happy.

The effect of all this, of course, was to sharpen the pulse of the office and inspire the staff. People wanted to work for him, enjoyed doing so and thus improved their performance. 'He was like the player-manager in a successful football team,' said Fynn. 'He would give the inspiring team-talk before the match but would also be available on the pitch to play a winning pass or score a crucial goal.'

The Brothers, meanwhile, remained aloof, quite happy for Tim to be the front man. They were more interested in making Saatchi and Saatchi bigger by corporate expansion. In other words, taking over other agencies. Despite their obsession with seeing the Saatchi name in the press, Charles and, to a lesser extent, Maurice, increasingly cultivated a reclusive image. Charles refused to give interviews, pose for photographs or meet clients. He never attended board meetings or advertising conventions because he was bored by them. 'Charles couldn't be bothered with the persistent phoniness of it all,' said Bell.[22] Even his own staff rarely saw him. Shut away in his sixth-floor office, he would see favoured colleagues and at lunch-time play chess or backgammon with friends and fellow gamblers like Trudi Pacter, the *Campaign* journalist. But as the agency became more successful, he grew increasingly remote. He did not have a title and Maurice only became chairman sixteen years after the agency was founded.

Opinions vary on whether the Brothers were genuinely shy or whether this was an ingenious marketing ploy to create an aura of mystery and intrigue about the agency. Charles was certainly socially awkward and had no interest in cultivating new friends and relationships, but Maurice was more convivial and understood that business success was partly based on connections and contacts. Yet he, too, preferred a degree of detachment, particularly when it came to placing news stories. 'Maurice doesn't like his fingerprints on things,' said Bell.[23]

The Brothers' invisibility made people talk about them even more: 'The less you see, the more you think is there,' said Paul Green, who has known the Saatchis since the late 1960s. 'It was a fairly conscious and calculated approach to develop that persona and image,' said Martin Sorrell, former finance director of Saatchi's. 'I think it was very carefully and effectively done.'[24]

A week after the Compton's merger, Bell had the opportunity to uphold the promises he had just made to his new expanded staff. Keith Holloway, marketing direct of the prestigious drinks company Schweppes, had decided that his advertising agency, J.Walter Thompson, was lacking creative inspiration. They had devised the famous 'Schh . . . You Know Who' campaign, but Holloway was dissatisfied with their recent work. Research showed that people now thought that that advertisement was only for tonic water and Holloway made JWT re-pitch for the account along with rivals Saatchi's and Dorland's.

Saatchis was on the short list because, after a virtuoso sales performance by Bell four months earlier, they had secured the account for 7-Up, whose franchise was owned by Schweppes UK. 'When we did our pitch,' recalled Roger Neill, 'he had no time for a briefing, so about five minutes before it, I met him close to Charlotte Street. As we walked the twenty yards to the office, I gave him four or five headlines. He walked in and gave a presentation in which he appeared to know everything about 7-Up. It was just amazing.'

That campaign fizzed and Holloway gave Bell and co. the opportunity to pitch for the whole Schweppes account. It was a tough assignment. 'Nobody gave us a chance,' said Bell later.[25] Saatchi's was still a relatively small agency with big dreams – a boutique rather than a chain of shops. It was up against the country's top market leader in JWT, and the best creative team in Collett Dickinson and Pearce.

Saatchi's approach was typically cheeky and inventive: a photograph of a rogues' gallery with the line: 'You can always spot a rotter by his total lack of Schweppes.' Charles Saatchi nearly spiked the ad because he didn't understand the colloquialism. 'What's a rotter? What does it mean?', he asked Bell, when he was shown the draft. Bell explained and Charles agreed. The ad was then presented by Roger Neill, who described the strategy and thinking, and by Bell, who outlined the campaign. 'Tim was brilliant,' recalls Neill. 'He just caught the mood of the room and went with it. I tried to get him to rehearse, but he never rehearsed, because he just couldn't do it. His whole approach was about instinct and seizing the moment.'

At first Neill was concerned that they had finished early – they had spoken for twenty-five minutes instead of the allotted hour – but knew they had won the business when he saw that Holloway and his colleagues were beaming. 'They had the creative spark I was looking for,' recalled Holloway. Schweppes was a successful client for ten years: Saatchi's captured the mood of the time and made Schweppes products the first adult soft drinks with the slogan: 'Drinking Schweppes straight.'

Winning the Schweppes account was a turning point for Saatchi's: it was their first major prestigious blue chip account and really put them on the map. And it boosted Bell's self-confidence. During meetings he would convey that conviction-thinking to clients. 'This is how we should do it,' he would say politely but forcefully. 'Trust me, it will work.' The ultimate optimist, he truly believed that anything was possible. Yet in business terms, Bell was as hard-headed as the next man. 'You have to be ruthless,' he told a friend many years later. 'That means you don't often see the other man's point of view and you're unreasonable. To get to that stage you have to be driven and have a very clear view of what you want. Most important, you have to really believe it's actually going to happen.'

However, some former colleagues argue that his unshakeable self-belief bordered on a cocky – if never malicious – arrogance. 'He always gave the impression that he thought he was destined for greatness,' said Holloway. 'He had that supreme self-assurance about himself and always looked worldly-wise, as if he knew a lot more than what he was saying.' For some he was developing an unhealthy ego. 'He could never recognize that occasionally he got things wrong,' said Alex Fynn. 'He always thought he was the best.'

When Saatchi's pitched for the Warner Lambert business in 1976, Bell was accompanied by Fynn and Ron Leagas, a board director. Bell dominated the meeting and then introduced his executive colleagues: 'We've got two senior people here who will be working on your business.' But, he said it in such a way that Leagas looked like a *maître d'* and Fynn a waiter, who had just got off the boat from Naples. This was apparent in his next remark: 'Alex, will you serve us some coffee?' For the rest of the meeting neither man could get a word in edgeways. 'There was no harm in it but the implication was always that he was the main man and everyone else was behind him,' recalled Fynn. This occasionally backfired because some clients were wary of a one-man show – however good the top of the bill. This time, they didn't get the account.

Bell also believed he could do other people's jobs. The problem for his critics was that he usually could – with the exception of the creative ones. On his own admission, Britain's most famous advertising man – apart from the Brothers – had little creative judgement. During meetings to inspect copy, he would say, 'Marvellous, fantastic,' to the copywriter or art director, but after they had left the room he would whisper to colleagues, 'Are you sure it's all right?' It was the one chink in his advertising armoury. 'Tim couldn't judge an ad to save himself,' said a former Saatchi's executive. 'He could neither judge them nor write them. His clients would get the impression that he wrote them, art-directed them and did all the work. Not that he would have said that, but he would give that impression. His judgement was sometimes dangerously out, and if you did the opposite from what he said you'd probably be right. But once you told him the work was great, then he'd go out and sell it superbly.'[26]

Later Bell seemed irritated by this flaw and clearly did not enjoy the creative process: 'It can be fantastically frustrating working with creatives. They're petulant, difficult and refuse to pay attention and have different priorities. Dumb insolence is a classic characteristic of creative people and they are very dismissive of everybody else ... They're completely blind to the consumer. That's something they have in common with newspaper editors and television men. All of them have this arrogance, that it is not necessary for them to know what the people they communicate with actually think ... The answer is not to deal with them but to deal with their work. Liking them needn't come into it.'[27]

THE EXHIBITIONIST

For most of the 1970s Tim Bell lived, ate, slept and dreamt Saatchi and Saatchi. After his separation from Sue, the agency was his whole life. He became a workaholic, often putting in sixteen-hour days. He had virtually no personal or domestic life, ate in restaurants and hotels, and had little idea about the value of money. 'Will three hundred pounds be enough?' he once asked his secretary on sending her to buy socks, shirts and basic clothing for him. He had a large comfortable flat in Hampstead but was rarely there. His life was chasing, winning and retaining clients for the agency. He was addicted to Saatchi and Saatchi.

Old friends had always thought he had an addictive personality. For years he had tried to give up his heavy smoking habit and had once even checked into the Champneys health farm in Hertfordshire. While he was there a TV camera crew were filming a documentary on health farms and asked him why he was there. 'Because my wife laughs at me whenever she sees me naked', he joked, quick as a flash. Like Charles Saatchi, Bell was also addicted to success. But, more significantly, he needed his achievements to be noticed and recognized. If his name was not in the newspapers or over the office door, material signs and possessions would serve as a substitute. After becoming managing director of Saatchi and Saatchi in August 1973, he celebrated by buying a red Ferrari. His friend John Hegarty, the art director, thought it over-the-top and asked him why he'd wanted it. 'Well,

John, I'll tell you', replied Bell. 'When I'm at a client meeting and I'm trying to sell one of your excellent ads and I've got a 23-year-old assistant brand manager from the client telling me what's good or bad and I have to take that crap because he's the client, the only thing that consoles me is that when we go home he gets into his Vauxhall Cavalier and I get into my Ferrari.'

His colleagues were sceptical about this explanation, and, as Bell himself later told *Campaign*: 'Ever since I was a teenager, I always dreamed of owning a Ferrari . . . I work very long hours and I like to drive to and from work in a luxurious, lovely car. I enjoy being stared at and seeing the car being admired.'[28] When *Campaign* showed these comments to psychologist Martin Raw, he replied: 'He [Bell] is very self-assured – at least superficially. He is obviously a success and doesn't mind showing it. This guy is at the top of the tree and knows it. Some people might become a little nervous about having reached the top of their profession. I would think that it certainly doesn't worry him. He probably enjoys his success.'[29]

For Bell – and the Brothers – fast, flashy cars have always been a passion, not so much for their speed or mechanical prowess but for their appearance. Throughout the 1970s he had various models as a company car, first a Porsche, then a Daimler and later a bigger and better Ferrari, a G400 automatic. In 1975 he possessed a Maserati Mexico, a rare luxury, and friends were amazed by its impact on other people. Mike Renvoize recalls feeling depressed late one Friday night. He went over to see Bell, then living in Wedderburn Road, Hampstead, who suggested going out for a hamburger. They set off in the Maserati and stopped at a set of traffic lights next to a Mercedes, which contained two attractive girls in the back seat. As soon as they saw the Maserati, the girls got out of the Mercedes and scampered over to join Mike and Tim. 'There's nothing like a sports car and a pair of long legs to get over a bout of manic depression,' Mike thought.

Even though he had a chauffeur, Tim loved to show off his beloved Maserati. One evening as they left work, Saatchi employees were amused to see their boss sitting in his car outside the office with the windows wound down and the stereo turned up. He just sat there, cigarette in hand, watching the scene around him. Later in his career he would arrange for his chauffeur to drive him from his office at 80 Charlotte Street to lunch at his favourite restaurant,

L'Etoile, at number 30 – all of 250 metres away. For six years he entertained clients, cabinet ministers and friends almost daily at the table in the right-hand corner window of the restaurant, visible to everyone passing by. He was such a regular customer that the waiters would order the wine for him. After lunch his chauffeur would drive him back to the office. When asked about this habit years later, Bell was endearingly honest: 'Oh, absolutely true. I liked to use the car phone, and to be seen arriving with a chauffeur. As a kid, I always hoped to be the sort of person who could walk into restaurants and be well known. I love famous people and there's nothing quite as exciting as sitting in a restaurant where all the people around you are fantastically well known and they all know you.'[30]

This exhibitionism asserted itself somewhat differently in one of the most controversial incidents of his life. In the early hours of 21 October 1977, three days after his thirty-sixth birthday and close to the peak of his advertising career, Bell stood naked in the bathroom of his second-floor flat at 13c West Heath Road overlooking Hampstead Heath, and exposed himself to several women while masturbating. At 8.35 a.m. he was arrested and a month later, on 19 November 1977, appeared at Hampstead Magistrates Court. According to the official conviction certificate, he was charged with 'wilfully, openly, lewdly and obscenely' exposing himself 'with intent to insult a female' under Section 4 of the 1824 Vagrancy Act. He was found guilty and fined £50 with seven days to pay. Curiously, this newsworthy case was never reported in the local newspaper, the *Hampstead and Highgate Express* and only his close colleagues at Saatchi's knew of it. To his credit, Bell never flinched when the incident, which later assumed an importance of some political magnitude, was raised. He admitted the conviction but denied that the event took place. He confided to a colleague that his lawyers, Butcher Brooks and Co. advised him to plead guilty to avoid a scandal.

THE GOLDEN GIRL FROM SYDNEY

Despite Bell's workaholic existence, life was always eventful and entertaining if you worked closely with him. He had a mischievous sense of fun and humour, and could be boyish and giggly. He would hold impromptu music competitions in his office. His favourite sounds were late 1950s rock 'n' roll and American doo-wop. He would ring up John Perris, the media director, play an obscure record over the phone and take a bet on whether he could guess the performer and title of the song. If Perris got it right, Bell would jovially shout, 'Bastard,' down the line.

The staff loved his attitude – work hard and play hard. Women, in particular, found it attractive and they liked Tim Bell. Six feet tall, slim, good-looking with long wavy bleached-blond hair, his charm contained a degree of vulnerability. All that combined with his quick wit and story-telling expertise made it easy to understand what women saw in him. He enjoyed seducing them, which sometimes landed him in trouble.

After separating from Sue, Bell shared a flat with his old friend and Saatchi's colleague Roy Warman, first in St Johns Wood and then in Wedderburn Road. It was, by all accounts, a riotous two years. In 1975 Bell was having an affair with a married woman whose husband was a south London nightclub owner called 'Barry'. 'Barry' discovered what was going on and threatened to kill him. With a mixture of courage and recklessness, Bell decided to meet the aggrieved husband but took Warman along for protection. They met in the bar of the Regent Palace Hotel, with Warman sitting nervously in the background while Bell was confronted by 'Barry', accompanied by one of his security guards. 'There was a lot of finger-pointing and chest-prodding,' recalled Warman. 'The message being conveyed to Tim was that he was going to end up wearing concrete boots. The whole thing was like a B-movie. Tim was nodding and looking around, making sure I was still there.'

The following year Bell met the first of two women who would change his life. At the end of a long, hard day in the office, two young account handlers, Steve Fox and Peter Buchanan, joined him for a drink at the Three Crowns, a pub on Babmaes Place just behind the Saatchi's office. When the three sat down with their drinks, they noticed a group of attractive girls with Australian accents, notably a striking blonde. 'I fancy her,' said Fox, and went over to chat her up but without success. Then Bell walked over. It wasn't long before he had persuaded her to meet him for dinner later that evening at Animos, a lively Greek restaurant in Charlotte Street. Her name was

Virginia Wallis Hornbrook. She was twenty years old and on her first trip to London; he was thirty-five.

In appearance, Virginia bore a remarkable and uncanny resemblance to Bell's first wife Sue. Both had long, golden hair and fine facial bone structure with a shiny smile. But there the similarities ended. The daughter of a prominent Sydney family – her father was a successful doctor – Virginia was status-conscious and much more materialistic than Sue. Born in 1956, she went to school at Ascham, Sydney, where she was a bubbly, effervescent teenager. 'You had better watch out,' her headmistress told her, just before she left school.[31] After a year at secretarial college, she went to the University of New South Wales. She stayed only a year but worked on the successful campaign to elect Malcolm Fraser as Prime Minister of Australia, and appeared on his behalf on television.

Bell was besotted by the stunning Virginia almost as soon as they met. Nothing was too good for her. He spent thousands of pounds on presents and gave her a Porsche for her birthday. When she returned to Sydney, he gave Bill Muirhead, his Australian colleague, lavish gifts to pass on to Virginia when he saw her. On one occasion he sent an airline ticket to a Caribbean Island, a diamond ring and a camera.

Virginia was more cautious about their relationship. There was the fifteen-year age gap and Bell was still married. He worked such long hours, and she was a young woman who wanted to be entertained. As she longed to spend more time with him, she became increasingly unhappy. It grew into a tempestuous relationship. Virginia was also homesick for Australia and returned to Sydney several times a year. Eventually, in late 1977, frustrated with occupying second place in his life to Saatchi and Saatchi, she left him and went home.

Bell was distraught, and when Virginia returned to London he agreed to set aside more time for her. In early 1978, the couple moved into a new house on Frognal Cottages in Hampstead, which Saatchi's bought for him. An indication of his commitment to her was the astonishing sight – to his colleagues, anyway – of their managing director pushing a trolley around the supermarket with his girlfriend. As for Virginia, she was ambitious for Tim's career and enjoyed his social scene: it was not too heavy a burden to attend the endless round of client-based parties and dinners, which often involved interesting celebrities.

Virginia Hornbrook was a beautiful young woman of mettle, independent spirit and strength of character, who proved a crucial influence and factor in Tim Bell's life. Yet within a few weeks, Saatchi and Saatchi's managing director would meet another strong woman, who would play an arguably even more significant role in it.

Chapter Three

Love Stories

'One can't help bragging about knowing *her*, the Prime Minister, because it's such a wonderful thing that you think about it all the time'

Tim Bell, *Harpers & Queen*, April 1989

'It was one of the great love stories of the twentieth century'

Michael Dobbs

In the winter of 1973, the Western world was gripped by the growing political drama known as Watergate, one of the most serious constitutional crisis in American history, which forced President Richard Nixon to resign his office. He had attempted to cover up his involvement in the obstruction of justice after a burglary at the Democratic Party headquarters in Washington D.C. As the full litany of dirty tricks, illegal phone taps, sabotage, slush funds and fraud emerged, two White House aides emerged at the centre of this web of political intrigue and scandal: Robert Haldeman, Nixon's powerful chief of staff, and John Ehrlichman, his pugnacious domestic-affairs adviser. 'Every president has his son-of-a-bitch and I'm Richard Nixon's,' Haldeman told the congressional inquiry. Known as Nixon's 'two German shepherds', they spent eighteen months in jail for perjury and obstruction of justice.

As the saga unfolded daily on television, the 32-year-old Tim Bell was fascinated by how Haldeman, a former J. Walter Thompson executive in charge of clients like 7-Up and Disneyland – had turned political fixer and successfully sold a right-wing candidate to the American public in the 1968 Presidential election. It was

Haldeman who had persuaded several of his colleagues at JWT – Dwight Chapin, Larry Higby, Ron Ziegler and Ken Cole – to leave the agency and work full-time for the Nixon campaign. They then all entered the White House as the President's Men. 'Tim was in awe of those guys', said Mike Renvoize. 'He thought they were wonderful, particularly the way they stage-managed events. It wasn't about politics. Which side you were on didn't matter to him. He admired them because they had the power and could exert influence at the highest level'. According to Renvoize, it was clear that Bell aspired to play a similar role – at the centre of the action. For most of his twenties he had been more interested in making money than being a party political activist, but in the 1960s he had canvassed for Tory MPs like Iain MacLeod, in Totteridge, Reginald Maudling in Barnet and even Margaret Thatcher in nearby Finchley.[1] 'I think he liked the *idea* of being an MP,' recalled Renvoize. Bell's stepfather, Peter Pettit, was, of course, a prominent Conservative, and through him Tim had met local and national politicians. He had also been a Tory member of Elstree Parish Council during the sixties while he lived in the area, and later joined Hampstead Conservative Association.

Bell's 'political' ambition was more to do with exerting influence than being elected to high office. The opportunity for fulfilling such a role came in 1978 when an ebullient television producer, with an extravagant taste for champagne and cigars, was appointed director of publicity at Tory Central Office. His name was Gordon James Reece. Not only did he revolutionise political communications, but he became one of Tim Bell's closest friends.

Born in Liverpool in 1930, the son of a car salesman, Reece was educated at Ratcliffe College, a Catholic public school where one of his contemporaries was Norman St. John Stevas, then plain Norman Stevas and later a Conservative Cabinet Minister. A vigilant Catholic, Stevas reported young Reece to the headmaster for alleged atheism. This was almost certainly unfair: later in life Reece became a devout Roman Catholic, sometimes attending church four times on a Sunday. 'Church services,' he said, in the 1970s, 'are so wonderful that they ought to charge for them . . . I think religion is the coming thing. People are ready for it.'[2]

After national service in the RAF, Reece read law at Downing College, Cambridge, but did not pursue a legal career. 'There was no money for young barristers in those days', he said later[3].

In 1960, aged thirty, he began to work as a reporter for the *Liverpool Daily Post* and then the *Sunday Express*. But it was not until he joined ATV as a television producer that he found his true talent. Characteristically, he started with religious broadcasts, then moved to *Emergency Ward 10*, and covered the 1964 election campaign in the ITN studio. In the late 1960s he produced programmes on ITV for Eamonn Andrews (*This Is Your Life*), the comedians Spike Milligan and Dave Allen, of whom he is proudest, and Bruce Forsyth.

It was during the 1970 general election campaign that he first met Margaret Thatcher, then a rising star as shadow education secretary. Reece was joint managing director, with the broadcaster Cliff Michelmore, of RM EMI Ltd, a video-cassette company, but was hired as a freelance producer to supervise the Tories' party political broadcasts. He was immediately impressed by her steely resolve and believed her strength of character could, eventually, be projected powerfully on television. The two worked well together and kept in touch.

Reece's opportunity arrived in February 1975, during Mrs Thatcher's successful campaign for the Conservative Party leadership. It was his idea that she appear on Granada TV's *World In Action* washing up in a pinafore at her house in Flood Street, Chelsea, just before the poll. It had such an impact that when William Whitelaw entered the contest for the second ballot, his advisers thought that as this photo-opportunity had secured her extra votes he should also be pictured in domestic pose. Thankfully the idea was shelved.[4]

Four months after Mrs Thatcher's election as opposition leader, Reece joined her staff at the House of Commons for a year as an 'adviser', on secondment from EMI, for which the party paid him a nominal fee. Although he counselled her on all extra-parliamentary activities, Reece became essentially her image-maker. The relationship prospered, and he did not return to EMI. Margaret Thatcher has always preferred charming, can-do, self-made men with a touch of flash to more traditional Tories. Perhaps because she is so serious and sober, she has a weakness for extrovert gregarious men from her own class background who look her in the eye, make her laugh and gently flirt with her. Reece fitted that bill and developed an almost unassailable place in her affections. 'Gordon was a godsend,' she recalled. 'His good humour never failed and he was able to jolly me along to accept things I would have rejected from other people.'[5]

Reece was anxious to make it clear that his brief was presentation not the issues. 'I am in no way a policy-maker', he said, in 1975. 'You know, the sort of chap who makes you sick – after a year's research thinks he can whisper in the ear of the king, or in this case the queen . . . My job is to present Mrs Thatcher to the country.'[6]

The former TV producer wasted little time in reshaping the leader's appearance and manner, particularly for television interviews. Within a few weeks, she was a new woman. Gone were the top heavy garden-fête hats, so beloved of Conservative ladies. Suddenly, there was a groomed, softer hairstyle. Here are some of the tips that Reece offered to her: 'It is important not to wear a lot of fuss on television. Edges look good but scoop necklines are out. The ideal outfit is a tunic dress with a shirt underneath. Go easy on lots of jewellery near the face. Stick to pastels. And look out for the background. If you are wearing a bright green dress and the background is bright blue, then it's a shambles. And instinctively this kind of conflict makes the viewer dissatisfied. Behave quite naturally. Hands can look wrong on television, so keep them out of the way. The greatest mistake on television is trying to act in front of the cameras.'[7]

Reece realised that Mrs Thatcher was not a natural performer on television. He remembered a party political broadcast in 1970 that was scuppered by her inept camera style. 'She was filmed in a park where she was surrounded by kids going up and down slides screaming,' recalled advertising executive Barry Day. 'Margaret looked extremely out of touch. She was saying, "I believe you should have a choice for your children," but gave the impression she hoped they wouldn't be sick all over her dress. She was very ill at ease with the camera and the children: it was amateur night.'[8]

Even after becoming party leader, Mrs Thatcher was never comfortable under the bright lights and cramped spaces of a TV studio. Her nervous tension showed up in her strident, high-pitched, hurried delivery, which came across during interviews. 'Winston was never on television', she then remarked, 'certainly never interviewed on it.'[9] In a memorable phrase, the BBC political reporter Michael Cockerell said that she 'reacted to television like an African tribesman faced with a tourist's camera: she almost seemed to believe it would take her soul away'. She was clearly uneasy about the whole process.

'It's not really me you're seeing, because so far I don't feel natural on television', she said, in early 1975.[10]

To her credit and unlike many senior Tories then, Mrs Thatcher was astute enough to understand the growing political significance of television, both in terms of communicating her message and long-term electoral success. She saw her political creed as a product in the market-place, which needed to be sold. 'If you have got a good thing to sell', she said later, 'use every single capacity you can to sell it. It is no earthly use having a good thing and no one hearing about it.'[11] But she was also aware of her own limitations and was not too proud to ask experts for help. She became Gordon Reece's willing pupil, which heralded many agonising and protracted sessions with her Svengali-like master. 'It was quite an education,' said Mrs Thatcher, looking back.[12]

Reece's seminars were based on the results of regular private opinion polls commissioned immediately after Mrs Thatcher's TV broadcasts. He concluded that the most difficult problem was His Mistress' Voice. It was high-pitched, rather shrill, and when she spoke in the Commons she tended to shriek. The elocution lessons she had had in her youth also gave her a contrived, exaggerated, upper-class accent that grated on the ear, and Tory supporters said it would lose her working-class votes. In the privacy of a closed-circuit studio, Reece spent many hours with her overseeing what were, effectively, reverse elocution lessons to make her speech more ordinary. He hired a voice tutor from the National Theatre to give her humming lessons to lower her tone and to teach her to speak more slowly. 'Gordon found me an expert who knew that the first thing to do was to get your breathing right', recalled Mrs Thatcher, in her memoirs, 'and then to speak not from the back of the throat but from the front of the mouth. She was a genius and a great help.'[13]

Thanks to the tuition, the pitch of Mrs Thatcher's voice dropped. Reece took her to meet Sir Laurence Olivier, in case he had any further useful tips. He complimented her on her delivery. On Reece's advice she began to speak closer to the microphone during speeches so that she would sound more intimate. One newspaper noted that this gave her voice a husky, even sexy quality. When this was published Jim Prior, then shadow employment secretary, telephoned her to ask if she had had a cold or a sore throat. 'No,' she replied rather indignantly. 'I've never been so insulted in my life,' she said later, laughing.[14]

The next task for Reece was the way television itself presented the new Margaret Thatcher. By 1977, as he had suggested, she had changed her hair, clothes and voice. Now he would attempt to control how and where that new image was transmitted. The previous year he had spent considerable time in the USA, studying the Presidential campaign between Jimmy Carter and Gerald Ford, and noticed the power and prominence of the 'photo-opportunity', the placing of the candidate in a variety of visually interesting and telegenic situations to highlight different aspects of their personality. Or, as the *Guardian* journalist Michael White put it, 'television with the sound turned down'.[15] He rationed her appearances on current-affairs programmes and drew up an 'enemies list' of broadcasters he considered too hostile or left-wing, notably Lew Gardner of Thames TV, and she refused to be interviewed by them.[16] Instead, she appeared on general-interest programmes like *Jim'll Fix It* to reach a broader, less politically committed audience.

However, there was one final element in Reece's communications revolution: political advertising.

'OVER MY DEAD BODY'

In January 1978, Reece moved from the House of Commons to Tory Central Office as the party's director of publicity. His job description was simple: win the election. But when he arrived at Smith Square, some Tory grandees were bemused and uneasy at his presence. At first there was tension: he had scant respect for the old guard bureaucrats and their 'awful Forties war-movie accents'.[17] They, in turn, were suspicious of his new ideas and flamboyant lifestyle, with his devotion to expensive torpedo-shaped cigars, handmade pink shirts, silk ties and handkerchiefs. But it was his passion for vintage Krug and Lanson that caused the most trouble. Lady (Janet) Young, then a deputy chairman at Tory Central Office, claimed he was charging exorbitant expenses for champagne. 'I did question it,' she recalled. 'He seemed to breakfast on champagne and gulls' eggs and I didn't think it was a good image for the party. It made fund-raising more difficult because it undermined our efforts to attract donations. How could we approach individuals and companies on the basis that we needed the money if our own money was being spent in this way?' She raised the matter with Lord McAlpine, the party treasurer. 'Something should be done,' she said.

'Do you have a car, Janet?' replied McAlpine.

'Yes, a small one.'

'But you have to buy petrol for it, don't you? You see, if you have a Gordon Reece you have to run him on champagne.'[18]

Reece's professional colleagues were more impressed with him, despite some initial misgivings. 'When Gordon first arrived I had never met anyone like him,' said David Boddy, then a press officer at Central Office. 'He appeared to do absolutely nothing. On the surface all he seemed to do was sit in his office, drink champagne and smoke cigars, but everything that was supposed to happen did happen and worked. He didn't understand the press too well but he knew how to communicate a political message and he was brilliant at it.'

Despite his deceptively laid-back manner, Reece had an eye for detail. More importantly, he was a lateral, strategic thinker, and he wanted to import some of the techniques he'd seen used during the Presidential campaigns by Lyndon Johnson in 1964 and Richard Nixon in 1968. He had also been impressed by the methods adopted by the Australian Liberal Party – the equivalent of the UK's Conservatives – during their successful election campaign in early 1978. These had used an advertising agency to great effect and its communications director, Tony Egleton, came to London for a meeting with Reece and Mrs Thatcher to discuss how a Labour government could be toppled. Afterwards Reece realised that reliance on the Tory press would not be sufficient: he needed extra firepower. But he was unhappy with the existing collegiate approach to advertising at Central Office: 'I've always thought a committee approach to running a political campaign is a very bad idea,' said Reece. 'One of the reasons is that they're all chiefs and there isn't a single Indian there. And when you end up trying to get rid of someone it's the Battle of Hastings, because he resigns in a huff and you have to explain it to the newspapers and it becomes a *cause célèbre*. If you've got an agency, you simply tell the managing director to change a chap because you don't get on with him, and he is changed.'[19]

In late February 1978, after having agreed the idea with Mrs Thatcher, Reece began his search for the right one. 'I was looking for an agency with a rising reputation, but not too big,' he reflected. 'One that was hungry, with creative people. Large enough for the media clout we required, but not a giant corporation . . . I wanted somebody who would say, "God, we could get really famous if we did this properly." '[20]

Saatchi and Saatchi, of course, fitted that design perfectly and particularly the last qualification. Their controversial public-service advertisements also gave them an edge. After a recommendation from Terry Donovan, the flamboyant photographer who knew Charles Saatchi, Reece went to Charlotte Street. His approach was characteristically informal and an almost casual one-hour round-table discussion took place with Maurice Saatchi, Ron Leagas, Roderick More and John Perris. Like Tim Bell, Reece liked to work on instinct and was feeling out Saatchi's. He was more interested in their general attitude and working methods than their specific ideas for the Tory account.

Maurice Saatchi saw the account in purely commercial terms. He told Reece, 'We would like it very much,' concluding, 'and we are all Conservatives here.' (That was not true, but perhaps he gambled that the truth would not be discovered.) The Tory publicity chief was impressed: 'There was a dynamism about the place,' he said. 'It was the coiled spring, the kettle bubbling. I felt I had to get them appointed.'[21]

The Brothers guessed correctly that Reece had already made up his mind but their top account handler, Tim Bell, was on holiday in the West Indies. Maurice rang Bell in Barbados that afternoon with Ron Leagas listening in on the squawk box. 'What do you think?' asked Maurice.

'Over my dead body do we take this account on,' replied Bell, who claimed that political party accounts had damaged other agencies, like Kingsley Manton Palmer, who had run Labour's campaign in 1964, and Colman Prentis and Varley, who had had the Tory account in 1959. 'It's a bad idea,' he said, clearly irritated. 'It will be completely disruptive to the whole agency and there won't be much money in it. I don't think we should do it.'

Bell's argument was that failure would be very public; the account would divert resources for no real commercial return; and existing clients might not approve because not all of them were Conservative supporters. 'I'm coming straight back,' he said Bell sharply. When

Leagas turned off the machine, Maurice dismissed Bell's view: 'Don't worry, it doesn't matter what he says.'

The Brothers were delighted by the prospect of the Tory account but before Reece could appoint Saatchi's, he needed authorisation from Lord Thorneycroft, then party chairman. The problem was that no one from the agency was available for the meeting at Central Office. Maurice Saatchi was out of town on Proctor and Gamble business, and Charles refused to go as he did not meet clients. It was Roderick More, a junior account executive, who met Thorneycroft. Reece, who had expected Maurice or Charles, introduced him 'as the top man who handles all these matters at Saatchi and Saatchi'. They talked about everything except political advertising and at the end of their conversation Thorneycroft formally awarded Saatchi's the account. As More and Reece walked out into Smith Square, they encountered a breathless, worried-looking Maurice Saatchi to whom More, rather bewildered by his meeting, was able to give the good news.

The Brothers wanted the Tory account because they knew that close association with the Party would generate free publicity, contacts, and more and bigger clients. Their own political stance was immaterial. After all, this was the agency that had devised the advertisement for the launch of *Cosmopolitan* magazine in January 1972. It consisted of photographs in two columns of prominent women: those on the left-hand side would read the magazine; those on the right, however, were unlikely to do so and their faces were crossed out. Beside the latter group a caption read: '*Cosmopolitan* isn't for every woman.' One of these women was Margaret Thatcher.

That Saatchi and Saatchi were working for the Tory Party was rich in irony and so was Maurice Saatchi's remark to Gordon Reece that 'We are all Conservatives here.' During the 1974 general election campaign, an account executive had said to Maurice: 'I can't imagine myself ever voting Conservative.' Maurice concurred: 'I agree,' he replied. Charles was more consistent in his views: he was apolitical. Contemptuous of all politicians and parties, he was iconoclastic and idiosyncratic. If anything, he was closer to being an anarchist. And in 1975 Saatchi's had worked for the Labour administration. They had been hired by Michael Foot, the left-wing Secretary of State for Employment and later party leader, to show how concerned the government was about the vicious circle of unemployment so the following ad was used: 'I can't get a job without experience and I can't get experience without a job. Vicious, isn't it?'

Saatchi's links with Labour actually went back to the general election of October 1974. Notley Advertising was then working for Transport House, and had been commissioned to buy advertising space and produce the party's advertisements but not to design them. Saatchi's took over Notley in 1975 and retained the client. By 1976, they wanted to expand the account and approached Percy Clark, then Labour's director of publicity. 'They offered to do our publicity and take over any future advertising campaign,' said Clark. 'We had to explain that our principles were that we did not use agencies to project our image, but we had no objection to giving them a campaign.'[22] Saatchi's were appointed to promote the party newspaper, *Labour Weekly*. Labour was happy with the campaign, so Saatchi's lobbied for the full business: 'It was quite clear that they were after the major thing, which was taking over the Labour Party's image,' said Clark. 'To use an expression in the trade, they "nursed" one of my colleagues with lunches and so on and were pressing the case that Saatchi's would make a good job of putting the Labour Party across.'[23] It was only when they were hired by the Conservatives that these links with Labour were severed.

For the Brothers 'business is business'. According to former Saatchi executives, they would do anything as long as it was legal. 'If taking hard drugs was made legal then they would have taken on the account,' said Alex Fynn. Bell took a similar view: the moral aspect of advertising was irrelevant. 'I'm not a priest or a public figure or an elected official,' Bell told the *Observer*'s John Sweeney. 'Outside the legal framework, society is made up of individuals and people should be allowed to make up their own minds about what they believe in and what they don't.'

The irony of Saatchi's holding the anti-smoking account for the Health Education Council (HEC) was not lost on the agency's employees: Bell was a heavy smoker and Charles Saatchi also indulged, usually on social occasions. In the early years, a TV camera crew recorded an interview with him about the anti-smoking campaign. Charles was nervous and needed several takes to deliver his rousing condemnation of smoking. Exhausted by the experience, he waited for the cameras to leave and then declared: 'Shit, someone give me a fag. I'm dying for a smoke.'[24] And when Saatchi executives attended meetings at the HEC, Alastair Mackie, its director-general, would thoughtfully bring out an ashtray for Bell.

In 1983 a new HEC director-general, David Player, asked Saatchi's to repitch for the account but they withdrew. Within a few weeks they had secured the Gallaher account for Silk Cut. Saatchi's went on to produce some award-winning advertisements, notably one by Charles that featured a pair of scissors slicing across a bed of silk. Some employees were aghast at the effrontery and hypocrisy. 'To me it was heresy, to them [the Brothers] it was business,' said Fynn, who had worked on the HEC account for thirteen years.

In the spring of 1978, though, Saatchi's were basking in the glory reflected from the Tory account. And no one did so more than Tim Bell. By the time he had returned to London from his Caribbean holiday, the Brothers had already officially taken on the Tory Party account and he had been assigned the client. This was partly because he was the senior account handler but also because he was by far the most politically motivated in the agency. 'I was a very committed Conservative,' he said later, 'but it's not something I ever discussed with the Brothers. We never talked politics at all. We were businessmen influenced by the political environment, and it never occurred to us to think about how to influence the politicians.'[25]

When Gordon Reece hired Saatchi and Saatchi in March 1978, he was convinced there would be an election that autumn and was anxious to set them to work. In his view, governments do well during the warmer months so he planned a summer offensive and scheduled a meeting.

When Bell and his team arrived in Lord Thorneycroft's office, Reece was impressed but some of the more strait-laced, old-school Tories were initially wary. Lady Young noticed that Bell wore an open-necked shirt, a silver necklace and almost shoulder-length hair. She mistrusted such brash, flash young chaps from an untried agency, who had never fought an election campaign or stood for public office and seemed to know nothing about real politics. It was also, she noted, going to cost the party a large amount of money. However, as soon as she saw the quality of the 'clever and effective' posters, Lady Young was won over.

Old Etonian Lord Thorneycroft developed a warm, fruitful working relationship with the agency. He appreciated their cavalier attacking style while they liked his genial personality and wry sense of humour. After he and Mrs Thatcher had paid a secret visit to the Saatchi's office in Charlotte Street, he was escorted into the underground car park. He gazed at the display of expensive cars. Among the Ferraris and Aston Martins was a large Cherokee jeep with bull bars on the front. 'Who drives that?' he asked.

'It belongs to Charles Saatchi,' said Roy Warman, who was with him.

'Get a lot of trouble with cattle in Hampstead, does he?' replied Lord Thorneycroft.

On another occasion he was walking down the stairs of Central Office with Lord McAlpine when he saw Bell walking briskly towards them. 'Oh, Lord, Alastair,' he said. 'There's that fellow Bell. He'll want some more money. You'd better take someone out to lunch.'

Mrs Thatcher needed little persuading to sanction the use of a full-time advertising agency in the election campaign – for the first time since Harold Macmillan had employed Colman Prentis and Varley in 1959. 'There was no question of the advertising agency devising what that message was, of course,' she later said. 'But politicians should resist the temptation to consider themselves experts in fields where they have no experience.'[26]

The expert responsible for liaising with her was, of course, Tim Bell. He had met her briefly during the 1966 campaign while canvassing in Finchley. However, his first proper audience with her, twelve years later, proved rather more auspicious. It took place in her room at the House of Commons in April 1978. Bell was excited as he walked up the stairs, high in the turrets of Westminster, and then along the corridor. Outside her office he encountered Airey Neave, her closest political adviser who had masterminded her bid for the Tory Party leadership. 'You're going to meet Mrs Thatcher, aren't you?' said Neave. 'You'll find it quite a daunting experience, but you'll just have to see how you get on.'

Bell walked another ten yards into the office and was greeted by two secretaries, Alison Ward (now Wakeham) and Caroline Stephens (now Ryder). 'Who are you?' asked one. 'I'm from er . . .' began Bell nervously.

'I know,' she interrupted, 'you're the man from Starsky and Hutch,' and ushered him into the opposition leader's room.

He shook hands with Mrs Thatcher, then sat down in the middle of a large brown sofa. She sat opposite him and set out her views in a characteristically blunt fashion. 'You will find that politicians have very large fingers and very large toes,' she told him, 'and you must be frightfully careful not to tread on them by accident, which they don't like. I, however, have no fingers or toes – and you will tell me the truth at all times, however painful you might think it will be for me.'

Bell was stunned but impressed. 'Fine, I'll be delighted to do that,' he replied. She then added a note of caution: 'If you paint a picture of me that isn't true and I get elected,' she said, 'then I won't be able to do what I want because people will expect me to do something else.' She told Bell she would not interfere with the creative work, but gave him one piece of advice – a lesson she had learned during her first election campaign in Dartford in 1951. Her Labour opponent, Norman Dodds, had compiled posters with the slogan 'Dodds Again for Dartford' leaving blank white space around the words. Her young Conservative supporters amended the posters to read: 'Odds Against Dodds Again for Dartford.' 'Don't make posters that people can write on,' she said, and smiled with the look of a seasoned political street-fighter.[27]

Mrs Thatcher concluded the meeting by asking: 'What's your favourite poem?'.

'"If" by Rudyard Kipling,' replied Bell.

'Mine too,' she said, as she produced a battered volume from her handbag. 'What's your favourite speech?'

'Abraham Lincoln's State of the Nation address when he said, "I fail to see how you will make the weak strong by making the strong weak."'

'That's my favourite speech too,' she declared, delighted, as she pulled out a crumpled copy of it. 'I think we're going to get on famously.'

After the meeting, Mrs Thatcher wrote to Bell emphasising how important communications were to her political strategy. She told him that she was aware that people would say there was something immoral about using an advertising agency in this way, but that she was quite happy to do so. 'She had got past the stage of whether it should or should not happen,' said Bell.[28] She knew what she wanted to say. She just needed to learn how to say it.

Saatchi's managing director had established an immediate personal rapport with Margaret Thatcher. Like Gordon Reece, he understood how important personal relationships were to her. 'He filled her with confidence,' David Boddy, who succeeded Reece at Central Office as director of publicity, told me. 'He never really argued with her, but could persuade her round to his point of view. He was never a yes man but could bring her round with that winning smile.'

She also liked his volatility. 'It's his great strength,' said Michael Dobbs, then Mrs Thatcher's researcher who worked closely with Bell. 'It enables him to give unconventional advice when the going gets tough. Mrs Thatcher liked having emotional people around her, people who could make her laugh and share her tears.'[29] Later she referred to Reece and Bell as 'the laughing boys', for their constant optimism.[30]

Despite Tim Bell's supreme self-confidence, he was isolated from the political environment and Establishment of the time. He was a novice. According to David Boddy and other former colleagues, he did not understand the issues and had only a light political touch – but he was an advertising man, not a politician. However, being an outsider and free of ideological baggage was, in fact, a distinct advantage. He was not shackled by the old prejudices of the party officials and could promote clear messages that ordinary people could understand. He knew what the middle-class voter aspired to because he was one of them, so his political naïvety turned out to be an asset.

'ATTACK, ATTACK, ATTACK . . .'

In April 1978, after Mrs Thatcher had shown the green light, the pressure was on. Bell immediately commissioned his own market research as he was unimpressed by the statistical rigidity of Central Office's work. He pored over the results with mixed feelings as he concluded that Mrs Thatcher would be difficult to sell. Despite Gordon Reece's media wizardry, she still looked and sounded like an archetypal middle-class Tory housewife when she needed to be marketed as the potential leader of one of the major powers of the Western world. However, the research confirmed that the

Conservatives still had substantial support on issues connected to individuals. As Bell and his colleagues compiled their first strategy document the issues crystallised: choice, freedom and minimum state interference. Disillusionment with the Labour government was also an important factor. They identified potential Conservative voters to target: the young first-time voters, women in council housing and traditionally Labour households and skilled manual workers. Bell even mentioned the relatives of trade-union leaders as the kind of people the party needed to attract: 'We'd been through the Winter of Discontent and the nightmare of the trade union grip on the way we lived our lives,' reflected Bell. 'We worked out audiences of people who we could persuade because of these circumstances – like wives of trade union leaders – because we figured that women were probably fed up with their husbands coming home and saying, "I'm on strike again, dear." Women seemed a natural audience.'[31]

Essentially, Bell and Reece focused their communications strategy on winning over working-class women, 'soft' Labour or Liberal voters and skilled manual workers. In their view, these people were more likely to be persuaded by impressions than arguments. 'You have to create impressions,' said Reece. 'That's what people vote on, not issues.'[32] He based this judgement on the assumption that many people do not think rationally about politics and are influenced by their emotions and prejudices. As voters carry in their heads simple images and themes, they are susceptible to propaganda and symbolic simplistic messages. Bell and Reece believed that most voters thought about public affairs in terms of stereotypes, largely because most found politics complex and remote compared to, say, the household budget. The image-makers concentrated therefore on basic emotional responses. In other words, the campaign would be about values not policies.

It was on this basis that Bell and his team planned to research consumers' (voters) emotional reaction to the product (election promises) and then reduce the objectives of the client (Tory Party) to their most elementary, almost tabloid level. In a presentation to Reece and Lord Thorneycroft, Bell outlined his tactics: 'We were not talking about incomes policies, tax cuts, industrial relations or public expenditure,' recalled Bell. 'We were talking about the emotional meaning of a Conservative vote.'[33]

This emphasis on people's gut instincts set the style of Saatchi's advertising. 'We wanted a tone which was warm, confident, non-divisive and exciting,' said Bell. "Warmth" just means talking *to* people rather than *at* them. The Conservative Party had long been perceived as a cold and unsympathetic party. This needed to be changed. 'Confidence', on the other hand, was an attribute we worked to re-create. Looking at the research over the previous twenty years, we found that the Conservative Party had lost its position as the party ranked by the electorate as the most competent and confident. It was, therefore, essential for us to talk in a confident tone, as though we knew that Conservative policies would work.'[34]

The agency knew that the public were disillusioned with the Labour government: 'Everything we did was directed towards increasing the salience of this dissatisfaction,' Bell said later. 'I make no apologies at all for saying that advertising, as a form of mass communication, is inevitably a blunt, crude, direct instrument.'[35] The chief exponent of that weapon at Saatchi's was Jeremy Sinclair. 'Our philosophy is to attack first,' he said. 'Attack, attack, attack . . . Even when they [the Tory Party] were in power we maintained the mentality of a marauding opposition. This was our instinct.'[36]

Bell's first opportunity to turn these ideas into hard advertising copy came in June 1978. Saatchi's had been asked to compile their first presentation to Mrs Thatcher for her approval of that summer's advertising offensive. Simple, clear, direct and aggressive messages had always been Saatchi's approach to advertising and now they were to be used to great effect. The most deadly nearly missed being deployed. It depicted a queue snaking into the distance outside an unemployment office, with the slogan, 'Labour Isn't Working.' The pay-off line, 'Britain's Better With the Conservatives', echoed 'Life's Better With the Conservatives' which had been used in the 1959 campaign. It was a brilliant advertisement but just one of twelve ideas proposed on the Sunday before the presentation. Incredibly, it was placed in the 'Possibles' file and effectively discarded by Bell and Charles Saatchi. Andrew Rutherford, the copywriter who had devised it, discovered that it was not going to be put forward and secretly reinstated the copy.

The next day Bell and Maurice Saatchi drove to Scotney Castle in Kent where Mrs Thatcher had rented a large apartment for the presentation. They were joined by Gordon Reece and Ronald Millar, the Tory Party leader's speech-writer. Bell's brief was an anti-Labour campaign and, ambitiously, Saatchi's had decided to attack them on a traditionally Labour issue. He showed Mrs Thatcher several advertisements, including 'Labour Isn't Working'.

She stared at it for a long time: the convention in party propaganda was not to mention the opponent directly. 'Why is the biggest thing on this poster the name of the opposition? We're advertising Labour,' she said. Bell and Maurice replied, almost in unison, 'No, we're demolishing Labour.'[37] They convinced her that it would undermine confidence in the Labour Party to a dynamic degree and she authorised its use.

After the presentation, Saatchi's needed to make the visual side work and persuaded a group of Young Conservatives from Hendon to pose as if they were standing in a dole queue. In August 1978, the poster was placed on only twenty sites nationally. But it had a huge impact.

Labour reacted furiously to the advertisement. Denis Healey, then Chancellor of the Exchequer, claimed that the dole queue in the poster was a 'fraud' because the people pictured were not unemployed but Saatchi and Saatchi employees. Although this was not far from the truth, his outburst gave the ad even more prominence, drew increased attention to the issue and, of course, generated considerable free publicity for Saatchi's. Bell loved the controversy. 'Healey made a great song and dance and it got shown on every television broadcast,' he said later. 'Then it got shown on discussion programmes. We must have had £5 million worth of free publicity.'[38] Not bad for an ad that had only cost £50,000.

'Labour Isn't Working' struck at the heart of the government, and Saatchi's quickly followed up with more controversial offerings. One ad on law and order stated boldly, 'Mugging Up 204 per cent, Criminal Damage Up 135 per cent – Is It Safe To Vote for Another Labour Government?' 'Many critics claimed exactly the same thing had happened under the last Conservative government,' Bell acknowledged. 'I must confess I didn't myself see how this negated the point of our advertisement.'[39]

By the first week of September 1978, Saatchi's were prepared for battle. Maurice had outlined their strategy in a one-page paper that started with the proposition: 'Governments lose elections, oppositions don't win them.'[40] Everything needed to be focused on exploiting people's dissatisfaction and disillusionment with Labour. 'Hit first, hit hard and keep on hitting' was his policy. First, though, they needed an arena to display their weaponry. On 7 September 1978, James Callaghan, the Labour Prime Minister, announced that he would not be calling an election in the autumn. Bell was 'savagely depressed', given the amount of work the Saatchi team had done.[41] That evening he attempted to restore their spirits over champagne with Gordon Reece at a West End restaurant. Mrs Thatcher shared the sense of anti climax and telephoned Bell at home later that night to ask how he was taking the news. Just as she was about to ask after Reece, Bell suddenly shouted, 'My God, I've been burgled.' So he had, but nothing was taken.[42]

BROADCASTING THE SAATCHI MESSAGE

It was up to Saatchi and Saatchi also to produce the Conservatives' party political broadcasts (PPB). It was not an easy task. Over time they had become dull, lifeless, consisting largely of senior ministers preaching to the party faithful. Saatchi's realised that if they were to persuade the unconverted, floating voter to watch them, the format needed radical changes: they became fast-moving, clearer and visually innovative.

However, some at Central Office were concerned that the draft scripts were not always in line with party policy. Dermot Gleeson in the research department checked their content and found that Saatchi's were occasionally producing material they believed the people wanted to hear, rather than what the manifesto stated: Saatchi's felt that conservative policies were not in line with popular thinking. Lady Young confirmed this: 'Yes, we had to keep a sharp eye on that,' she said.

Bell and his colleagues had been heavily influenced by an advertisement used by Lyndon Johnson during his successful 1964 campaign to be re-elected as President. The film showed a little girl picking the petals from a flower one by one. After the last, a mushroom cloud appeared and the voice-over said, 'If you want your children, don't vote for Barry Goldwater. Vote as if your life depended on it.' Bell thought the ad brilliant. 'Tremendous

Tim Bell's mother, Greta Findlay, with his step-father, Peter Pettit, at the family home in Totteridge, north London, in 1961

Nicholas Soames, then Minister for Food, makes his point during a party in late
April 1992, while Bell's close friend, Sir David Frost, looks on

LIKE FATHER, LIKE SON. Tim's father, Arthur 'Paddy' Bell, in 1956 when he was 50 years old. After divorcing Bell's mother, Paddy emigrated to South Africa where he became a radio celebrity. Tim (pictured left at the same age) bears a striking resemblance to his father

Bell's step-father, Peter Pettit, on becoming Mayor of Marylebone in 1961. A solicitor and Conservative councillor, Pettit was an accomplished if reserved man

FIRST LOVE. Suzanne Melodie Cordran, whom Tim married in 1965. A model and designer, she appears here in an advertisement for maternity wear. The couple separated amicably in 1974 but did not divorce until 1985. In appearance, Sue bears an uncanny similarity to Tim's second wife, Virginia

Tim Bell (far right) with friends at a wedding in Barnet. His close friend, Mike Renvoize, is second on the left and Sue, his then wife, is third on the right

A NEW ADVERTISING. Bell (centre) with Charles Saatchi (left) and his younger brother Maurice (right) in 1970, the year Saatchi and Saatchi was launched. Behind them is the famous poster of the 'pregnant man' which established the agency as one of the most innovative and controversial of their generation

The Saatchi brothers in 1988 at the height of their fame and corporate success. It was also the lowest point of their relationship with Tim Bell after the rows during the 1987 election campaign

SPOILS OF SUCCESS. As managing director of Saatchi and Saatchi, the flamboyant Bell was financially well rewarded and he took every opportunity to show off the fruits of his labour. Here he is (*left* and *below*) in 1978 posing by one of his beloved cars, a Ferrari

Bottom Picture: Bell with Mike Russell-Hills, a film director who made commercials for Saatchi and Saatchi, in 1978. The two spent a lot of time together socially in the late 1970s and early 1980s

SELLING THATCHER. Sir Gordon Reece, former director of communications for the Conservative Party, holding Saatchi and Saatchi advertisements in Central Office during the 1979 General Election campaign. Later knighted by Mrs Thatcher, Reece became one of Bell's closest friends emotional imagery,' he said. 'What the ad did in a very simplistic way was to crystallise the total political argument in a single issue.'[43]

Saatchi's first PPB depicted Britain going backwards under Labour with shots of people walking backwards, of Stephenson's Rocket steaming backwards and the world's first jet-liner landing in reverse. The final sequence showed Michael Heseltine saying. 'Britain is going backwards. Backwards or forwards, because we can't go on as we are. Don't just hope for a better life – vote for one.'

Bell himself was more involved in the PPBs than the press advertising, particularly when it came to filming Mrs Thatcher. As early as the autumn of 1978, the two had established a close mutual regard. 'He could make her do things in relation to her image that others couldn't,' recalled Adrian Rowbotham, who directed many of the PPBs. At first she was co-operative but nervous and did not enjoy being filmed. To help her relax, and melt her almost frozen expression, Bell would sit behind the camera and smile at her. If that didn't work he pulled faces. She found the whole process difficult and depended on Bell, particularly for her facial expressions while delivering a speech. During filming she would rattle off a series of questions at him: 'How do I sit? Where do I put my hands? What facial expressions should I adopt? Am I going too slow or too fast?' And 'Is the tone right?' was a favourite.

He also provided private counsel for Mrs Thatcher's studio television interviews. She was a competitive, combative interviewee: if the questioner asked her something that was designed to make her look fallible or weak, she could not resist the opportunity to hit back hard and attempt to undermine them. It would then become a battle between her and the interviewer. Bell realised this was a mistake: 'You ought to be talking to the audience and not to the interviewer,' he would suggest.

As a way of rehearsal, Bell and others would visit Mrs Thatcher the evening before a major TV interview. Suddenly, she would say: 'OK, be a nasty interviewer.' Bell would then ask hostile questions. 'Sometimes if you are playing nasty interviewer and she gives you the strong answers, you end up apologising for having asked such a nasty, stupid question,' he recalled. 'It's only afterwards that you remember it's a game, but she is very tough about television. She knows she is talking to millions of people, that the images are very quick and open to misinterpretation, so she's very conscious of being accurate. That's one of the reasons why she speaks so slowly.'[44]

As 1979 dawned, Bell and Saatchi's were handed a perfect propaganda coup in the form of the 'Winter of Discontent'. A wave of public-service disputes hit the country after the government imposed a 5 per cent limit on pay increases. Strikes involving lorry drivers, dustmen, ambulancemen and even grave diggers resulted in chaos. On 10 January 1979, Prime Minister Callaghan returned from a summit in Guadeloupe and told reporters: 'I don't think other people in the world would share the view that there is mounting chaos.' Although his comment was misreported by the *Sun* on their front page as 'Crisis? What Crisis?', many people disagreed with him.

Saatchi's immediately tried to take advantage of this by producing a double-page spread in all the popular newspapers: 'Why Every Trade Unionist Should Consider Voting Conservative.' They also attempted to catch the mood of the electorate with a poster campaign: 'Cheer Up! Labour Can't Hang On For Ever', and '1984 – What will Britain Be Like After Another Five Years of Labour?' And then there was 'Labour Still Isn't Working', which showed a queue of patients trying to get into a hospital.

A week after Callaghan's complacent remarks, on 17 January 1979, a conservative PPB revolving around Mrs Thatcher was due to be transmitted. Under Bell's guidance, Saatchi's had filmed a broadcast on the windswept roof of a building on Tottenham Court Road in London. But when it was shown to Ronald Millar and Chris Patten, head of research at Tory Central Office, they were unhappy. 'It had no theme, no passion, and above all no relation to a country in turmoil,' recalled Millar.[45] They believed that the leader should strive to transcend party politics. Instead, she should make an emotional appeal for national unity at a time of crisis, with the underlying theme that she was the best politician to make that happen. With that in mind, they rewrote the script and showed it to Bell and Lord Thorneycroft, who agreed to the changes. Then the four men met Mrs Thatcher in her office in the House of Commons. She read the new text carefully. 'You know what you're doing, don't you?' She frowned. 'You're asking me to let Callaghan off the hook.'

'No,' said Thorneycroft gently. 'We're asking you to put country before party.'

She agreed – on two conditions. First, it must be filmed in her room at the Housed Commons. 'But TV cameras have never been allowed inside the House,' protested Bell. 'Leave that to me,' said Thorneycroft. Second, the room must be filled with spring flowers. Millar was unhappy about this because it was out of tune with the mood of austerity he wanted to project. But Bell instantly agreed. When Millar glanced at him, Saatchi's managing director said quietly, 'Don't worry,' and winked.

The next morning the room was full of flowers. 'What's this? The Chelsea Flower Show?' Millar hissed.

Out of the corner of his mouth, Bell whispered, 'Look at the camera angle.' When Millar peered through the lens he smiled at Bell's guile. It was pointing straight down at Mrs Thatcher in the tightest of tight close-ups and virtually all the flowers were out of shot.[46]

The broadcast was a success. Gone was Mrs Thatcher's bossy, hectoring tone. Instead, she spoke for the full nine minutes and forty seconds in a reasonable, persuasive manner, projecting herself as a potential national leader and stateswoman as opposed to an ambitious party politician. 'We did not write the script for that broadcast,' said Bell, 'but we did produce it and give advice on how the material could be most effectively presented. Although I am not a political scientist, my feeling is that this broadcast won her the election. The Labour government had been caught in a position where it had to pretend that nothing was going wrong at all . . . The Conservatives could therefore present themselves as the party of the nation.'[47] The market research and even Callaghan acknowledged, if only privately, that this PPB had been a turning point. Now the Conservatives were ready for the official campaign.

A TABLOID STRATEGY

In terms of newspaper coverage and press advertising, Saatchi and Saatchi had been much influenced by the Tories' 1959 campaign. The strategy employed by Bell's old agency Colman Prentis and Varley had been to point out that it was permissible for working-class people to be Conservative. 'It was the first campaign that I can remember,' said Bell, who was eighteen at the time. 'It shocked the nation because it showed pictures of what were then called working-class people – milkmen, postmen, miners – and underneath, a piece of copy saying, "I Am a Conservative" or "You're Looking At a Conservative"'. This was supposed to be an astounding piece of news because it was assumed the Tory Party represented the ruling class . . . I thought it was a very important part of reaching out to people who had previously been ignored.'[48]

By 1979, Bell was even more impressed with the successful 1959 campaign and read a book on it – *Communication and Political Power* by David Windlesham, from which he learned how traditional class alignments and loyalties could be broken down by an astute communications plan. As Saatchi's and the Conservative Party would be targeting working-class people, they would focus on the mass-circulation tabloid newspapers – 'the only audience that matters', according to Gordon Reece.[49] Advertising would be placed with them, and Bell and Reece assiduously courted the editors of two newspapers they had singled out for special attention: Larry Lamb of the *Sun* and David English of the *Daily Mail*. Mrs Thatcher's media advisers were particularly conspicuous at the *Sun's* offices at Bouverie Street, just off Fleet Street. They would drop by regularly for informal meetings with Lamb, usually in the evenings over large quantities of champagne. Known by *Sun* executives as 'Greece', the Tory Party publicity director would often stay late with the editor to witness the paper being printed. Lamb was encouraged to expound on his merits as an editor and his paper's at communicating with its readers, and how he understood the 'folks' thesis. Bell and Reece would nod sagely.[50] 'Quite frequently we did meet to discuss what we were up to,' recalled Lamb, 'discuss each other's plans and seek advice on whether we thought we were going the right way . . . Politically, at that time, I thought it was a very worthwhile thing to do, to strive to get rid of the Callaghan government.'[51]

Bell was profoundly influenced by the *Sun* and spent hours with Lamb studying the Tory Party's draft advertisements written by his colleagues in Charlotte Street. 'We had more of an effect upon what Saatchi's were doing', said Lamb, 'because we were able to say, 'Well, that may well win you an advertising award at the next session, but it ain't gonna pull in any votes." And I think Tim would recognise that we were, perhaps, closer to reality in the sense that we had the people who were capable of being switched.'[52]

Between September 1978 and the election the following May, the *Sun's* editor was also invited for several discreet private meetings with Mrs Thatcher at her house in Chelsea. 'Gordon Reece was very anxious to know what the *Sun* was thinking and which way it was going and she did indeed seek advice,' said Lamb, who strove to explain the minds of the common people to the opposition leader. 'I told her that there was a great bulk of working-class people who were going to vote Tory for the first time, and I was one of them.' His father had been a colliery blacksmith from the West Riding of Yorkshire.[53]

Bruce Matthews, then managing director of News International, owned by Rupert Murdoch, says that Bell's main purpose in befriending Lamb was to ensure that the *Sun* really did support the Tories and deliver those working-class votes. It had been a broadly Labour paper during the two elections in 1974 and had called for a coalition government of national unity. Now that it was the second most popular paper behind the *Daily Mirror*, its endorsement was of crucial importance.

It was not difficult to persuade Lamb, who had already made up his mind, as had Murdoch. But they had to be sure. 'She'll carry out her promise,' Bell told the paper's senior editors. In return the *Sun* was given the inside track on the Tory campaign and informed political gossip, according to Peter Stephens, Lamb's deputy and later editorial director. For example, Reece disclosed to Lamb that Mrs Thatcher regarded the Labour Prime Minister as a formidable opponent and shrewd operator: 'Margaret Thatcher regards Callaghan as the Baldwin of modern politics,' he had said.

Mrs Thatcher was deeply grateful for Lamb's support. He even wrote parts of her speeches. 'The *Sun* was one of the biggest influences in 1979,' recalled Bell. 'I think Larry had a considerable conviction about Mrs Thatcher. I think he saw her as a crusader and saviour of the people and all the things he believed in. His view towards her was not so much collaborative as deeply admiring and respecting . . . She had a very good relationship with editors at that time. They found her easy to talk to, and she was interested in their readership.'[54]

'We regarded Mrs Thatcher as the Tory most likely to succeed and we were desperate that she should succeed,' recalled Lamb. 'The print unions were ruining our business and the Labour Party were ruining the country . . . We were very anxious that the Callaghan government should cease to govern and – in so far as we had a strategy – it was a day-by-day, piece-by-piece, bit-by-bit endeavour to ensure that he didn't continue to govern . . . Toppling governments is a lot of fun, particularly if you think you get it right.'[55]

The *Sun*'s support was, indeed, unequivocal. Their front-page banner headline on polling day boomed, 'Vote Tory This Time. A Message to Labour Voters – It's the Only Way To Stop the Rot'. A year later Larry Lamb was awarded a knighthood on Mrs Thatcher's recommendation. Despite his fervent support for Mrs Thatcher, Rupert Murdoch was angry that Lamb accepted it. He did not like honours. 'I would never accept a knighthood,' Murdoch told Matthews at the time. 'Well, maybe I would on my deathbed.'

Around the corner at Northcliffe House on Tudor Street, the offices of the *Daily Mail*, Bell and Reece were equally assiduous at keeping editor David English happy. His paper was important in delivering the middle-England vote by alerting its readers to the perils of supporting Labour. On 26 April 1979, just over a week before polling day, the *Mail*'s front-page headline was 'Labour's Dirty Dozen'. It then listed twelve Labour 'lies' about the Conservative post-election plans as if it were a *Mail* scoop. In fact, it was a Tory Party PR gimmick and the article has been lifted straight from a Central Office handout.

It was not a tough assignment for Bell and Reece: English was a man committed to the cause. Two days before the big vote, political correspondents gathered outside Tory Central Office waiting for Gordon Greig, the *Mail*'s political editor, and David English to come out after their recorded interview with Mrs Thatcher. When they appeared, Greig played them the tape. The reporters were astonished to hear English coaxing answers out of Mrs Thatcher: 'Give me more, give me more,' he implored as she answered rather too cautiously for his liking. And when she responded, he said, 'Yes, that's good.'

Bell was helped by Mrs Thatcher's increasing ability to adapt to the tabloid campaign by changing her use of language. 'She did seem to have a sort of innate finger on the pulse of the things that mattered to ordinary people,' said Bell. 'She talked about holidays, cars, schools, houses and owning your own home and not spending more than you've got in your purse . . . She expressed herself in very ordinary language in a way they saw things. It was unusual political language and a departure from the way the Tory Party leaders had approached the electorate in the past.'[56]

As the intensity of the campaign increased, so did the temptation to run negative advertising and attack Labour remorselessly – after all, Saatchi's had plenty of ammunition. At first Mrs Thatcher was tempted. But she realised that this would open the floodgates to a month of mud-slinging and would prove counter-productive. When Bell showed her a poster portraying Callaghan as the captain of the *Titanic* selling tickets for the ship's next voyage, she vetoed it. A recommendation that she accuse the Labour Prime Minister of hypocrisy for having two houses was also quickly rejected: 'But, dear, you don't understand', she said sweetly. 'We want everybody to have two homes.'[57]

On Thursday 28 April 1979, a week before polling day, Maurice Saatchi and Tim Bell were in Lord Thorneycroft's room at Central Office, nervously waiting for the latest opinion polls that would be published in the next day's newspapers. Suddenly, a breathless Keith Britto, deputy head of the research department, arrived and announced that there was 'a really bad poll. It says we're 4 per cent behind. I can't prove it, but I believe it's a rogue one.' Labour had been saying that the Tories were going to increase VAT as soon as they were elected, and clearly this had had some impact.

Despite Britto's reservations as to the genuineness of the poll, Lord Thorneycroft was downcast and looked round the table at the other glum faces. 'What shall we do?' he asked. Maurice and Tim remained silent, profoundly depressed. 'It's like this,' continued Thorneycroft. 'You're in the ring. Your opponent has landed a punch directly on your nose, and blood is pouring down your face. What do you do?' Silence from the Saatchi team. 'There's only one thing to do now,' he said rousingly. 'You have to land a blow on your opponent's chin that knocks him out.'

For Maurice Saatchi it was a turning point, and that final week the advertising reached a new aggressive pitch. 'From that moment we understood that political campaigning is, above all, an adversarial activity,' he later reflected. 'This is a robust world. A world of trial by combat in which you would hit or be hit. Not a world for the squeamish or faint of heart. In the years to come we applied that lesson about immediate impact to our campaigns with enthusiasm, indeed with relish, probably because it accorded with our nature. We learned a lot about marketing strategy form military strategy too.' In a speech that provided a rare glimpse into the Saatchi psyche, Maurice revealed that Sir John Fisher, the First Lord of the Admiralty at the turn of the last century, was the agency's inspiration. 'He had an excellent motto for how to conduct a military campaign and we adopted it for our campaigns,' said Maurice. 'It was "Hit First, Hit Hard, Keep on Hitting"'[58]

Bell agreed with this approach and combined it with a heavy emphasis on visual metaphors. 'What we brought was the concept of imagery, as opposed to words,' said a member of Saatchi's team. 'Politicians live off words and they don't think about imagery.'[59] Reece and Bell were always conscious of this and always looking for new stunts. For example, they helped Harvey Thomas to organise a youth rally that featured pop stars and various celebrities extolling Tory virtues. Showbiz and glitz was never far from the minds of Reece and Bell.

When Margaret Thatcher entered 10 Downing Street on 4 May 1979, Saatchi and Saatchi felt their controversial tactics fully justified. So did the new Prime Minister. A week later she invited Tim Bell, Jeremy Sinclair and Maurice Saatchi to a party at Downing Street to toast the election victory. Bell, in particular, had become 'One of us'.

ONE OF US

Working for Margaret Thatcher and the Conservative Party changed Tim Bell. His gregarious, generous nature remained but he was now smitten with high politics and seduced by the aphrodisiac of power. He was mixing with cabinet ministers and, through them, with high-powered industrialists and celebrities. And back at the Saatchi and Saatchi office he did not hide his fascination for the political world. When long-standing clients called, he would respond: 'I'm sorry I can't talk to you now, I have to go and see the Prime

Minister', or 'I'm now working on the Conservative account'. This created tension because no client wanted to be regarded as second-best to another account and, indeed, many were not even Tory supporters. But it was a measure of Bell's changing priorities and his penchant for name-dropping.

He also became much more ruthless and a celebrity networker, according to Roy Warman, as the press began calling him 'Mrs Thatcher's favourite adman'. 'Don't spend your time with pygmies', became a favourite Bell phrase. On one occasion in the early 1980s in response to something Warman had said about a particular MP, Bell rejoined sharply, 'Ignore him, he's just a pygmy, fucking pygmy. What are you doing listening to him?' This was a different Tim Bell from the one of the 1970s who had spent much of his time turning pygmies into giants. 'This sort of talk was part of the political world,' said Warman. 'It's classifying people into those who are useful and those who aren't. Either Tim had changed his perception of the world or he was using borrowed language.'

Another former Saatchi's colleague, Paul Bainsfair, also noticed this change. Bell had been sucked into the world of the 'great and the good' and his colleague felt that he now saw political influence as a more exciting arena than advertising. However, his political love affair was with power and the Prime Minister, not with the Conservative Party, and an indication that Bell meant more to Mrs Thatcher than just the executive who handled the Tory account came on 12 May 1979, just over a week after the election. Bell was invited – along with Gordon Reece, Ronald Millar and Lord McAlpine – to Chequers for dinner.[60] He was now part of her inner circle, a vanguard of unofficial advisers who would help her implement the Thatcherite revolution.

The shopkeeper's daughter from Grantham considered herself an outsider. She distrusted the Tory grandees and the civil service. Instead, she preferred to rely on a coterie of loyal confidants and aides, who could operate outside the constraints and conventions of the government machine. 'She did feel that you either belonged or didn't belong,' said Sir Charles Powell, her foreign affairs private secretary from 1984 until 1990. 'Basically she was a revolutionary. She was carrying out a revolution in this country, though of course not single-handedly, and all successful revolutions are carried out by small bands of people. I think in a very strange mirror image you could find something of Lenin there. Somebody who is dedicated to an idea and a clear picture of what she wants to achieve and feels you need a vanguard of people to help you push it through.'[61]

The coterie was particularly important in the early years of her administration, when she did not have a natural majority in support of her policies in cabinet, but in response to complaints expressed by elected colleagues, the Prime Minister would say, 'I have a line to the people'. For the next eleven years that line was Tim Bell. Soon after entering 10 Downing Street, Mrs Thatcher realised that she would have difficulty in remaining in contact with the electorate and saw that Bell, who had the common touch, could bring news from the front. That was why she called him 'my man on the Clapham Omnibus'. Bell summed it up neatly when he said to Harvey Thomas, another media adviser and Thatcher confidant, 'You know why we get on so well with the old bat? None of us wanted to be politicians'. Because Bell, Reece and Thomas were from the outside and had been hired for their professional expertise, they could afford to be outspoken. Mrs Thatcher knew that, with them, there were no hidden political agendas. 'Tim was closer to her than the rest of us because he had a bluff, gruff front combined with his charm,' said Thomas. 'Gordon was smooth and a bit more detached and I helped make it work. Tim was a bit of both and we all understood each other.'

It was Tim Bell's special personal relationship with the Prime Minister that set him apart from other confidants. Publicly, Mrs Thatcher has said little about him. 'He had a feel for politics and a sense of fun,' was her only remark in her memoirs.[62] But others were more explicit. 'Tim would do the most appalling things and get away with them,' recalled Michael Dobbs, who worked closely with both Bell and Mrs Thatcher, 'because she loved him and he loved her. You could tell just by the way they looked at each other. He would kneel at her feet, tell her how wonderful she was and then show her some advertising which the chairman of the party had thrown out several times and had instructed him never to show to the Prime Minister. It was one of the great love stories of the twentieth century.'[63] Bernard Barnett, editor of *Campaign* from 1978 until 1984, goes further. 'She was besotted by him,' he said. 'There is no question about it and that was partly why she saw him so much. I attended at least two receptions at 10 Downing Street and you could see how he flirted with her but he was also very respectful . . . She also trusted him completely, which was surprising when you think how indiscreet he can be'.

The key to the success of his relationship with her was that Tim Bell treated Margaret Thatcher like a woman. Her austere outlook on life caused her ministers to behave formally in her presence. Most had never worked for a woman before and the grandees like Ian (now Lord) Gilmour and Francis (now Lord) Pym found it very difficult. 'She used her feminine wiles when it suited her,' said Bell. 'She would throw little temper fits, she could be sweet and coquettish and would do all sorts of things to get her own way. And men found that slightly uncomfortable.'[64] 'They were brought up by a nanny and they did not expect to have one running the rest of their lives.'[65] The late Julian Amery, the former Tory MP and aviation minister, quipped. The truth was that they had no idea how to deal with her, so they treated her like a man.

Bell, though, fawned on, flirted with and flattered her – but he did it without being obsequious. He would always make one minor criticism to ensure that he did not appear too sycophantic. He would listen to her intently, then say: 'Margaret, I do love that outfit you're wearing. It really does suit your figure. But can I just say one thing. Your jacket is a little long.' Mrs Thatcher, whose only interest in life, apart from politics, family and money, is clothes, was always receptive to this line. 'No one gives her compliments,' he told a Saatchi's colleague. 'I do. I always compliment her on her hair and dress and her aides hate it. I give her flowers and I once fell on my knees pretending to beg her to say yes to one of our ads.' Her political cohorts apparently hated this informality.

Above all, Bell could make her laugh. Just before the 1983 general election he and Michael Dobbs were at Chequers waiting for her to come into the reception room. Bell was flicking through the Sunday colour magazines. When Mrs Thatcher came into the room, he began to read out her horoscope entry (she's a Libra) saying, 'Look, it even says in the stars that you're going to win.' She loved it.

While Mrs Thatcher adored her media guru, he found her spell-binding and magnetic. It was her clear-minded, intuitive sense of conviction and self-belief that he found so attractive and, of course, the immense power at her disposal. She was charismatic but there was another side of her that appealed to him. 'She's like your mother,' said Bell. 'You come home having made a fool of yourself and she puts her arms around you and says, "You're a silly fool, aren't you?" and gives you a cuddle.'66

Bell was starstruck. 'One can't help bragging about knowing *her*, the Prime Minister,' he said, 'because it's such a wonderful thing that you think about it all the time.'67 Nicholas Coleridge, managing director of Condé Nast, received the full force of his feeling when he remarked, over lunch at the Ritz Hotel, 'I hear you had Boxing Day lunch at Chequers with the Prime Minister,' Bell was nonplussed. '*Boxing Day* lunch? Boxing Day?' he exclaimed, as if it was the most devalued, periphereal invitation on the social calendar. 'Oh, no, we got *Christmas* Day lunch at Chequers, the Christmas lunch. Boxing Day is just for the cabinet and people who give money to the Party and flavours of the month. Christmas Day is for family and friends.' He beamed benignly around the dining room before continuing, 'Oh, yes. Her Christmas Day lunch is the one to be at. It's a minute version of the New Year's Honours List, but sadly less lasting.'68

It helped, of course, that Bell was a quintessential Thatcherite: self-made from a middle-class background with a successful career in a service industry. 'He seems to be a construct in a way,' said an American media expert, 'as if someone asked, "Who is a Thatcher man?" and up jumped Tim Bell from the shooting gallery. In a strange way, he's like a Thatcherite Lord Goodman.'69

Bell's advice to her was always on the communication of policy. 'If you put this in your budget, this is how it will look or be reported in the media,' or 'If you implement this legislation, this is how people are likely to respond'. He never directly drafted or wrote any of her speeches but he did contribute phrases, ideas and themes. 'This is the line to take,' he would say and even, because of his close personal relationship, 'Come on, Margaret, you know you can't say that.' Gordon Reece would only remark, 'If you think that's right, Prime Minister.'

However, working for her had its lighter moments. Late one night Bell and Ronald Millar were working on a speech when Mrs Thatcher wanted to use a favourite quotation from a well-loved novel. One of the characters, constantly said something like, 'That man couldn't organise Pussy.' Bell had to explain why she couldn't use it. 'I told her it wouldn't look good if during a speech or TV interview she said Jim Callaghan couldn't even organise pussy,' said Bell. But he was too embarrassed to tell her exactly what 'pussy' meant in common parlance. 'Eventually, I gestured to her nether regions and said, "It's your . . . you know what." To this day, she thinks I meant her handbag,' said Bell laughing.[70]

THE APHRODISIAC OF POWER

By early 1980, Bell was living his life at an incredible pace, racing around running Saatchi and Saatchi as well as discreetly advising the Prime Minister. Perhaps it was not surprising that he was convicted for drunk driving on his way to Chequers. On 20 March he was found guilty at Ampthill Magistrates Court in Bedfordshire and disqualified from driving for a year. At the court hearing his barrister said that his client needed his driving licence so that he could see the Prime Minister at Chequers. But it was to no avail.

It was not long before his reputation brought him to the attention of other national leaders. Later that year Bell was approached by Charles Haughey, the Irish Prime Minister, who was in trouble politically and looking for advice. Bell met secretly with Haughey and his then Foreign Secretary Brian Lenihan in Dublin. 'You're Mrs Thatcher's image-maker,' said the Irish Premier. 'I think I need a new image. What kind of image do you think I should have?'

'I don't really do that sort of thing. That's not the way it works,' replied Bell.

'What do you mean?'

'Well, we believe you can move away false perceptions, diminish weaknesses and heighten strengths, but really the job is to find the real person and bring that out in front of the people. I can only represent you as you really are and present your best assets.'

Haughey paused before saying: 'Well, do you know anyone who does do new images?'

Despite his stated reservations, Bell was hired.

Bell's relations with Mrs Thatcher's civil service advisers were not so cordial. He had virtually nothing to do with Sir Bernard Ingham, her press secretary, throughout almost all her time in 10 Downing Street and only met him twice. Ingham, the hard-nosed Yorkshireman who had spent a lifetime in newspapers and government public relations, was dismissive of Bell's role and activities, and there was a fair amount of tension between the two. 'I have very little impression of the extent, and still less the effect, of interventions with editors, whether sanctioned or otherwise,' Ingham said. 'I sometimes think these people's own PR was better than the PR advice they administered. But Bell was able to create an aura of magic about him which he used to good effect.'

Mrs Thatcher kept civil service and external advice on communications in separate channels, so it was rare for Bell to know what Ingham was doing and vice versa. However, they came into conflict with each other when Bell advised Mrs Thatcher to hold Presidential-style press conferences during the parliamentary recess. 'I think perhaps we should have a press conference in June,' she suggested to Ingham, on a couple of occasions. 'What about?' Ingham asked, who argued against the idea. 'It will help us get our message across,' Mrs Thatcher said, rather half-heartedly. But her press secretary was resistant. 'I thought it was unnecessary,' he recalled, 'because most people were fed up with politics by the summer and it would do no harm for a quiet period particularly if the Prime Minister was in good nick. It would also set up expectations and would appear artificial and transplanted.' She was persuaded to drop the idea.

Ingham also opposed Bell's suggestion that Mrs Thatcher be interviewed by Michael Aspel on his lightweight, celebrity-based show on ITV. Ingham said that for the Prime Minister to involve himself in such a programme would trivialise and cheapen the office she held. 'Well, they [Bell and Reece] want me to do it,' said Mrs Thatcher, and this time she went ahead. Bell accompanied her to the television studios and escorted her to the Green Room where she met the other main guest, Barry Manilow. It was like a meeting of two superstars, which is how Bell viewed the Prime Minister. Bell hovered around backstage while she was being interviewed. Mrs Thatcher gave a sparkling performance and Ingham's fears were laid to rest. 'As it happens, it turned out well and she went down a storm,' he reflected, 'partly because it wasn't adversarial and there was more substance.'[71]

However, it was not always sweetness and light between the Prime Minister and Tim Bell. By 1981 he had begun to exploit his access to

10 Downing Street in acquiring and preserving clients for Saatchi and Saatchi. Impressionable and easily pleased industrialists loved being close to the Prime Minister's inner circle.

One of Bell's most prized clients was British Leyland. He had secured the business in the mid-1970s and developed a close relationship with its chief executive, Michael Edwardes. The other advertising agency on the account, Leo Burnett, was fully aware of Bell's reputation as a presenter. In late 1979 when Edwardes summoned the two agencies for a review of the business, Leo Burnett spent days preparing for the meeting. 'I was immensely confident,' recalled Roger Edwards, its then chief executive. 'I knew he couldn't beat me. Then when Tim walked in, he went over and said, "Hello, Michael, Margaret sends you her best regards," I was completely floored.'[72]

Tony Cummings, British Leyland's then marketing director, was also enamoured by the trappings of political power. During a lunch in early 1981 with Bell and his Saatchi's colleague Bill Muirhead, they were discussing the election campaign. 'So you've been to 10 Downing Street?' said Cummings.

'Yes, many times,' replied Bell. 'Would you like to go?'

'I'd love to go.'

'Sure, no problem,' said Bell.

Muirhead was amazed. 'You're such a bullshitter,' he thought. But he was curious as to how Bell was going to fulfil his promise, particularly when Cummings rang up asking when his visit to 10 Downing Street would take place.

The opportunity arose three months later, in June 1981, when Bell came up with the idea that Mrs Thatcher should attend a charity performance of *Anyone for Denis*, the hilarious but biting satire of her husband. The play, starring John Wells, went further than his 'Dear Bill' letters in *Private Eye*, holding Denis up to ridicule but without the affection. Bell and Robert Fox, the theatrical producer, believed that Mrs Thatcher could boost her popularity by appearing in the audience and showing that she was 'a good sport' and 'could laugh at herself'.

Unfortunately, she was deeply offended by the play, which, according to her daughter Carol, portrayed her husband as 'a prototype little Englander, full of ghastly, off-hand class and race prejudice'.[73] What was worse, Bell had organised a reception afterwards at 10 Downing Street, during which both the Thatchers felt a combination of embarrassment and annoyance. They hid their feelings behind gritted teeth. It did not help that Paul Raymond, the Soho pornographer and property magnate, insisted on attending the party, pointing out that he did, after all, own the Whitehall Theatre where the play was performed.

The event was a disaster, alleviated only slightly by newspaper headlines that bestowed a sense of humour on the Prime Minister. For Bell it had backfired badly. He told Carol Thatcher that the evening was 'one of the greatest mistakes of his life'.[74] The only benefit, of course, was that Tony Cummings, British Leyland's marketing director, finally got his invitation to 10 Downing Street.

Four months later, the strength of Bell's relationship with the Prime Minister received its toughest test yet. On 14 October 1981, a week after the Tory Party conference and at a time when she was very unpopular, Bell's private thoughts about the Thatcher family were published in *Event* magazine, the now defunct rival to *Time Out*. Bell had attended a birthday dinner party for the comedian Kenny Everett at which he regaled the guests with a mixture of indiscreet anecdotes about Mr and Mrs Thatcher and made highly critical comments about their son Mark. One of the guests was a journalist and tape-recorded most of his remarks.

He told a few amusing stories about the Prime Minister's tendency to use ill-advised language but the most embarrassing related to her husband's drinking habits – 'practically a whole bottle of gin' in one evening – and his irritation with her speech-writing method: 'Words, words, it's all bloody words. Bloody waste of time.' He painted a portrait of Denis Thatcher that was not unlike the version in *Anyone for Denis*, skying golf balls from the front lawn of Chequers for his Special Branch detectives to retrieve from the undergrowth. Worst of all, were Bell's criticisms of Mrs Thatcher's beloved son. 'He is a twit,' he told the dinner-party guests. 'In my opinion, he has absolutely nothing to offer the world.'[75]

When the magazine was published, Mrs Thatcher was not amused and Bell was deeply distressed. He lay awake at night, worrying about what his gaffe would do to his relationship with the Thatchers. Eventually he asked a close colleague at Saatchi's what he should do. 'I would talk to Denis and apologise,' he was told. He also sought the advice of Gordon Reece, who agreed. Bell then wrote a grovelling letter of apology. By return of post came a handwritten note from the Prime Minister's husband: 'I doubt that you said it. If you did, you didn't mean it. Please come to tea in Downing Street at four.'[76] After returning to Charlotte Street from his meeting, Bell was a greatly relieved man. He promptly relayed Mr Thatcher's own remarks about his son. 'I have a great sympathy for you,' he told Bell. 'I know he's a prat, but I don't want the whole world to know that.'

For almost anyone else, the injudicious remarks about the Thatchers' private lives would have meant the end of any relationship. If a prime minister is to trust an unofficial, external adviser, discretion is a major priority. It was testimony to the strength of their bond that Mrs Thatcher felt confident enough to forgive Bell. Or, perhaps, it was all down to one of his favourite maxims – 'I can fall in the sewer and come out smelling of roses.'

Chapter Four

Breakdown and Divorce

'Governments listen to me. Why won't those two arseholes?'
Tim Bell, referring to Charles and Maurice Saatchi, in 1983

'You don't understand how it makes you feel. It makes a good
man great'
Tim Bell on taking cocaine,
to his close friend and colleague Roy Warman

Tim Bell's close personal relationship with Margaret Thatcher
was resented by the Brothers, particularly Maurice. It rankled
that the Prime Minister addressed him as 'Mr Saatchi' and Bell as
'Tim'. 'Mrs Thatcher thought Tim Bell was Saatchi's,' said Cecil
Parkinson, Tory Party chairman from 1981 until 1983. 'I sometimes
used to think she thought Tim did all the artwork and generally
put things together, whereas Tim was the man who presented
the work and explained it, and was brilliant at it.'[1] However, the
Brothers' irritation did not deflect them from their central quest:
global corporate expansion and domination. Working for the Prime
Minister and the Tory Party was important, but their priority always
remained the same: to be the biggest agency in the world.

That was not Bell's preoccupation. He wanted Saatchi and Saatchi
to be a large powerful international agency but he also wanted it to be
the best and most respected, and the Conservative account was a way
of achieving that. By January 1979, that had become a full-time job,
so the Brothers appointed a new managing director to run the agency
on a daily basis while Bell became its chairman. A remarkable board
meeting took place: the directors were astonished to see Charles

Saatchi – who never attended such meetings and had become an almost Howard Hughes-like figure – enter unannounced, carrying a crown neatly placed on a red velvet cushion. Without a word, he walked over to Ron Leagas and silently placed it on his head. He then strolled out. It was Charles's way of appointing him managing director.

Publicly, Bell welcomed the decision. 'Well done, congratulations,' he told Leagas, as he shook his hand. But privately he was irritated by the way it had been done. After all, only an emperor can crown a king. And Bell wanted to be an emperor. Charles realised this and the next day a more elegant crown was brought into Bell's office and placed on his desk to signal his appointment as chairman. 'That incident was an indication of the insecurity and fragility of their relationship,' Leagas told me.

After the 1979 election victory, Bell returned to the office and developed a successful working relationship with Leagas but it was not long before the strength of his personality and talent re-established him as the pre-eminent executive of the agency. He was also acquiring more prominence and power because the Brothers were concentrating on the long-term corporate development of the company, and the daily management of the agency fell on Bell's shoulders. 'It was Tim's agency,' said a former Saatchi's executive. 'He was running it. He was getting and keeping the business. The clients never even saw the Brothers, let alone did business with them. As far as the clients were concerned, it was Tim's show because they only dealt with him. So did most of the staff.'

In June 1981, with the takeover of Dorland's, Saatchi's became the biggest agency group in the UK. Bell now wanted to share some of the fruits of the agency's success, which he had engineered. He had received several offers to leave and set up on his own but he remained loyal, although he could have taken most of the clients and staff with him. His shareholding was now worth close to £2 million.

However, his name was not above the door and he was not even on the board of the holding company, although he ran and was chairman of the main operating subsidiary. He felt excluded from the arena where strategic decisions were taken about the future of a company he had done as much as the Brothers to build.

In essence, he was desperate to become the 'Third Brother'. 'I am the "and" in Saatchi and Saatchi,' he used to say. 'I'm really the third brother,' he would tell clients. 'It's Saatchi, Saatchi and

Bell.' But he could not understand the strength of the special bond between the Brothers, and even devised bizarre theories to explain it. 'Tim once told me over a drink about the mystery of why Maurice and Charles held their shareholding in a joint company in the Isle of Man,' recalled John Perris, former media director of Saatchi's. 'He said it was because they both came from a tribe whose tradition was that the eldest brother killed the father to become the head of the family. The second oldest brother would then kill his elder brother to be head of the tribe. He said that because Charles assumed that Maurice would try to kill him, he put the shareholding in a jointly owned company, so this would not happen.'

Bell's position was like being married to a twin but not realising that the twin would always be closer to their sibling than to their spouse. Saatchi and Saatchi was a Jewish family business and Bell was not a blood brother.

There were other sources of contention. One was that Charles was irritated by Bell's familiarity. It was always 'Charlie this' or 'Charlie that', which irked him. 'Charles is a very powerful man and liked yes men,' said a former Saatchi's creative director. 'I once read an interview with Picasso who said, "I only like people who do what I want," and I thought to myself that was exactly Charles's attitude. He respected people who stood up to him during arguments, but on fundamental issues he needed to be in full control.' Essentially, the Brothers were content to delegate authority but never power and Bell was increasingly less of a yes man. He was growing significantly more independent, confident and, to the Brothers, dangerous, by building a strong power base among the staff and clients. And he received flattering publicity as 'Mrs Thatcher's favourite adman' and the 'Third Brother'. It annoyed Maurice and Charles intensely but they had only themselves to blame: they had deliberately shunned personal publicity – apart from off-the-record briefing and leaking to *Campaign*. It had been inevitable that, as the agency became more successful, Bell, the front-man they had, appointed would draw the spotlight.

Now that he had become a threat to their power, the Brothers began to marginalise him. Charles admired Bell's talent and charm but claimed that he was afraid of his instability, 'Charles's behaviour was instinctive not premeditated,' recalled Leagas. 'It was honed and based on power games but no more than a rapid step up from the school playground.' It resulted in increased internal bickering and after a year of this, Leagas left to form his own agency. 'There were just too many in-built tensions,' he said. After his departure, Bell became both chairman and managing director – but an almighty battle of wills was developing.

According to former colleagues, Charles was 'instinctively Machiavellian' and began to play 'mind games' with Bell.[2] An emotional and sensitive man Bell was wide open to such a tactic. 'Their management policy was divide and conquer,' recalled Roy Warman and for Bell that meant that one day he would be told, 'You are the greatest. You make this agency tick', and the next he would be castigated, 'Look what you've done to us.'

As the agency grew corporately and expanded internationally, the Brothers' ambitions outdistanced their dependence on Bell. They wanted to take on the world, which was of limited interest to him. There were plenty of others to help in such a venture, so there was less need for Bell. The Brothers had outgrown him: he had remained an adman but they were interested now in a multi-service communications business.

Bell wanted more money and, crucially, recognition of his status with a seat on the board of the holding company. But Charles, in particular, was contemptuous and insensitive to his demands. 'We made him rich, but he wanted to be richer,' he said. As chairman and managing director of the agency, Bell deeply resented being treated in such a cavalier fashion. The Brothers' response was 'Stop being so emotional and pull yourself together.' They agreed with businessmen like Bob Woodruff, chairman of Coca-Cola, who said, 'You can achieve anything so long as you don't care who gets the credit.' Which is easy to say when you're at the top. 'They did treat him badly,' said Bernard Barnett, editor of *Campaign* between 1978 and 1984, 'but you have to remember that the Brothers were not good man-managers. They led by example, not by nurturing talent where they had no skills. The problem was that they did not appreciate what Tim contributed to the agency's success and Tim needed that recognition because, at the end of the day, he was insecure just like the rest of us. There was also an element of a middle-class boy who had become rich, successful and famous quickly and could not cope. He ran himself too fast and did not pace himself.'

Bell reacted by trying to strengthen his power base. In 1982

Saatchi's approached Boase Massimi Pollitt to acquire them at a time when the Brothers were nurturing the City. The plan was that Martin Boase would be chairman of the whole company with Bell as chief executive and the Brothers in the background. But there was more to it than that: Bell wanted Boase, a highly respected advertising figure, to help him create an axis against Maurice and Charles. 'Look, if you come in at least it will be balanced. It will be us against them,' confided Bell. 'Yes, there was an element of that,' Boase recalled. Bell was desperate for reinforcements to bolster his position but his potential ally wisely rejected his offer. They were faced with a strength of feeling that was based on Jewish family blood and even Bell's charm could not overcome that.

The crisis for Bell was the way in which Saatchi's acquired the prestigious and valuable British Airways account. The deal's origins lay in late 1981 soon after Lord King became chairman. One of his first executive decisions was to clear out the finance and promotion departments and bring in his own people.

Brian Basham, BA's PR consultant who also represented Saatchi's, was curious about why King was so anxious to purge both departments. 'I've been doing some background research,' he told King. 'It seems to me you've got good accountants and an advertising agency [Foote, Cone and Belding] who've done some decent work. Why are you going for a new agency?'

King paused and said, 'Do you know the story of the man and his mule?'

'No,' replied Basham.

'Well, a chap goes to the stall in the market and tries to saddle his mule. But the mule kicks him and causes so much trouble he can't saddle the mule. Another chap saw what was happening, picked up a large plank of timber and whacked the mule square between the eyes and almost knocked it out. Its owner was horrified and asked why he did it. The passer-by replied, "Look at your mule's eyes. He's now paying you attention".' Lord King then added with a glint in his eye, 'That's what I'm doing here. I'm getting their attention.'

Lord King looked at several advertising agencies and was eventually introduced to Maurice Saatchi by Ian Watson, then city editor of the *Sunday Telegraph*, over lunch at the Ritz Hotel. King knew little about

Saatchi and Saatchi. He hired them partly because he did not want an American agency to promote BA, but mostly because they had the Tory Party account and he was part of that political cabal. Cecil Parkinson, then party chairman, was a close friend and they had done business together. Hence Saatchi's was the natural choice.

Nevertheless, Maurice and Charles conducted the negotiations in unprecedented secrecy and consciously kept Bell, their managing director, in the dark. Every other Saatchi executive was excluded too, notably the copywriters, as the agency was not required to pitch for the account.

Meanwhile, Bell was trying to save the British Caledonian account. 'They were the client from hell,' said Bill Muirhead, the account executive. In 1982 British Caledonian decided to review the business but after an intense campaign, Bell and Muirhead retained it. It was a considerable achievement.

A month later, Muirhead was having lunch with British Caledonian's marketing director, David Coultman, and Alastair Pugh, managing director, at their office at Gatwick airport. Towards the end of the lunch Muirhead was told, 'We have it on good authority that you're now working for BA.' He strongly denied it because if this had been so there would have been a conflict of interest and the agency had just retained the Caledonian account. When he returned to Charlotte Street, he confronted Bell. 'Don't be stupid. That's ridiculous,' Bell replied.

The next day Muirhead went to see Maurice. As soon as he saw his face, he knew it was true. Then Charles walked into the room, grinning broadly without saying anything. 'Why didn't you tell us about BA?' asked Muirhead.

'Well,' replied Charles, 'we didn't want to say anything until we were sure.' He then paused and quoted the proverb: '"After all there's many a slip 'twixt the cup and the lip."' In other words, the Brothers had not quite landed the account but any indiscretion could lose them the deal. The clear implication was that Bell could not be trusted with the information.

In fact, Charles had already spoken to Bernard Barnett, editor of *Campaign*, as they would naturally be the recipients of the story. 'What does Tim know about it?' asked Barnett, who was concerned about it leaking.

'He doesn't know,' replied Charles.

'Can you keep it like that?'

'I won't tell him.'

Campaign ran the story on its front page – 'British Airways Poised To Switch £42 m to Saatchi's' – without speaking to Bell, who found out from John Perry, the newly appointed BA director of public affairs, over dinner at L'Etoile. Bell was hurt, angry and humiliated but managed to disguise his shock. 'That's fantastic,' he said. 'I didn't even know we were talking to you.'

Maurice and Charles claimed that they could not tell Bell because he was working on the Caledonian account. That, however, was just a convenient excuse: they could easily have withdrawn from British Caledonian. The agency had never shown any scruples in dumping as account for a more lucrative client: the previous year they had discarded Bon Duelle, a French food company, in favour of the more prosperous Ross Foods, despite having promised Bon Duelle, in writing, that they would never desert them for a rival account. A conflict of interests was not the reason why the Brothers had excluded their managing director from the BA deal. The reality was that Bell was being frozen out – and British Caledonian, of course, was soon discarded by Saatchi's.

The BA débâcle was the beginning of the end for Bell. Despite the phenomenal energy he put into the agency, he was being sidelined. The pressure became almost intolerable.

BACK ON THE CAMPAIGN TRAIL

Soon after the British Airways episode, Bell's attention was diverted by the impending general election campaign. Although he was again at the helm of the Saatchi's team, a new regime was now in place at Tory Central Office. His great friend Gordon Reece had moved to California to work for Armand Hammer and been replaced by David Boddy, who concentrated on building good relations with lobby correspondents; and a new marketing department, set up by Christopher Lawson, a former marketing director at Mars, would be in charge of advertising. Thus was born the 'Hemel Hempstead

Mafia' as Boddy, Lawson, Cecil Parkinson, the new party chairman, and Norman Tebbit, the employment secretary, were all from the Hertfordshire town.

A backlash against the Reece appproach soon swept Central Office, where it was felt that politics had been reduced to photo opportunities, buzz-words and American-style PR stunts. Lord Thorneycroft had allowed Reece and Saatchi's a free rein to run the show but some senior Tory officials believed that the relationship had become a little too cosy. Lord McAlpine, the party's Treasurer, who reported directly to Mrs Thatcher, had been happy to spend millions of pounds on Saatchi advertisements. In his eyes the agency could do no wrong and he had also developed a close personal rapport with Bell. Indeed, his office was filled with framed prints of Saatchi advertisements, notably 'Labour Isn't Working'. He believed that two factors won general elections for the Conservatives: Saatchi's advertising and the Prime Minister. Bell shared his opinion but it was hotly contested by Bernard Ingham, the press secretary at 10 Downing Street, and cabinet ministers such as the chancellor, Nigel Lawson. McAlpine's view of donations to the party was made clear in a response he gave to a question about the distribution of party funds: 'I raise all this money to win elections,' he said. 'It's better to be a bankrupt party in government than cash-rich in opposition.' And he believed Saatchi's were a useful aid to fund-raising. McAlpine would point to their successful posters and ads as tangible evidence that the money spent by donors to the party had brought invaluable returns.

Cecil Parkinson, however, decided that a strong dose of professionalism must be administered and that the party's message should be projected more seriously. Suddenly, advertising was downplayed and downgraded, and the emphasis shifted to the press. The party's communications strategy would now be run by an inner cabinet at Central Office, and Saatchi's would be more accountable. Party funds were in short supply and Michael Spicer, a Tory MP who had been an economist, was made deputy chairman to bring fiscal prudence into the relationship between the part and Saatchi's. These reforms created considerable tension between Central Office and Bell, who had enjoyed a high degree of autonomy under the previous regime.

The first shot across Saatchi's bows was fired by Christopher Lawson when he met Bell and Saatchi's in January 1982. He told them that, as far as he was concerned, the Conservative Party no longer had an advertising agency and that Saatchi's would have to repitch for the business. 'Agencies like to run their clients and tell them what to do', recalled Keith Britto, Lawson's deputy. 'We needed to make them realise there were alternatives out there.' Privately, Lawson had no intention of sacking Saatchi's but he wanted to give them a jolt and deter any complacency.

Bell reacted badly, arguing that the agency had served the party well in the past and could do so again. He was also unhappy about being out of the political loop. But within weeks he was back in the fold and able to rebuild his relationship with Parkinson. One of the key priorities was to keep Mrs Thatcher happy and as Bell was as much a friend as an adviser to her, he was the ideal figure to play that role.

On 5 January 1983, Bell's renaissance was established when he delivered a presentation at Chequers on the style of campaign for the election to the Prime Minister, Cecil Parkinson and senior Central Office officials. He had commissioned several focus groups of between twelve and fifteen people around the UK, chosen by a polling agency, who met privately and regularly to talk about a wide range of issues. They were not political activists but ordinary voters who were unaware on whose behalf their discussions were being held. Their meetings had been video-recorded, and that afternoon at Chequers, Bell played the tapes to Mrs Thatcher and Parkinson.

Bell delivered mixed, but largely encouraging, tidings. People blamed high unemployment not just on the Tories but on a wide range of factors, notably the world economic recession, and a strong thread of patriotism had also emerged due to the Falklands War.

However, time after time the main topic of conversation among the focus group members was Margaret Thatcher. Here, Bell did not flinch from delivering bad news to the Prime Minister. She was regarded as by far the best and most effective party leader but many voters considered her harsh, authoritarian and autocratic, with scant regard for the plight of ordinary people. 'When she first came to power, being bossy was a problem because she hadn't earned her spurs,' he later reflected. 'Britons didn't like being hectored and lectured to by this headmistressy character who had yet to prove herself.'[3]

The Prime Minister was a little startled by the criticism in Bell's presentation but she respected his judgement.[4] 'Tim had a more sensitive set of antennae than most politicians,' she said later. 'He could pick up quicker than anyone else a change in the national mood. And, unlike most advertising men, he understood that selling ideas is different from selling soap.'5

Bell ended by proposing a number of advertisements, most of which the Prime Minister rejected out of hand. She was uneasy about Saatchi's occasional tendency to be flippant. 'She did not want politics reduced to entertainment,' recalled Bell. 'If you are too jokey you might trivialise the message. And she would sometimes veto an advert, just to let you know who was in charge.'6

However, several campaign themes emerged: 'Share the Blame' to deal with unemployment and 'Stay the Course', which was a pre-emptive strike against the inevitable opposition jibe of 'It's Time For a Change'. Mrs Thatcher's favourite was 'Britain's On the Right Track. Don't Turn Back', which hinted at the Falklands victory. That became the pay-off line at the end of every party election broadcast.

Three months later, on 7 April 1983, Bell returned to Chequers for an all-day session on the general election strategy. This time the manifesto was in its final stages and campaign fever was running high. Key Central Office personnel attended as well as Ferdinand Mount, head of the Prime Minister's Policy Unit, David Wolfson, from her political office, and Ian Gow, her parliamentary private secretary. Together they discussed the style and content of the campaign which focused increasingly on the Prime Minister herself.7 Bell was asked to devise a specific plan to rubbish Labour's past record on unemployment, a vulnerable area for the government.8

When Saatchi's planned their strategy, their first instinct was simply to promote, in a positive way, the government's record since they had been in power. But when Bell and his Saatchi's colleagues – Peter Wallach and Michael Dobbs – began to discuss the campaign, they decided it would be more effective to combine this with the 1979 formula of attacking, knocking copy. In other words, a balanced battle-plan. Bell also believed that nine minutes forty seconds was too long for party election broadcasts and reduced them by five minutes, on the basis that in advertising ninety seconds is a long time. On the press side, he was in regular contact with Sir David English, editor of the *Daily Mail*, and Kelvin McKenzie now editor of the *Sun* briefing them on the latest Tory policy and passing on stories –

non-attributably, of course. These papers were even more partisan than they had been in 1979, so much so that during the 1983 election, fifty-seven of the *Mail*'s editorial staff formally protested about its 'one-sided' coverage.[9]

When Mrs Thatcher and her colleagues agreed that knocking copy should be retained, Saatchi's were delighted and straight away devised an advertising campaign to show why Labour voters should switch to the Conservatives. One showed a photograph of the opposition leader Michael Foot, carrying a stick and walking his dog on Hampstead Heath. The caption ran: 'As a pensioner, he'd be better off under the Conservatives.' Another proposed poster featured 'Wedgewood Benn: As a rate-payer with three properties, he would be better off under the Conservatives.' Other prominent Labour politicians were portrayed 'As a parent . . .', 'As a taxpayer . . .'. They were rejected, according to a Saatchi's creative source, 'because Parkinson and Thatcher thought they would create sympathy for the opposition by provoking the British tendency to switch support to the underdog.' It was deemed too risky. 'We didn't want it to be too personalised because we didn't think it was necessary,' said Michael Spicer. 'Michael Foot was already making a mess of the campaign and there was a feeling of "Let's not blow it when we're so far ahead."'

When the Foot advertisement was shown to Mrs Thatcher by a recalled Gordon Reece and Tim Bell over champagne at 10 Downing Street she said, 'That's not the way I do things. I'm not going to indulge in personal attacks.' But that did not prevent *Newsline*, the Tory Party's official newspaper, from describing the Labour leader as 'amnesiac, clapped out and half-witted – a self-opinionated old invalid'.[10]

The most notable advertisement was a direct line-by-line comparison of eleven Labour and Communist policies with the caption: 'Like Your Manifesto, Comrade.' In another, the Tories offered a dozen bottles of claret – Roy Jenkins' favourite drink – to anyone who could describe the SDP–Liberal Alliance's policies. The only reaction was that within hours of the poster being plastered up, Central Office was besieged by Alliance supporters – and alert claret drinkers – clutching copies of the party's manifesto and claiming their cases of hooch.

Back in the Saatchi and Saatchi operations room, an evangelical and animated Bell stood behind a huge desk in his office with a bank of telephones and photographs of Mrs Thatcher on the wall.

He had a hot line to Cecil Parkinson: 'Cecil!' he would shout. 'I've got some great news. We've just had some research come in.' To Bell, the Tories were not just another client, they were a cause and he believed in them. 'How can anyone vote Labour?' he would say to any colleague who happened to be in his office. 'Let me show you this,' and he would run round his desk and point to a chart showing how inflation had been reduced in the past three years. When a planner said that a member of the Saatchi's research panel was not convinced and would still vote Labour, Bell was stunned. 'How can that be? I just don't understand.'

The 1983 campaign was tense: Mrs Thatcher's moods swung from high to low. Bell found it much more difficult to get advertisements approved because Parkinson was more selective and vigilant than had been the case in 1979. He had more success with the party election broadcasts (PEB): they were not, perhaps, as creative or innovative as they had been in 1979 but they were more serious, fact-driven and politically more effective. The highlight was a sharply edited film montage of the 'Winter of Discontent'. This showed angry picket lines, closed hospitals and terrifying headlines of the previous Labour government while the viewer heard haunting background music and the actor Anthony Quayle's doom-laden baritone voiceover: 'Do your remember . . .?'. It was more like a horror film than a PEB.

Bell was particularly astute at coaching the more tight-postured and nervous cabinet ministers when they recorded their contributions to PEBs. On 2 June 1983, Norman Tebbit, then employment secretary, was being filmed on unemployment. It did not go well until Bell told him: 'Try talking as if you're flying a VC-10 and telling the passengers you're about the land the plane.' That did the trick.

As with newspaper advertisements, some of the filmed material was not used. The most notable was a short biographical portrait of Mrs Thatcher known as *The Grantham Tape*. Modelled by Bell on what he described as a 'fantastic' campaign commercial for Gerald Ford in the 1976 Presidential election, the film opened with a shot of Mrs Thatcher's parents corner shop in Grantham. It moved rapidly through her early life before the presenter intoned: 'At fifty she became leader. She had not wanted it, but her party did.' The eulogy continued with archive film of what were deemed Mrs Thatcher's single-handed foreign policy triumphs – negotiating in Europe, winning the Falklands War, relieving the Iranian Embassy siege and playing the world statesman. 'We are a superpower again, due to one woman,' concluded the film.[11]

Both Bell and Mrs Thatcher were immensely proud of *The Grantham Tape* but she believed the party would object to its Presidential style so it was never shown. Another film, *The Spoilt Child*, a critique of the welfare state written by Antony Jay, also remained on a shelf in the cutting room.

Mrs Thatcher nearly always wanted to change the scripts. On Sunday 5 June, four days before polling day, she arrived at a studio hired by Bell in Maddox Street to record the final election broadcast. Adrenaline was surging through her as she had just attended a triumphant Young Conservatives rally at Wembley where celebrities and sports stars paid homage to her in an American-style extravaganza. Bell, her speech-writer Ronald Miller, and Peter Wallach had decided to try to portray her in a warm, compassionate way to combat the prevailing view of her as austere, heartless and ruthless. But when Millar read out the first draft of the script she didn't like it. 'It's no good,' she said. 'It doesn't tackle the issues. I want facts, not moods. Facts, facts, facts!' Wallach, Millar and Bell retired to another room to redraft it. Left alone, Mrs Thatcher walked over to the camera crew. 'I'm sorry, gentlemen, that the filming has been delayed,' she said. 'The script needs to be rewritten and it's taking a little longer than usual for me to get my own way.' She then offered them a drink.

She was not happy with the second version either and suggested a change with which Wallach did not agree. 'The logic won't work that way, Prime Minister,' he said.

'Make it work,' replied Mrs Thatcher, with a steely glare. Wallach returned to Millar and Bell. 'I've a funny feeling that the Prime Minister is looking straight through me,' he said.

'That, Peter, is because you no longer exist,' said Bell. Which appeared to be true because the next time they met Wallach had to be introduced to her.

Despite the Prime Minister's reservations about portraying herself as more compassionate, Bell remained anxious to soften her Iron Lady image and believed the Boadicea line was being overdone. He warned her against sounding 'too headmistressy', but she took little notice. So he tried a different tactic to project her more human, feminine side. He arranged to take her to the opera on the Wednesday night, the day before polling. Amazingly, she agreed, but her aides vetoed the idea, arguing that it would not be politically expedient for her to be seen out with her media guru on the evening before the election.

Throughout the 1983 campaign, and in line with the new spending restrictions under Cecil Parkinson, Bell found it difficult to get advertisements accepted. But on the last Thursday before the vote, a rogue opinion poll had appeared to indicate that Labour was closing the gap between them and the Conservative lead. Bell and Gordon Reece suggested that the Conservatives commission an unprecedented three-page advertising spread to be published in all national newspapers on the Sunday before polling day. Entitled 'If' (after Mrs Thatcher's favourite poem by Kipling), the first page gave ten reasons for voting Tory, the second gave eight reasons for not voting Labour and the third demonstrated one reason for ignoring the Alliance – a blank page because of their alleged lack of policies.

Bell wanted to proceed but he needed authorisation from Christopher Lawson, Cecil Parkinson and the Prime Minister. Lawson was opposed to the advertisements purely on the basis of cost, which would amount to about £1.5 million. 'I thought it was a waste of money and unnecessary because all the private and public polls showed we were streets ahead,' he recalled. But Lord McAlpine – who, as Treasurer, would have been expected to jib at spending such a vast sum on advertising at the end of a campaign that saw his party 20 per cent ahead – supported Saatchi's.

Parkinson was intrigued but uneasy about the cost and agreed with Lawson. He rang Bell and delivered the bad news. 'I'm sorry, we can't do it,' he said. 'People will think we have money to burn if we take out a whole page in a newspaper to print one sentence. I'm sure the PM will agree when she sees it.' Parkinson showed the ads to Mrs Thatcher who concurred: 'We can't waste money on three-page advertisements.' Bell refused to accept the decision and tried to change her mind. 'This is risky. It could cost you the election,' he said dramatically. But Parkinson refused to budge. 'I really think it will be damaging,' he said.

'Well, then, we'll pay it for ourselves,' responded Bell angrily.

'Look, Tim, it's just a bloody advertisement,' countered Parkinson. 'You're not Michelangelo and this isn't the ceiling of the Sistine Chapel.'[12]

However, Saatchi's chairman refused to give up and tried to persuade the Prime Minister directly. But he was not nearly as influential in 1983 as he had been in 1979 and during that last week he was often excluded from key meetings. At one point he was barred from 10 Downing Street when even Mrs Thatcher would not see him. The final decision was made in the Prime Minister's private plane on the tarmac in London on the final Friday just before she flew to Edinburgh. 'I really think that to spend hundreds of thousands of pounds on blank pieces of paper is going too far,' she said, and asked Michael Spicer to confirm the cancellation. He left the plane and called Bell: 'The PM says it's not on. Remove the ads.' Bell was furious but the decision stood. Lord McAlpine had the last word on Parkinson's veto. 'If we win on Thursday, you'll be a hero,' he told him, 'but if we lose by one, you should emigrate without delay.'[13]

After the campaign, when Saatchi's bill arrived at Central Office, Spicer was astonished. 'What on earth is going on?' he asked Keith Britto. In his estimation the 'amount due' of £3,624,000 was a massive £750,000 in excess of agreed budgets, and included invoices for the ads for the last Sunday's papers that had been neither commissioned nor used. Saatchi's view was that they had been approved by Lord McAlpine, the space had been booked and they faced penalty charges from the newspapers. But the agency had included the full newspaper fees plus a commission of 15 per cent. They also hinted strongly that as they were expanding corporately they needed the money.

However, Spicer, a hard-nosed economist, was adamant that the ads had not been authorised and that the money had not been spent. Therefore, the invoice was not valid. Yet the Prime Minister backed the agency. She was grateful to Saatchi and Saatchi and would not query the invoice. But Spicer handed it to Britto, who spent the next three days meticulously checking and cross-referencing the items. He found several discrepancies in Saatchi's expenses as well as the uncommissioned advertisements. Eventually, after a series of tough meetings with Bell and Michael Dobbs, the party refused to pay the full amount and Saatchi's wrote off the £750,000 'arrears'.

Charles Saatchi believed that the fortunes of his agency and the Tory Party were inextricably linked. This was curious because, although Maurice was by now a committed admirer of the Tory Establishment, Charles was no Conservative and closer to being an anarchist. Saatchis, in fact, did a sizeable amount of work for the Tories for which they were never paid because Charles Saatchi recognised that, like the BA account, some clients were prestigious and beneficial for the long-term prosperity of the agency. According to former managing director Roy Warman: 'It's absolutely true that the Tories did not pay the proper price for everything we [Saatchis] did. I know that we did things that were not charged for and time for work we did was not always properly accounted for. That I am absolutely sure of. Whether these items were identified as write-offs I don't know. In 1979 the campaign went on for a long time. It was a bit like repitching for the account every three months without the client paying for the new business pitches. Whether these costs were identified as write-offs in accountancy terms is a moot point. The fact is they got an awful lot for a great deal less than they paid for.' A lot of unsolicited development work for the party was not charged for, and invoices for the production costs of the PPBs and PEBs were not paid. In 1981 the agency had even produced the party's political broadcasts for free. Instead of hiring a studio, they used the free production and editing facilities available at the BBC to all political parties for their broadcasts.[14]

The financial arrangement between the party and the agency was laid bare when Lord McAlpine asked Maurice Saatchi in the summer of 1978 how much money his party owed the agency. 'It's up to about half a million pounds,' Maurice replied.

'Phew,' replied the Tory treasurer. 'We haven't got that amount. Now, we're entirely in your hands. We can pay you in a year's time. There won't be any interest, of course.'

Maurice agreed. He had calculated that the agency was big enough to carry the debt – but it made a dent in that year's figures and was a sharp blow to the idea that the account could be run on a commercial basis.[15]

This frustrated some senior Saatchi executives, and after the 1979 election Terry Bannister had suggested they should consider resigning from the account. Saatchi's had been charging for third-party costs – newspaper ads and production costs – but not for their time. 'We were not treating it as a commercial account,' said Bannister. 'We were not making any money from it and I wanted it re-examined.' Bell, however, was bound up in the glamour of high politics and thought Bannister crazy even to raise the idea.

MELTDOWN

After the 1983 general election triumph, Bell was in a hyper, exultant mood. He was living on a high. 'Tim's an obsessive,' said a former Saatchi's executive. 'He's not moderate about anything. The joke at Saatchi's was that he rattled. There was a pill to go to sleep, a vitamin pill in the morning and so on. It's quite a dangerous personality to have.'[16] During meetings he talked even faster than usual and at exorbitant length. At a Proctor and Gamble presentation, one of their executives whispered to Ed Wax, a senior Saatchi's executive: 'Gee, this guy talks like a Spanish commercial, and he's smart too.' However, what many of his colleagues discovered was that the rapid-fire delivery and extreme mood swings were caused partly, though not on that occasion, by his cocaine habit, which had been an open secret among close friends for some time. Bell first started taking the drug in 1978 when he began to spend a lot of time socially with jazz and rock musicians, and film directors who made commercials. Bell never denied it but took no action when *Private Eye* repeatedly referred to his cocaine habit and always maintained he could control it: 'I was never addicted to cocaine,' he told me in 1993. When asked about it by an Australian journalist, Bell replied that 'whatever the fault, one never cries "Foul"'.[17]

Cocaine, or a 'mood enhancer' as it was known in the advertising industry, was not difficult to obtain. In some production companies it was almost like standard currency, available at about £60 per gram. 'There were plenty of drugs and drink knocking around', recalled Tim Mellors, former creative director at Saatchi's in the early 1980s. 'I don't know how much was actually done in the building. I'm sure there must have been some, but I didn't see the police arresting anyone in there. Cocaine was the drug of choice for the 1980s and in some of the clubs cocaine and champagne would be passed around.' According to Mellors, the attraction was the fast lifestyle: 'It was a mile a minute talking and lots of jerking about behaviour,' he said. 'The kind of braggadocio element that drugs like that do to you'.[18]

As his relationship with the Brothers worsened, so did Bell's reliance on cocaine . The crunch came when Saatchi's bought Compton's USA and he was again excluded from the negotiations. What made it worse was that the chairmanship of the new worldwide company went to Milton Gossett in New York. 'That was my job and they gave it to somebody else,' he said.[19]

Bell was enraged, but Charles tried to reassure him: 'Don't worry, he's [Gossett] going to retire in two years.' In fact, he stayed eight.[20] Instead, Bell was made chairman of Saatchi and Saatchi International. It sounded grand but because his responsibilities excluded the USA, where two-thirds of the group profits came from, it soon became clear that he had been sidelined. Officially, he was in charge of Europe, Australia and the Far East, where there was relatively little business – and on occasions Charles and Maurice even prevented him having access to overseas clients. In advertising terms, he had been exiled to the Third World. To compound the feeling of isolation, Bell was moved away from his power-base at Charlotte Street to a new, barren, open-plan office at Downing House in Maple Street. 'It was effectively a departure lounge,' said a colleague. 'It looked like an isolation ward,' said another.

What made it worse was that he had to report not to the Brothers but to Milton Gossett. They did not get on. In his frustration, Bell would stay in the office as late as 2 a.m. to telephone New York and accuse them of 'getting at' him. The only major international client was Proctor and Gamble, which was controlled by Gossett and this annoyed Bell intensely. He would call the multi-millionaire to harangue him and they would have bitter transatlantic rows.

Everyone knew that Bell's new post was meaningless, and as he needed and thrived on bustling activity, he became increasingly frustrated. This of course, was what the Brothers wanted. The ever-loyal Roy Warman would stay late in the office with Bell, who was often close to tears, drinking Scotch and lashing out at the Brothers. 'Governments listen to me,' he would say. 'Why won't those two arseholes?'

By the late summer of 1983 Bell was barely recognisable as the man of his heyday in the late 1970s and early 1980s: his behaviour and personality had changed significantly. This was partly because of the deterioration of his relationship with the Brothers but also because of the effects of cocaine. 'Erratic' and 'unreliable' are the words most of his former close colleagues use to describe him during this brief but traumatic period. He would leave meetings at twenty minute intervals. He would come into the office late – unheard of in the past. His speech was often incoherent and slurred. His eye movements were exaggerated and he was often paranoid – he had a bodyguard throughout the 1983 election campaign. 'Although I didn't deal with him frequently, I had a lot of time for Tim and he was the inspiration behind the agency's success,' recalled Peter Suchet, a Saatchi's account director between 1978 and 1988, 'but he was finding it difficult to function and was quite troubled during this period. His behaviour was unpredictable and you could never tell how he was going to react. He would keep people in his office and talk to them for hours on end for no apparent reason.'

His self-esteem was at its lowest and cocaine was an escape from the misery. 'Why do you take it?' Roy Warman once asked him. 'You don't understand how it makes you feel,' replied Bell. 'It makes a good man great.'

By September 1983, he was close to being out of control, although there is no evidence that he was addicted to cocaine. 'Yes, everybody knows about it [the cocaine] so I don't mind talking about it, because that's the way I remember him strongly,' said Margaret Bischoff, a planner who worked closely with him at Saatchi's during this period. 'When I joined he was quite far along that road already . . . Once, I sat there trying to write a presentation. He came in and sat down for ten minutes. Then he sort of jumped up and he was completely gone. He was so hyped. He couldn't sit still, you know, and just couldn't concentrate any more. He started writing something or saying what we should do and then he sort of jumped up and put some music on. Then he went out and came in again and just had no concentration. In the end, we put it together and he was a brilliant presenter.

'He once talked about it [cocaine]. He felt he was much more brilliant when he took it and he felt he didn't have any particular brilliance without it . . . Afterwards, when he had been off for quite a while and he was back in the office and everything stabilised, we went out from time to time to have lunch together and he once said, "I feel so boring without the coke," and I asked him, "How do you feel now? Do you feel better now that you're off it?" and he said, "Well, I sometimes feel I'm so boring." I mean, good God, he was the last person to be boring, but I always felt he was very insecure and he didn't have that much self-confidence – or not as much as he could have had, really, with all his achievements. He was a brilliant man, and given that he was so brilliant he had no reason to be insecure or lack self-confidence, but I guess it had to do with his relationship with the Saatchi brothers.'

The cocaine however also induced an artificial self-confidence that made Bell believe that everything was possible. One meeting with a client went on for four hours because he could not stop talking. During another, when the client was proving troublesome, he rose from the table and declared to colleagues, 'I'm going to tell them to sack their marketing department.' When told that this would not be prudent, he shouted, his eyes bulging, 'I can do anything I want.' According to Margaret Bischoff, 'There was not one meeting when he could stay quiet and concentrate for a long period of time. After one hour he went out and you were sure he was going to take some more stuff to keep him going.'

Bell was visibly in decline. He had been moved into exile in the new office far away from the action – 'Death by ignoring,' as one colleague called it; his judgement had gone; he was hiring people at random and at exorbitant salaries. His management style was increasingly eccentric. On one occasion he sent ten Saatchi executives on a one-day course at an Ascot hotel on 'Signs of Alcohol Addiction'. Roy Warman and Terry Bannister refused to go, saying it was a waste of time, and pointing out, half-jokingly, that it was Bell himself who should have been at the head of the queue. But the other eight went. At lunchtime they were informed: 'Wine is available but not advised', so they took the available option and drank all the best with little marked effect.

Perhaps the lowest point came on 22 September 1983, during a meeting for all the new agency's international managers, at a hotel by Lac Helmen near Geneva. In front of fifty Saatchi executives from all over the world, Bell spoke from 9 a.m. until 10.30 but according to those present, it was 'intellectual gibberish, incoherent and just plain wrong'. The charts didn't make any sense and the figures did not add up. It was sad to see the legendary Bell in such a state. His body was slumped, his eyelids heavy and his speech slow and ponderous.

After the interval, however, the old Bell, miraculously, was back. The words tumbled out coherently, the eyes were clear and the energy had returned. Now he was making sense. 'There are three things we are going to do to make our new global company work,' he said. 'We're going to globalise the creation of ads. One ad will run all over the world, controlled by Jeremy Sinclair. Then we're going to make all our TV commercials in one place, to be controlled by John Staten. Finally, we're going to centralise our media under one person and make global deals with media multinational tycoons like Rupert Murdoch. That will be run by John Perris.'

Bell's problem was that he had a dependent character: he had leant on either his girlfriend Virginia, Margaret Thatcher or the Brothers. The crisis point arrived when Virginia left him and returned to Australia. That, combined with his ostracism by the Brothers, drove him to despair and chronic depression. He was staring into the abyss.

Close friends like Bill Muirhead were extremely worried and tried to get help, and even Charles Saatchi was sufficiently concerned to call him every day and arrange for the company doctor, Robert LeFevre, to make an emergency visit to his house in Hampstead. Fortunately, that evening in October 1983, Margaret Bischoff and Michael Dobbs were with him until the doctor arrived at midnight. For the next four hours he poured out his heart, railing against the Brothers and everyone else. 'I wasn't sure if he would survive then, because I think he was at the brink somehow,' recalled Bischoff. 'He had stopped taking cocaine and he said he was under medical control. The doctor came along at midnight and was supposed to come again. We sat there and kept talking to him so he had somebody to talk to . . . Before, he felt that he was still in control, but at the time Michael and I were up at his house, he was aware that it was "five minutes to Charlie", as we say in Germany [close to crisis point]. And that it was absolutely adamant that he stayed away [from the cocaine]. And he felt he could now, with the help of the doctor . . . We just talked about everything. The Prime Minister was on his mind very much at that time. He was very frustrated with Maurice and Charles that day, that they either took his problem too seriously or too much against him.'

After that evening, Bell recovered, due partly to his extraordinary will power. He also received professional medical help. Within a few weeks he was a different man, although he found it hard – perhaps understandably – to accept that he had had a problem. 'Are you better now after your treatment?' asked Keith Macmillan, the *Campaign* photographer. 'You shouldn't believe everything you're told,' replied Bell defensively.

One of the most decisive factors in his rehabilitation was Virginia's return from Australia. 'She had a very positive stabilising affect on

Tim,' David Miln, former director of new business at Saatchis, said. 'He was distraught when she left him and that was a major factor in pulling himself together.'

By late 1983, it was clear that Bell was on his way out of the agency. Others were laying plans to appoint his successor as Saatchi's became even more corporate in outlook. 'You know how the business works,' Maurice told Roy Warman. 'You know how to make money. Tim has been good at getting clients and driving on the business, but not making profits for the company.' Bell set up a meeting for the twelve group account directors at the Regent Palace Hotel in central London. He told them that he was stepping back and that the agency needed management changes. He hinted quite strongly that he would be difficult to replace. He then told his colleagues that they were all to be assessed by Warren Lamb, an industrial psychologist, whose speciality was re-evaluating management techniques. Lamb would come into the agency, attend meetings and sit with the executives. His strategy was based on a three-track notion of investigation, intention and commitment. The idea was greeted with sniggering around the table. 'We weren't that enthusiastic but saw nothing wrong with it,' said one of those present. But Bell was adamant. 'We're going to do this to help shape the future,' he said.

The psychologist duly sat in on meetings and produced profiles of each group director. The outcome was that Roy Warman, then commercial director, and Terry Bannister, a group account director, were made joint managing directors. For the next six months they reported to Bell as a form of dress rehearsal before they took over.

In December 1983, Bell made one final attempt to secure the recognition he thought he deserved and become a director of the holding company. He approached Charles and argued that most of his colleagues felt he should have joined long ago. It was a highly contentious issue. The Saatchis had always kept their board tight. Even though it was a large public company, there were only five directors: the Brothers, the chairman Kenneth Gill, finance director Martin Sorrell and company secretary David Perring.

Charles was furious. 'You'll never, ever, go on the public company board,' he told Bell. 'No advertising people go on the board. If they did, then every time we make an acquisition we'd have to put the person [from the newly acquired agency] we bought on the public company board. It's just going to be Maurice and me and the money men.'[21]

After fourteen years of Charles's outbursts, Bell was used to them but this time he was hurt and upset by his remarks, particularly the words 'never, ever'. For years to come he resented Charles's reaction to his request and his anger grew when other advertising people joined the board of the Saatchi holding company. He decided to leave. It was just a question of how, when and where.

Chapter Five

High Stakes
at 10 Downing Street

'You can't use him [Tim Bell], he works for the Tories'
Geoffrey Kirk, former director of communications of the National
Coal Board, to Ian MacGregor, during the 1984–5 miners' strike

In January 1984, Tim Bell decided to rest at home for a month and contemplate his future. Nineteen eighty-three had been probably the worst year of his life. He had been close to losing everyone and everything he held most dear. Even his apparently impregnable relationship with Margaret Thatcher had suffered – he saw her only three times during the election campaign. Virginia had left him, although he had persuaded her to return, and he was now resigned to parting company with the Brothers. These people has formed the bedrock of his personal and professional life.

After a holiday in Kenya with Virginia in February, Bell returned to work with his mind made up. 'I don't want to work here any more,' he told Charles. Despite their differences, Saatchi's founder tried to keep him: 'Why don't you set up a public affairs consultancy?' he replied. 'You're very good at that. We'll finance you. You can own 45 or 50 per cent of it, or whatever you like. It will be yours and we'll own a chunk of it, and it'll be really be good.'

That, of course, was not what Bell wanted: 'It felt like you've been somebody's wife', he said, 'and now you're told you can be the maid.'[1]

However, as events unfolded it was public relations and political crisis management that brought about a radical shift in Bell's career.

Inevitably, this occurred through his close association and friendship with Prime Minister Thatcher, which he had re-established after the relative frisson of 1983.

The headlines in the early weeks of 1984 were dominated by Mark Thatcher's business activities. The source of the controversy was his consultancy with Cementation International Ltd. In 1981 Cementation, a wholly owned subsidiary of Trafalgar House plc, was lobbying hard for a 300 million contract to build a new university in the prosperous Gulf state of Oman. Despite the potential interest of other construction firms, the Sultan of Oman awarded the order, without it going out to tender, to Cementation. It then emerged that Mark had been in Oman at the same time as his mother had visited the country and both had lobbied separately for Cementation to secure the lucrative deal.

When the story broke in the *Observer*, so did the political and media dam: all the newspapers, radio and TV followed up allegations of under influence on the Prime Minister's part and questions in Parliament were asked almost daily. Mrs Thatcher was under considerable pressure. She countered that she had been merely 'batting for Britain' and helping to secure valuable export orders for UK firms. She had pushed for Cementation, she argued, because they were the only contractor involved. But she persistently refused to answer whether she knew that her son had a financial interest in the outcome of the deal. Mark admitted that he had been briefly hired by Cementation and 'played a very small part in a very successful British contract'.[2] But his usual response was laced with paranoia and showed signs of a persecution complex: 'It's become "Get Mark Thatcher Time" in certain sections of the media,' he said. 'And they don't care how they do it.'[3] This was usually delivered with an ill-mannered, arrogant smirk.

As the Oman scandal showed no sign of disappearing from public view, the Prime Minister and her inner circle became increasingly concerned about the political damage it was causing. Something needed to be done – and no one was more conscious of the potential peril than Tim Bell.

Privately, like all Mrs Thatcher's admirers, Bell thought her son was not only inept but dangerous. His views, as we have seen, were recorded for posterity in 1981 during that birthday dinner for Kenny Everett. He was also critical of Mark receiving sponsorship funds for his motor racing activities from Japanese rather than British firms. 'He had gone into the arrangement with his eyes wide open in the full knowledge that he would profit from it,' said Bell. 'Margaret would never have interfered, but I'm sure her staff would [in stopping the deal].'[4]

Publicly, Bell defended him. 'He is tenacious, hard-working and has never courted publicity,' he said. 'I respect him enormously . . . He does have a clipped manner and a lot of people think he is being rude. This is not the case. In fact he has a sense of humour and introduces himself as "charmless Mark".'[5]

Despite his staunch public rearguard action, Bell was a shrewd strategist and knew that Mark's commercial activities were politically explosive. 'Tim thought he was a bomb just waiting to go off,' said a political source close to him at the time.[6] Hence Bell co-ordinated a public relations operation on Mark's behalf to limit the damage caused to the Prime Minister by the disclosures of the Oman deal. Wisely, Bell did not accept any payment. 'I just advise him as a friend,' he said.[7] In fact, he did it as a favour to Mark's mother.

On the evening of Friday 9 March 1984, Bell telephoned David Boddy, who had worked closely with him as director of publicity at Tory Central Office, and asked him to come to his house in Hampstead the following afternoon. The topic for discussion was the media treatment of Mark Thatcher. Bell told Boddy that the Prime Minister had 'requested his assistance' in dealing with the press and television coverage of her son. Boddy, who had just left Central Office to set up his own company, Capital Publishing, agreed and was hired by Bell on a contract worth £18,000. Bell secured the funds to pay him from Conservative-supporting sources or 'friends of the party', as one source described it. Under Boddy's leadership, a small group was then formed. Apart from Bell, this consisted of Michael Dobbs, his personal assistant at Saatchis, and Rodney Tyler, a freelance journalist who was a consultant to the agency on a retainer of £1,000 a month.[8] Sir Gordon Reece, whose cigar smoke was often in evidence during a political crisis or campaign, was also consulted. Their brief was to engage in 'crisis management'. The basic idea was to keep Mark out of the newspapers, remove him from the media agenda, and when there were press enquiries, to ensure that questions were answered and statements written and released.

At first Mark co-operated. He called in when arriving at Heathrow airport so that photo opportunities could be arranged. There followed a series of articles and front-page stories with pictures of the Prime Minister's son, particularly with his American girlfriend – 'Top Mark' ran a *Sun* headline. When it was decided that Mark should make an apologia for his actions, it was through the medium of an exclusive double-page interview with Rodney Tyler in the *Mail on Sunday* – 'Mark Says I Am Sorry'. Five weeks later, on 13 May 1984, readers of the *News of the World* were treated to another exclusive story about him and his Texan girlfriend, oil heiress Karen Fortson: 'Our Love – By Mark and his Girl'. Words and pictures by Rodney Tyler. Tyler arranged for Fleet Street photographers to be at Heathrow when Mark and Karen flew in from Paris with her mother and twin brother. He then accompanied them to Chequers for Sunday lunch.[9]

Bell played a discreet role. He spent huge amounts of time on the telephone to Mark, advising him on the most minute details of his rehabilitation. But the Prime Minister's son did not respond well to the pressure: he began to act irrationally and showed signs of stress. His moods swung dramatically, from anger to despair, which resulted in bouts of unstable behaviour. One night he attended the Miss World dinner at the Grosvenor House ballroom. After the main course, he suddenly stood up and started to throw sugar lumps at journalists covering the beauty contest, shouting obscenities at them. 'He was on the verge of cracking up,' said a PR aide, who witnessed this spectacle.[10] It did not help that he was surly and suspicious of David Boddy, who was being paid to help him. He was always late for appointments and never responded to questions with a straight answer, which made it impossible for Boddy to do his job. He had to talk privately to Steve Tipping, Mark's business partner, to find out what was going on.

The major problem for the crisis-management team was that Thatcher and Tipping refused to disclose any detailed information or answer questions about the Oman contract. 'The press are out to get me,' was all that Mark could muster, so Boddy was reduced to issuing bland, meaningless denials. This, of course, made it impossible to defuse the situation and kept him in the firing line.

When it was realised that the media damage-limitation tactic was not sufficient, Bell joined Gordon Reece and Mark's parents for a meeting at the family home in Chelsea. They decided that something drastic had to be done. Denis suggested that he could talk to David

Wickins, a business associate and family friend, about arranging a job for his wayward son, preferably far away. He did so, and a lunch at Chequers was arranged at short notice, which Bell also attended. They agreed that Mark should leave the country.[11]

Moving to Texas was a smart PR coup for Mark Thatcher. It removed him from the media and political spotlight and the story faded away. David Boddy's thankless task was virtually complete and he submitted his invoice of £18,000 to Bell. But he only received £5,000 and never saw the remaining £13,000. It was never disclosed who bankrolled the 'Save Mark' operation. When asked, Boddy replied: 'A group of senior Conservatives. They were not based at Central Office but they were connected with it . . . I decided to cut my losses and forget it [the unpaid invoices]. I thought that when Mark next got into trouble we wouldn't be available to help him.'[12]

After the Oman affair Mark Thatcher was, indeed, periodically in trouble and it was Bell who fielded the calls from journalists and acted as his unofficial spokesman. Over the years he has become more impassioned in his defence of the Prime Minister's son, who has made millions by trading off his name in the arms, oil and construction business. Although Mark became universally unpopular even in the staunchly pro-Thatcher press, his PR adviser has remained stubbornly loyal, and when asked by Russell Miller of the *Sunday Times* why Mark had refused him an interview, Bell exploded, 'Why on earth should he talk to you? What possible benefit could it be for him when he knows from the start that he is going to be rubbished? If you receive nothing but abuse it is hardly surprising that you don't want to talk to them. I don't blame him . . . He won't talk about what he does for the simple reason that it is none of your business. I am sure if you were a potential client he would be happy to talk to you for hours about his company . . . It is the newspapers that have created all this hostility. He has no reason to thank the media for anything at all. He is attacked for trying to help his mother when you might think he would have been applauded . . . It is called straightforward media harassment and it has been going on for ten years. The real story is why on earth the media has been doing this, but I know you'll never print that. I think what has been happening is that the media has been trying to get at Mrs Thatcher through her son. It is nothing more or less than a vendetta.

'Sometimes I have advised clients to settle their differences with the media by giving interviews, but I don't think it's a good idea in his case because there is absolutely no goodwill towards him at all. If you think there is something there that you can find – some way of getting at him – you will do it. All the old rumours and cuttings are dredged up, all the rubbish about arms dealing. Hopefully, you will make a mistake and then we will be able to sue the pants off you.

'It may be that he is rather brash, rude, brutish in the way he behaves, maybe he boasts too much, but he is basically an ordinary bloke trying to get on with his life. I can promise you that if you knew the bloke you wouldn't find him the remotest bit interesting.'[13]

Bell would repeat this routine whenever journalists probed the source of Mark Thatcher's wealth: 'invasion of privacy', 'nothing in it' and 'way of getting at his mother'. When I wrote *Thatcher's Gold*, a biography of Mark Thatcher, I went to see Bell in his Mayfair office with my co-author Paul Halloran. He was loquacious and indiscreet but also nervous, almost twitchy. 'Mark does not want this book to be written any more than I would want one published about me,' he told us in May 1993. 'It's just not in our interests.'

Five months later Bell was called upon again when evidence surfaced that Mark Thatcher had profited from Al-Yamamah, the multi-billion-pound arms deal with Saudi Arabia that his mother had negotiated and signed. Bell had often denied this allegation on Mark's behalf, but there were now a multitude of sources for the story. 'I have never said that Mark was not involved in Al-Yamamah', he told Paul Halloran. 'All I've ever done is repeat what he's told me.'

It was a measure of Bell's allegiance to the Prime Minister that he would take on the burden of representing, unpaid, her son, who everyone agreed was 'the client from hell'. It was also his first experience of political firefighting on behalf of 10 Downing Street. The Thatcher years would be dominated by monumental struggles of will between the Prime Minister and her cabinet as she strove to transform Britain. To help her implement what her former private secretary Charles Powell described as 'a revolution', there was always a role for someone close to her, but outside the official party and government machines, to act as a private agent of influence. And Bell was a willing and well-placed candidate.

'IT'S A WAR'

Almost as soon as the skirmishes involving her son were over, the Prime Minister faced a new political battle on a different front. On 6 March 1984, the National Coal Board (NCB) announced the closure of 4 million tonnes of capacity, which meant the shutting down of twenty collieries and the eventual loss of 20,000 jobs. Led by the indefatigable Arthur Scargill, 140,000 miners walked out on strike and embarked on what was to prove a colossal and titanic struggle of force, endurance and wits.

Lasting just under a year, it was the longest and bitterest industrial dispute in British history and there were severe casualties. The strike cost one murder, thirteen other deaths, thousands of injuries, nearly 10,000 arrests and over £7 billion of taxpayers' money. But its significance was as much political as social and economic. For it matched Scargill and the miners, the Praetorian Guard of the trade union movement, against Mrs Thatcher's government, which was determined to smash organised labour as a weapon of political action. The stakes were high on both sides.

The appointment of Ian MacGregor as chairman of the NCB in September 1993 was a clear sign that confrontation was inevitable. A seventy-year-old American, MacGregor had a track record of clinically closing and stripping down major segments of an industry in the pursuit of profitability. He had done this as head of British Steel and was now prepared to do the same to mining. But he knew that first there would have to be a decisive conflict with the militant National Union of Mineworkers (NUM). 'A strike is inevitable,' he told Malcolm Edwards, the NCB's marketing director, three months before the dispute. 'If there is going to be a fight, we should get on with it. It's going to be a long job.' Cabinet ministers like Nigel Lawson, energy secretary from 1981 until 1983 and then chancellor of the exchequer until 1989, also told colleagues that a strike was unavoidable and, indeed, necessary: 'The problems of the coal industry could not be resolved without the decisive defeat of the militant arm of the NUM, even if that meant facing up to a strike, for which we would need to be properly prepared,' he later acknowledged.[14]

The political stakes were high and nobody was more conscious of that than Mrs Thatcher. She had been in the cabinet during the 1972 and 1974 coal strikes and had witnessed how the Heath government was brought down because public opinion favoured the miners' cause. The sympathy was genuine, although former NCB executives claimed it was tinged with outdated sentimentality for miners' working conditions. The point, though, was that the Tory government had been isolated and defenceless against the combined force of the miners' determination and the public's attitude. Heath went to the country in the midst of what he believed was industrial insurrection and asked, 'Who Governs Britain?' The electorate's answer was: 'Not you.'

A decade later, the fear of a repeat performance was at the forefront of Mrs Thatcher's mind and she implemented contingency plans to ensure that she would win not only the strike but also the battle for public opinion. She sanctioned a relatively generous redundancy package for miners, passed tough employment legislation that favoured employers during industrial action and, crucially, appointed Peter Walker as energy secretary, a brilliant publicist with a sympathetic, moderate face.

The 1984–5 strike was really about the battle for public opinion and the government was presented with two bonuses: the union's refusal to hold a ballot made the strikers look undemocratic; and the violence on the picket lines made them appear lawless. 'Presentation was absolutely the key to success or failure,' said Malcolm Edwards. 'The government was in a state of extreme agitation when it came to anything to do with the media.'

When the strike started the government had to demonstrate that it was in control, but the real issue was how to communicate that to the public. They soon discovered that presentation was not one of the NCB chairman's strengths. 'Ian MacGregor was commercially brilliant,' said Edwards. 'The cleverest man I ever worked with. But he had zero understanding and even less love for the British media. He found journalists intrusive, irrelevant and irritating. He was used to strikes in Wyoming where there was little media attention and if there was a trouble-making newspaper it would be, how shall I say, dealt with. Because there had been little national media in the USA, he had been subject to less scrutiny and so in the past he had a fairly easy ride.'

The UK media, in contrast, is intensely centralised and the spotlight was on the septnagenarian American. Industrial correspondents like Geoffrey Goodman of the *Daily Mirror*, Paul Routledge of *The*

Times and John Lloyd of the *Financial Times* were experienced, resourceful and knowledgeable and MacGregor could not understand the necessity for the searching analysis to which he was subjected. 'He did not like journalists,' said Edwards, 'and thought there might be sinister reasons why they asked questions in the way they did.' Ministers soon realised that in the propaganda stakes MacGregor was no match for Scargill. The coal board boss looked like an old man, while the miners' leader was rigorous and alert. MacGregor was inarticulate, hesitant and spoke in a ponderous American drawl while Scargill was sharp and eloquent. MacGregor came across as an outsider who appeared almost contemptuous about how his actions were received, whereas Scargill was a Yorkshireman defending jobs and local communities. According to Bernard Ingham, MacGregor was a 'total PR disaster'.

There was also a strategic problem with the NCB chairman: he wanted to get the miners back to work because he was convinced that, once back in the pits, they would stay there, disinclined to rejoin the strike. Consequently, he was not too concerned about the wording of any negotiated settlement document. Former colleagues say that MacGregor planned to implement his policy regardless of the precise details and clauses of any piece of paper. In this event Mrs Thatcher and her ministers were afraid that, in the post-settlement press conferences, Scargill would articulate compromise as victory, which would be politically catastrophic.

As cabinet ministers discussed the 'MacGregor problem', the pressure was on to find a solution. One of the most publicity-conscious was Lord Young, who had just been brought into the cabinet as minister without portfolio and who met MacGregor periodically for breakfast. Young realised that the NCB boss had never mastered the art of dealing with the media and, in April 1984, a month into the strike, suggested that he should appoint an outside public-relations adviser. MacGregor was interested because he was dissatisfied with Geoffrey Kirk, the NCB's public-relations director, although he was highly respected by the industrial correspondents. 'That set all my alarm bells ringing,' said MacGregor later. 'This was not going to be a dispute settled in the classic way in a week or two, after which Mr Kirk could go back to his cosy chats in the media. This had all the makings of a gloves-off job. I wanted a man who could handle the rough and tumble.'[15]

That morning Lord Young telephoned Norman Tebbit, the trade and industry secretary, for advice. Tebbit consulted his special adviser, Michael Dobbs, who suggested Tim Bell. Young knew Bell from his days as chairman of the Manpower Services Commission (MSC) when Saatchi and Saatchi had been their advertising agency, and thought it an astute idea. 'I took to Tim straight away,' he said. 'Puffing away on an inexhaustible supply of cigarettes, he is imaginative, enthusiastic and the archetypical "can do" man.'[16] The Prime Minister enthusiastically went along with the appointment and Bell was brought into the action.

The hiring of Bell was not greeted with such glee in the NCB's own communications department. 'You can't use him, he works for the Tories,' shouted Geoffrey Kirk, who saw the dispute as an industrial not a political struggle. He thought that Bell's appointment sent out the wrong signal: that the strike was about helping the Conservative government rather than the mining industry.

After his first presentation to the NCB on media strategy, Bell approached Kirk: 'I hope you don't feel put upon by us appearing out of the blue like this. We're not here to take your place, but to help. I hope we can get along and work together'. But the PR director was firm: 'I do resent you being here and I am not going to speak to you or co-operate with you in any way, shape or form.'[17]

MacGregor took no notice of Kirk's opposition and immediately and regularly took Bell into his confidence. 'Tim, we're not going to give away the store,' he told him. Bell privately sniggered at such language but liked and respected MacGregor – 'a great man'[18] – and referred to him as 'Mac'. 'A sweet, lovely man, never forgets birthdays,' he told friends. But Bell was fully aware of MacGregor's limitations as a communicator and advised him on which TV programmes he should be interviewed. 'Ian MacGregor didn't like going on television,' recalled Bell. 'He found the whole thing extraordinarily distasteful. He felt he just couldn't develop an argument and get his point across. He also talked in clichés which people were not familiar with. This made it very hard for people to follow exactly what he's talking about. He would say things like: 'It's like playing a salmon, the ghillie plays the salmon.' When he talked like that, of course, the audience got completely lost.'[19]

At first, to use a MacGregor phrase, nobody knew where the dust was going to settle but a routine established itself. The NUM would make progress by, for example, ensuring that little coal was sent by rail. Then they were in retreat when the Nottinghamshire miners voted to work normally. There were no decisive strategic victories or defeats, just heavy casualties on both sides. Early in the dispute MacGregor, according to Bell, was 'like a piece of granite' and inflexible. 'Wait, wait, wait,' he would say. His attitude was based on his past experience of long, bitter, violent disputes in North America where the workers had been ground into submission and he did not realise that it was politically and industrially expedient to be seen to be negotiating. Neither did he understand the importance of its propaganda benefits. He had no desire to settle the dispute quickly and believed that delays could only enhance his negotiating stance. 'It's true that MacGregor was not worried about it lasting a long time,' said Michael Eaton, the NCB's public spokesman. 'He used to refer in a sardonic way to a strike in Wyoming that lasted six years so he had no real sense of urgency, but some ministers were concerned about the social consequences of the violence.'

Although he was now on the point of leaving, Bell set up his own operations room in his bleak Saatchi's office in Maple Street. He retained the old Mark Thatcher PR team of David Boddy, who briefed political correspondents, and Rodney Tyler, who placed and even wrote stories himself. On 3 April 1984, just before starting work for Bell on the NCB account, Tyler wrote a feature for the *Daily Express* headlined 'Scargill's Seven Shadows – When King Arthur Hears Voices, These Are The Voices He Hears'. The article, heavily ironic, given Bell's role, continued: 'Every King needs a Court – a group of tried and tested cronies to advise and guide him, flatter and applaud him. None more so in his present bitter battle than miners' leader Arthur Scargill.'

A month later, on May Day, Tyler secured an exclusive interview with Ian MacGregor for the *Sun* – 'Scargill Doesn't Scare Me'. This page-long piece portrayed the NCB boss thus: 'He is not Scargill's lurid bogeyman at all. He is more like many of his miners than King Arthur himself. He has their toughness and inner strength.' Apart from six short introductory paragraphs, the article was one long quote from MacGregor.

The next day Tom Condon, the *Sun*'s industrial editor, telephoned Geoffrey Kirk at the NCB and complained that his own staff had not been consulted about the interview. 'We didn't know about it either,' replied Kirk. The interview had been arranged by Bell, Tyler and the *Sun*'s editor directly with MacGregor without the knowledge of his own press office.[20]

Such incidents increased the tension inside Hobart House, the NCB's head office. But it was the arrival of a new member of MacGregor's unofficial inner circle that caused the most angst among board executives. His name was David Hart and, working alongside Bell, he exerted considerable influence on the chairman. An enigmatic and shadowy figure, Hart's forebears were Polish Jews who had made, lost and retrieved a fortune. His father became wealthy as a merchant banker at Ansbacher's and left his two sons huge trust funds. After an unhappy time at Eton, David Hart dabbled unsuccessfully in film-making before making nearly £1 million as a property speculator. In 1974 he went spectacularly bankrupt after an orgy of over-spending.

After rebuilding his career he managed to secure limited access to the court of Margaret Thatcher, largely through the sheer exuberance of his right-wing libertarian views as expressed in regular features in *The Times*. Hart, like Bell, is one of life's enthusiasts with a flamboyant lifestyle and prone to grandiose political and social gestures. The Prime Minister was a little wary but enjoyed and made use of this latest evangelist for Thatcherism. Four days after the 1983 general election, she wrote to him: 'May I thank you very much for your help during the General Election campaign. I am *most grateful* for the contribution you made.'

In May 1984, Hart visited Shirebrook, Derbyshire, in his chauffeur-driven Mercedes and witnessed the effect that violence on the picket line had had on the people in that divided village. He took the side of the working miners and believed that the intimidation of them and their families was not only systematic, but the direct responsibility of Arthur Scargill.[21] The experience had a profound impact on him and he resolved to immerse himself in the struggle. For Hart, the dispute was solely political and little short of Marxist insurrection with Scargill playing the role of Lenin. 'It was a political event,' he said later. 'It had nothing much to do with the mining industry. It was not about wages and conditions. It was about Scargill's view of how the British political landscape should look versus Mrs Thatcher's and most of the British people's.'[22]

Hart secured a meeting with MacGregor partly through his political connections but principally because his brother had worked with MacGregor at Lehman Brothers in New York. MacGregor asked Bell to join them at his flat in Eaton Square, Belgravia. 'Who is he?' enquired Bell minutes before Hart arrived.

'Some kind of freelance journalist, public-relations consultant, plenty of money,' replied the chairman. 'I've checked him out. He's got connections to the front office.'

'Peter Walker?'

'The Lady.'

At that moment Hart walked in and, after being introduced to Bell, came straight to the point. 'Stop trying to achieve a settlement,' he said bluntly. 'It's a waste of time. You're not fighting an industrial dispute, you're fighting a political war. You're fighting for the freedom of the individual against the tyranny of the collective. It seems to me there's only one viable strategy and that is outright victory . . . Seems to me that means only one thing. Getting the miners back to work without a settlement. Now I have detailed plans in order to achieve that. Would you like to hear them?'

MacGregor turned towards Bell. 'Tim?'

'I like it. I like you, Mr Hart,' said Bell. 'Let's hear your plans.'[23]

MacGregor's new adviser argued that the way to break the strike was to launch an offensive on three fronts: first, a massive propaganda campaign to encourage miners to return to work; second, organise and finance working miners to catalyse this process; and third, wear down the NUM by legal action, using the government's new employment laws.

At another meeting in Hobart House, with Bell and MacGregor, Hart went into more detail. 'The Gulliver Plan will mean that the union will be held down by dozens of tiny ropes,' he said, 'legal actions brought by the working miners themselves. They will be tied down by so many writs they won't be able to move.'

'Legal action is costly,' replied Bell. 'They won't be able to pay.'

'Oh, I'll raise the money. There's plenty of people who want to help with the struggle.'[24]

Bell and Hart became good friends and developed a formidable axis in MacGregor's private office. 'Tim's a mucker,' Hart would quip. Bell, who was very much the senior partner in the relationship, enjoyed his new colleague's company and sense of humour, but was often wary of his more extreme plans. 'Bell had a genius for knocking down an idea without causing offence by joking about it,' said a former Hart aide. 'He would make light fun of Hart's more outlandish proposals and this diverted attention away from them.'

Most significantly, though, Bell agreed with Hart's diagnosis that it was a political strike and that a negotiated settlement should not be pursued. At first, however, they had difficulty in convincing MacGregor of this. 'The motives for the strike are political not financial, chairman,' Bell would tell MacGregor over the telephone. But because of his past experiences of coal strikes in North America, MacGregor believed that industrial action was ultimately always about money and that the dispute could be resolved by offering the miners financial inducements.

By June 1984, MacGregor had been won over by Bell, and also by Hart, whom he described as 'my intelligence officer in the department of economic warfare'.[25] But his increasing reliance on these outsiders angered his own industrial-relations department. Its director, Ned Smith, wanted a negotiated settlement in the long-term interests of the coal industry, and bitterly resented Bell and Hart who he viewed as 'clandestine advisers'[26] and little more than maverick interlopers. He believed that their strategy of legal action and working miners' committees would prolong the strike because it would harden the attitude of striking miners.

Smith first clashed with Bell over his idea that MacGregor should dispatch a letter to every miner headed, bizarrely, 'Dear Colleague'. Its purpose, MacGregor said, was 'to plant in their minds the idea that going back to work was possible'.[27] The industrial relations director was horrified. Based on his own soundings in the industry, Smith advised that a personal letter from MacGregor – who was widely thought of as 'an American butcher' among striking miners – would be counter-productive. However, despite his department's success in persuading miners to defeat the NUM in two ballots before the strike, he was now told that he was 'not a professional communicator'. On 22 June 1984, the letter was sent out albeit amended by Smith. Bell was unperturbed by such hostility: 'Smith and Hunt [his deputy] could not understand that it wasn't about getting a settlement,' he said afterwards.[28]

Two weeks later, on 4 July, the NCB launched their advertising campaign with a series of full-page spreads in the national newspapers under the banner headline of 'How The Miners On Strike Have Been Misled'. There was no attempt to question the men's loyalty to their union but to persuade them to re-examine what they had been told by their leadership. The advertisement also suggested that the strike was 'killing future growth' in the industry. It quoted ICI as having said that the dispute had led the company to have 'second thoughts' about converting its Wilton plant to coal – ICI, however, promptly retorted that the strike was only one of several reasons for its delay.[29]

Unknown to Geoffrey Kirk, the advertising campaign had been covertly instigated and guided by Tim Bell. Some of the ads were drafted at Saatchi's and MacGregor, conscious of Kirk's hostility to his PR consultant, would pretend they were his own ideas. He asked Kirk to persuade the official agency, the CM Partnership, to use them.[30] Bell played a similar clandestine role with the National Working Miners Committee, an organisation set up and funded by David Hart. Their ads – placed in *The Times*, the *Daily Express* and the *Daily Mail* – had been designed by Bell, who also wrote one of the committee's promotional brochures. A typical one was headlined 'Come Off It, Arthur!' . . . and continued, 'Scargill claims he is fighting to save jobs. But while he's trying to picket us out, pits and coal faces are being lost . . . Don't let Scargill tear the union movement apart.' Bell quietly briefed old friends like Sir David English of the *Daily Mail*, and Kelvin McKenzie of the *Sun*, and Andrew Neil of the *Sunday Times*. Occasionally, he was accompanied by MacGregor who much preferred the informal atmosphere of off-the-record briefings to setpiece interviews which he found too confrontational. 'I found it valuable to learn their perception of us and what we were up to,' he said, 'and, most importantly, how they felt the public were reacting to us and our case. This role, played particularly by Tim, helped us more as the strike went on.'[31]

Perhaps Bell's strongest ally in the propaganda war was the *Mail on Sunday* with headlines like 'Say No To Mob Rule' and 'Coal Boss Hits Out At Union "Nazis"'. This was a little surprising as the editor, Stewart Steven, was independently minded with left-of-centre leanings. But he had decided to champion the cause of the Nottinghamshire working miners. His industrial correspondent, Christopher Leake, took up their banner, notably with a front-page story on a self-styled strike-breaker called 'Silver Birch'. Bell, whose main strategy was to get the miners back to work, exploited this and cultivated Leake, making himself available to take calls from him, briefing him and providing stories and tips.

TENSION IN THE WAR ROOM

As the strike continued throughout the summer, the NCB's PR offensive had demonstrably not worked. The number of miners returning to work was a trickle not a flood. Private opinion-poll research commissioned by Bell showed that although attitudes were changing it was happening very slowly. And the running and strategy of MacGregor's own private office, now dominated by Hart and Bell, was being much criticised by his own senior executives like Ned Smith and Geoff Kirk. In siding with his private entourage and overriding advice from professional managers with decades of experience in the coal industry, MacGregor was adopting a high-risk policy.

The situation reached its lowest ebb on Thursday 18 October 1984, when NACODS, whose members were responsible for safety down the pits, voted overwhelmingly to strike, for the first time in their long and moderate history. MacGregor's response, induced by Hart, was to say that 'goddamn NACODS' could 'take their chances' like everyone else. Cabinet ministers were distraught: if the strike went ahead all the pits would close. After another disastrous TV appearance, MacGregor was increasingly viewed as a liability. But it was too late to ditch him.

MacGregor himself seemed aware of the crisis as, that evening, he called a summit of both his inner circle – Hart and Bell – and the industrial-relations team – Ned Smith and his deputy Kevin Hunt. The meeting took place at MacGregor's flat at 54 Eaton Square. As soon as Smith saw Hart and Bell, he threatened to walk out. 'Chairman, you know I won't talk to these people,' he said. 'I won't have them in the office.'

'Maybe that's why you're here,' replied MacGregor. 'Sit down and listen to what they have to say.'

'All right, I'll listen,' said Smith.

'My point is this,' said Hart. 'There's nothing special about these people. They're ordinary miners. They go to some sort of masonic ceremony. They roll up their trousers, hop around on one leg and suddenly they're members of the National Association of Colliery Overseeing, arse-licking, nose-picking—'

'Overseers Deputies and Shot-firers,' interrupted Bell, sitting to his right.

'That's the one. But we don't need them. If it comes to it, we can work those pits without them.'

'Look, my friend,' said Smith growing increasingly angry. 'Not you, not anybody, not the Royal bloody Engineers can work those pits without NACODS. They're responsible for pit safety by law.'

'The law can be changed,' said Hart. 'We can't have a bunch of militants holding a pistol to our heads.'

'Militants? NACODS? This is bloody nonsense. Most of them vote Tory.'

'Well, my information is that some of them are Communists, or at least Communist-inspired.'

'Don't talk daft,' interjected Hunt, who was also exasperated. 'Communist my arse.'

'Are you calling me a liar?' asked Hart

'Listen, don't start,' said Hunt, losing patience, 'or I'll have your ears off and you'll be out that bloody window.'

'Calm down, chaps,' Bell intervened characteristically.

But Smith had had enough. 'Come on, let's get out of here.'[32]

The next day, 19 October, Smith resigned because he would not be party to a NACODS strike that could be easily averted. He believed, unlike Bell and Hart, that a settlement with them was of crucial importance. A week later events proved him right when NACODS reached an agreement and ministers breathed a huge sigh of relief.

After Smith and Hunt had stormed out of MacGregor's apartment, Bell and Hart stayed on drinking Scotch and coffee late into the night. They were unperturbed by the passionate arguments of the industrial-relations executives, and MacGregor was more concerned about the severe pressure he was under from energy secretary Peter Walker about the NCB's 'bad PR'. Arthur Scargill had continued to outgun MacGregor on television with a barrage of confident, articulate statements, which undermined the back-to-work campaign. MacGregor thought the value of PR overstated but acknowledged that there was a problem.[33]

In fact, MacGregor's bumbling TV performances had been on the Prime Minister's mind, too. She had asked Bernard Ingham to recommend a new public spokesman. He suggested Ken Moses, head of the Derbyshire coalfields, and Michael Eaton, director of the north Yorkshire area. Her parliamentary private secretary, Michael Allison, was Eaton's local MP and knew him.[34]

The task of selecting the right man was left to Tim Bell. 'It's called the latitude of acceptance theory,' he later reflected, rather mysteriously. 'We needed a figure that was friendly and trustworthy, who was sympathetic both to the strikers and management.'[35] As Bell studied the videotapes of the TV appearances of Eaton and Moses, he was looking for someone presentable, personable and knowledgeable who could counter Scargill in the media on a daily basis. It was a close call, but Bell went for Eaton's pleasant, independent air, his friendly, reassuring face and clear Yorkshire accent. He was twenty-two years younger than MacGregor and had worked in the industry all his life. Bell also noticed that Eaton blinked less than Moses which, to the Saatchi and Saatchi received wisdom, suggested greater sincerity. He recommended the Yorkshireman to the Prime Minister, who approved his choice.[36]

Eaton was appointed, appropriately, on the NCB's worst day in the dispute, 18 October, the day that NACODS voted to strike. That morning he was telephoned by MacGregor and asked to come immediately to London. When he arrived at Hobart House at 4.30 p.m. he walked straight into the chairman's office and was greeted, not by MacGregor, but by a stranger. 'Hello, I'm David Hart. I'm an adviser to the Prime Minister, but under no circumstances should you disclose that information to anyone.' Eaton then saw the chairman who spoke to him briefly and asked him to meet his other aide-de-camp. 'Get close to Tim Bell,' he said. 'You'll get a lot of help from him.' Hart then took Eaton to his basement office at 4 Brook Street, Mayfair, for an informal talk with Bell, who said little. Hart, of course, could not stop himself. 'We must win the strike for the nation,' he said in typically grandiose terms. 'The miners must be brought to heel.'

At first Eaton was suspicious of Bell: 'Since I didn't trust MacGregor, I was initially wary of Bell because he was so close to him,' recalled Eaton. But, while he thought Hart disruptive and opportunistic, he was won over by Bell's professionalism. 'At no time did he talk about who he was connected to or who he knew or what other people were saying,' said the former NCB front man. 'He was very discreet. That meant he was trustworthy, because if he didn't disclose other people's private conversations then he was more likely to keep our meetings private.'

Bell approved of Eaton. He looked the part: for the PR veteran the visual image has always been as important, if not more so, than the message, and a TV spokesperson needs to be particularly sympathetic. 'It's not enough just to appeal to reason,' said Bell, warming to a familiar theme, 'you've got to appeal to the heart as well.'[37]

Eaton saw Bell almost daily. As MacGregor's media adviser had a low-key role, he did not want to meet at Hobart House so their meetings usually took place round the corner at the Goring Hotel in Grosvenor Gardens where Eaton was living during the strike. By now Bell was working virtually full-time on the strike. 'He didn't appear to have much else on,' recalled Eaton. He and Bell agreed that negotiations would never resolve the dispute: the deadlock needed to be broken by persuading strikers to cross the picket lines, and so the numbers of miners returning to work was the usual topic of conversation. That meant direct communication with the miners – over the heads of their union and through the media – involving effective television interviews, heavy briefing of sympathetic editors and, above all, advertising.

The new media strategy was implemented quickly and dramatically. On Friday 19 October 1984, the day after Eaton's appointment, Geoffrey Kirk was putting the finishing touches to some weekend advertisements about the threatened NACODS strike. Suddenly, he was instructed by MacGregor's office to take the ads – and, indeed, the whole NCB contract – away from the CM Partnership and hand them over to a new agency, Lowe Howard-Spink. Kirk was appalled. 'Lowe Howard-Spink had never done any work for us,' he said later. 'They had never submitted any work to us and had never put any in any competitive presentations of their work. We knew nothing about them.'[38]

The abrupt switch had been recommended by Tim Bell, who joined Lowe Howard-Spink as chief executive three months later. With Eaton, he now played a more prominent role in overseeing the creative work aimed almost exclusively at the working miners. But it was not a completely smooth relationship: Eaton knew that nearly all miners read either the *Mirror* or the *Sun* and was therefore shocked that the new advertisements only appeared in the *Sun* and the *Daily Telegraph*. 'Why don't we put them in the *Mirror*?' asked Eaton. But he was met by a hostile response from Bell, who, rather unconvincingly, said they should try to influence other sectors of public opinion.

The switching of the advertising agency was the final insult to be flung at Geoffrey Kirk. He had been in total charge of advertising and communications for the NCB for twenty-five years and had established an unrivalled reputation among both NCB management and journalists for his knowledge and understanding of the industry. Now it was increasingly evident that MacGregor was disregarding his advice in favour of Bell's. On Tuesday 28 October, Kirk was told to take indefinite leave. 'Geoffrey Kirk was sacked, he didn't resign,' said a former senior NCB executive. 'The chairman regarded him as a fifth columnist and as too independent and not compliant enough. MacGregor's management style was uncorporate, personal and autocratic. He did not like to consult the board.'

The treatment of Kirk was regarded by all sides – Tory cabinet ministers, NCB executives and journalists – as a massive blunder, and Bell was at the heart of the issue. 'I don't know what function they [Hart and Bell] have been performing with Mr MacGregor,' said Kirk, who died in a boating accident in the midst of writing a book on the strike. 'It is up to him whose advice he takes. My problem is that he evidently doesn't take it from me.'[39]

Bernard Ingham was also unhappy about Kirk's summary dismissal. 'I thought Ian MacGregor was a PR disaster from the day he was appointed, way before the dispute,' he said. 'If he had listened to people who knew the coal industry he would not have got into such trouble, but he sidelined the professionals like Geoffrey Kirk who really understood what was happening, who had no love for Arthur Scargill, but he would not listen.' Ingham also knew that the Kirk episode was largely based on MacGregor's preference for Bell and Hart but there was little he could do. Mrs Thatcher had sanctioned Bell's appointment and she could not be seen to be interfering in what was really an NCB or, at best, an energy department matter. She also had a high regard for Peter Walker, who was seen as 'a resourceful minister' and who was running his own news-management operation by regular briefing political correspondents and editors.

Kirk was replaced by his deputy, Norman Woodhouse, who was much more respectful of MacGregor. The day after his appointment, MacGregor told him: 'I want you to work with Tim Bell. He is very helpful to me. If you want a referee to blow the whistle here I am.' This meant that he would arbitrate if there was any dispute between Woodhouse and Bell but the two got on famously. 'He [Bell] did not confide in me, but we had a close rapport,' recalled Woodhouse.

FINAL COUNTDOWN

By late December 1984, the strikers' resolve had begun to crumble. Bell immediately wrote a report on a strategy for the vital months of the early New Year. Based on the correct assumption that the return to work would escalate, he recommended that Eaton and MacGregor's message should be that the coal industry had a bright future in which everyone could participate: 'We must make miners who might go back to work believe that our offer is final. We must make them see that our industry can and will carry on, that the opportunities are enormous and that it is unrealistic to believe that all this must be held back because a group of people – who are not faced with redundancy – will not consider a move to other areas.'[40]

An extra irony came after the strike when Lowe Howard-Spink, the NCB's advertising agency, which Bell later joined, was hired by the Nuclear Electricity Information Group. 'If we revert to coal, the miners can hold the country to ransom again,' said Frank Lowe in 1986. 'The Electricity Council feels it has a responsibility to this country and it needs to put the case forward for an alternative source of fuel.'[41]

Meanwhile, Bell continued to act as MacGregor's minder for television interviews and advised the American to wear light-coloured suits so that his dandruff would not show. It was the type of detail he had learned to observe from working with Gordon Reece. But it was what MacGregor might say rather than how he looked that most concerned ministers: the chairman needed constant vigilance, especially before a studio grilling, and his PR consultant would be on hand to brief and prepare him.

As the industrial dispute swung the NCB's way, the government was anxious to ensure that Arthur Scargill could not extract any political mileage from the outcome. Hence, and unknown until now, a covert channel of communication needed to be set up. Who better than Mrs Thatcher's favourite media man to perform that function? 'Tim Bell was a very important link between the Prime Minister and the Coal Board,' said Malcolm Edwards, the NCB's marketing director. 'The tactics had become a priority by that stage and there was a great anxiety at Downing Street to know what was going on. Mrs Thatcher was particularly keen to be appraised and informed on a regular basis. Bell played that role but not directly. He was a key figure.'

Bell's role was to liaise with, report and relay messages to 10 Downing Street through the Prime Minister's political aides as he could not be seen to be working for her directly. Eaton knew about the arrangement and used him as a sounding board to discover Mrs Thatcher's likely views. 'I'm sure the Prime Minister would think that or like that,' Bell would respond carefully. Michael Eaton recalled, 'I knew Tim was very close to Margaret Thatcher and he had her private telephone number in her flat but he didn't flaunt it like Hart. If I wanted something said in the House of Commons or publicly, I used Tim Bell because I knew he could pass it through the system through Michael Allison, the Prime Minister's parliamentary private secretary who I knew, or Stephen Sherbourne [her political secretary who Bell knew and later employed]. I was quite confident that the proper message was getting across because I would then hear Mrs Thatcher repeating my words in the House. It was a very useful operation.'

Bell was also valuable because he was one of the few people who could talk straightforwardly to both the Peter Walker, who was on the left of the Tory Party, and Mrs Thatcher. On Wednesday 12 February 1984, barely a month before the end of the dispute, the TUC council asked to meet Peter Walker. He discussed it with the Prime Minister, and agreed to go as he believed that a refusal would make the government look obdurate and callous. The energy secretary put his case before the TUC and stressed his own family links with the mining industry. Their response was to propose a joint NCB–TUC formula for a settlement that would not undermine the government's position.

Walker agreed to this and a draft was drawn up. On the morning of Monday 17 February, Norman Willis, TUC general secretary, and Walker met the Prime Minister for an hour to discuss the terms. They agreed that the document should be put before the TUC that evening. Walker left 10 Downing Street and convened a lunch with MacGregor, Bell and David Hunt, the coal minister. They made two minor changes to the draft, which MacGregor accepted.

When David Hart found out he went ballistic, and told MacGregor that Walker was trying to reach a settlement by making major concessions.

That afternoon Bell arrived at the Department of Energy to inform Walker that MacGregor had changed his mind about the settlement terms. This infuriated the energy minister, who was only placated when 10 Downing Street sent a firm message to MacGregor that the Prime Minister was satisfied with the formula reached at the lunch discussion. That night the meeting at the TUC proceeded and a final version was agreed. But for the next two days – Tuesday and Wednesday – Bell had to act as an emissary between Walker and MacGregor as they blamed each other for the breakdown in communications.

As it happened, the NUM rejected the TUC agreement, but it was a prime example of how Bell was used as a middle-man between the NCB and the government.[42]

Bell had been completely immersed in the drama and magnitude of the strike. He saw it in almost apocalyptic terms. Towards the end, as the violence increased, he had lunch with Roy Warman. Sitting at his usual window table at L'Etoile, Bell suddenly declared: 'What this country and government don't understand is these people [the striking miners] are dangerous. I've had death threats. It's a war out there.'

On the day that all the striking miners went back to work, Bell and David Hart celebrated the defeat of the NUM with MacGregor in his Eaton Square flat. As the end of the dispute announced was on television the chairman said, with more than a trace of relief in his voice, 'No more, no more Arthur Scargill, ever.'

'Largely thanks to you, Ian. Well done,' said Bell.

'Time to celebrate,' interjected Hart, as he handed round drinks and prepared a toast. 'Gentlemen, the freedom of the individual.'

'The right to manage,' said MacGregor.

'To Margaret,' said Bell.

'To Margaret,' repeated Hart.

'The Lady,' declared MacGregor.[43]

Publicly Bell claimed that the strike was about the employer's right to run the industry uninhibited. 'If you believe in wealth creation,' he said afterwards, 'and that wealth creation lies with the managers – be they owners or executives – then you are bound to oppose the concept of the workforce having unnatural power and that's really what it was about . . . The core issue was whether or not decisions about making the business efficient and profitable were to be made unhindered by the management.'[44]

Privately, however, he never lost sight of its political purpose, which was the suppression of trade-union power. He later said that the strike's effect was to smash what he called the remaining Marxist cells in the unions except for the NGA (printworkers) and NUPE (health service and local authorities). 'It destroyed the NUM as a political force and was also a necessary step to preserve the monetocracy and meritocracy of Thatcherism,' he concluded.

FAREWELL TO THE BROTHERS

The miners' strike was a watershed in Tim Bell's career. It was his first taste of public relations and political crisis management, but it also provided the opportunity for him to leave Saatchi and Saatchi. From late October 1984, Bell had worked closely with Frank Lowe, chairman of Lowe Howard-Spink Campbell-Ewald, on the NCB account. Lowe had heard from both sides about the falling out between Bell and the Brothers. Encouraged by Tony Good, his corporate PR adviser, Lowe realised he had a unique opportunity to hire the best presenter and salesman in the business, who would perfectly complement the creative strength of his agency. Without telling Bell, he rang Charles Saatchi and asked whether he would mind if Lowe made an offer to Saatchi's wayward genius. Charles had no objection and Lowe offered Bell a job, as group chief executive of Lowe Howard-Spink.[45]

Bell's departure from Charlotte Street after fifteen years was bitter, acrimonious and emotionally wrenching. 'I was just broken-hearted,' he said later. 'It seemed to me unnecessary. I don't know why they turned on me, why we came apart and why I got written out of the future. They've never been able to tell me.'[46]

Even though they had effectively forced him out, it was almost as though a brother was leaving a Sicilian family. 'Once you were not there, you no longer had a role in their life,' Bell later reflected. 'Their whole lives revolved around the company. They chose not to speak to you because there was no occasion to do so.'[47] Other departing executives had the same experience: when John Hegarty, the talented creative director, informed the Brothers he was leaving, Charles promptly walked out of the meeting without saying a word. 'He didn't speak to me for four years.' Hegarty remembers.

When Bell left, the Brothers did not make life easy for him. His four-bedroom Edwardian home in Hampstead was owned by the Saatchis and they made him buy it from them at the 1985 price, which was many times its original value as it had been purchased in 1978. Charles also made him sign a contract under which he was paid a £24,000-a-year retainer as a consultant on the Tory Party account for one more general election. This ensured that he was unable to take the business elsewhere. The final gesture, which rankled with Bell, a man so conscious of his status, was how his departure was reported in *Campaign*. For fifteen years Charles Saatchi had ensured, in return for other stories, that almost anything about the agency appeared on page one. Now, it seemed, he wanted another favour. *Campaign* obliged. Bell's move – a front page *Campaign* story by anyone's standards and which ran in most of the national papers – appeared on page three under the headline 'Bell Ends Rumours By Taking Lowe Job'.[48]

Publicly, Bell said little: 'They built the agency. I ran it.'[49] When his move to Lowe Howard-Spink was announced in January 1985, most advertising executives were surprised: they had expected him to form his own agency. But his close colleagues and friends understood: Bell needed a Charles Saatchi-type figure to work for, someone he could serve and to whom he could look up. Frank Lowe was the closest to that and his similarities with Charles were uncanny. Both had worked together at Benton and Bowles and then Collet Dickinson Pearce, where they established reputations as inspired creative copywriters. Both shunned personal publicity. Like Charles, Lowe had set up his own agency driven on by soaring ambition and a huge ego. And, also like Charles, Lowe's catalyst for commercial success was a reverse takeover of an ailing agency, in his case Wasey Campbell-Ewald. Needless to say, Frank Lowe was one of the few admen admired by Charles Saatchi. They were, and remain, close friends and avid competitive poker players.

Although Bell had extraordinary self-confidence in his professional abilities, it was not all-consuming. 'Like most people in the advertising business – probably most people in life – he was very insecure', said Martin Sorrell, Saatchi's finance director between 1976 and 1982. 'He needed continual boosting and reassurance, massaging and reinforcement'.[50] So he went to work for Frank Lowe. When asked why he didn't set up his own operation, he replied: 'That's for later on.' For now, he was looking at new ventures and challenges.

Chapter Six

The Corporate Persuader

'Don't do a press release when a good leak will do'
Tim Bell, speaking at a
Marketing Society lunch, 8 December 1995

Tim Bell joined Lowe Howard-Spink on a tidal wave of optimism and goodwill. On Friday 27 January 1985, the day after he moved into their Knightsbridge office, the share price of the holding company closed at 295p, a staggering increase of 45p on the previous day. Saatchi and Saatchi's stock remained static as the general market rose. Frank Lowe delivered what Bell had always craved and Charles Saatchi always denied him: equal status, a firm promise of his name on the door and a directorship of the holding company. A group chief executive, Bell signed a five-year contract worth £120,000 a year and generous share options. What's more, he was given a freer, more creative role: 'At his Saatchi I was an operator,' he said. 'At Lowe I will be a builder.'[1]

In many ways Bell was, ironically, returning to his advertising roots and an earlier incarnation of Saatchi and Saatchi. He was joining an ambitious young agency bursting with creative talent founded and galvanised by an unconventional, volatile personality in Frank Lowe. Born in 1941 – just two months before Bell – Lowe was sent to boarding school at the age of four. After Westminster School, he went straight into advertising with J. Walter Thompson – like Bell, he started as a traffic boy. In 1969 Lowe joined Collett Dickinson Pearce and carved an almost unrivalled reputation for producing ingenious advertising as managing director from 1972 until 1978. His most notable campaigns were for Benson and

Hedges and later Heineken ('refreshes the parts other beers cannot reach').

After resigning from Collett's, Lowe spent a frustrating three months in Hollywood, trying to raise $6 million to make a film with an Iron Curtain theme. But he was faced with a wall of ignorance, despite being a close friend of the producer David Puttnam and director Alan Parker. He then returned to what he knew best: advertising. In May 1981, Lowe set up his own agency in a blaze of publicity with Geoff Howard-Spink and clients like Fiat Motors, Olympus Cameras and Whitbread. Based on a perceptive understanding of English culture, Lowe Howard-Spink's creative work won many plaudits, but their new business record was poor and they made an erratic start. It was only their daring reverse takeover of the sleeping giant Wasey Campbell-Ewald in September 1983 that gave them credibility in the big league. Now their total billings were up to £50 million with plans for further expansion. A mere eight months later the agency went public. At first the flotation was a disaster: the share value was below the tender price and 64 per cent of the shares remained with the underwriters. But, eventually, the agency's stock rose steadily.

By late 1984 Lowe Howard-Spink ranked eighteen in the UK with total billings of just over £56 million and they needed to bolster the share price by bringing in someone to acquire and maintain new accounts, particularly abroad. Bell, of course, fitted that bill. 'Tim is much more experienced in the field of international clients and expansion, in mergers and acquisitions, than I am,' said Lowe at the time. 'Now that he is taking care of issues such as expansion, it gives me a chance to get more involved in the creative area.'[2] Despite the glaring similarities with mid-1970s Saatchi's, the new chief executive downplayed the common ground: 'We are not trying to do a mini-Saatchi,' said Bell. 'We want controlled growth and my job is to be a catalyst – to develop and motivate.'[3]

When Bell moved into his new office at Bowater House, opposite Harrods, the optimism generated by the dramatic share-price hike continued. His relationship with Lowe, based on their complementary talents, was strengthened by a mutual appreciation and affection. Lowe said that his new chief executive was 'one of the most talented and influential figures to have emerged in advertising since the war', while Bell described his chairman as 'the competitor I've most respected'.[4]

However, within a few months tension and friction emerged. One problem, according to former colleagues, was that it was unclear as to whether Bell was Lowe's partner or deputy or just in charge of new business and expansion. The idea was that they would be an unbeatable combination. They shared some characteristics – guile, cunning and the desire to be admired – but it was not enough to prevent their egos clashing. Their management styles were very different. Bell's approach continued to be open, accessible, ebullient, creating trust and loyalty. He still walked casually around the floor in his socks and would change into his dinner jacket in front of employees while bouncing ideas off them. As at Saatchi's, employees warmed to him as he stood there with a foot on a chair and a cigarette in one hand, regaling them with anecdotes (usually involving Margaret Thatcher), and he could still motivate staff into giving that extra 20 per cent while working long hours under pressure. Lowe, however, prowled rather than walked and managed on the basis of fear and respect rather than affection. Like Charles Saatchi, Lowe was introspective, reclusive and shy with a tendency to brood. He rarely granted interviews or posed for photographs. 'He was very smart, driven and incredibly manipulative,' said a former group account handler. 'He was brilliant at going into a meeting and getting exactly what he wanted'. It is difficult to dispute that Frank Lowe has modelled himself on Charles Saatchi.

The Bell–Lowe relationship did not work mainly because they thought fundamentally on how accounts should be handled, and specifically about the selling and production of advertisements. Bell believed in serving the clients, while Lowe wanted to service them. Essentially, this meant that the former Saatchi's chairman would do almost anything to please his clients and keep them happy. His approach was to explain, charm, cajole and develop mutually affectionate relationships with them. It was matey, informal and seductive. If an advertising idea was rejected, the Saatchi reaction was private contempt for the client and take the money.

At Lowe, by contrast, servicing clients meant remaining true to creative standards. Account handlers managed conflict and were required to deliver a hard sell. The system was tightly controlled. First, there would be considered, detailed briefs, and then total creative freedom with Lowe himself being the final arbiter. Finally, the presenters were expected to go to the clients, sell the advertisement and not return to the office until they had done so. If the client remained hostile, they needed to be persuaded otherwise. It was not a cosy relationship.

While Charles Saatchi had delegated client responsibility fully to Bell, Lowe was much more interventionist. Inevitably tension arose, even more so when they – unwittingly or not – overlapped on the same accounts. Lowe and Bell would then test each other by playing corporate games, using third parties, or get at each other by criticising their respective favoured employees. They also had huge rows. Yet there was an inherent strength in their relationship: within hours of a disagreement, a rapprochement would be reached. 'It was a bit like a rowdy marriage,' said one former Lowe account executive. 'They had these massive arguments, sometimes over relatively unimportant issues. But their loyalty to each other was stronger than an allegiance to anyone on the outside, so they could attack each other but heaven help anyone criticising from the outside.' Lowe also tried to appease his chief executive by fulfilling his promise of putting his name on the letterhead. In November 1985, the agency became Lowe Howar-Spink and Bell.

Still, senior colleagues began to notice that they talked together less and less frequently, even though their offices were next door to each other. The catalyst for their separation and eventual divorce came on their first anniversary. On 17 January 1986, *Campaign* published their annual 'Agency of the Year' award. They chose Lowe-Howard-Spink and Bell because it had 'added £18 million of billings without any losses, kept up its creative standards and become an acknowledged expert in the growing area of takeover bid and public issue advertising'. The article noted: 'It is no wonder that the agency's shares now stand almost 100p higher than they did a year ago.'

Staff and executives were delighted by the prestigious announcement. But when the page-long feature was faxed to Frank Lowe in New York, he stared at it with a mixture of despair and anger. The huge headline in the bible of the advertising industry ran 'Lowe: The Year of Bell', with a large photograph of Bell on the opposite page. The award essentially attributed Lowe's agency's success to his chief executive: 'His link-up with Lowe has completely galvanised the agency,' the piece stated, asserting that, before his arrival, 'Lowe had failed to match the high expectations it aroused when it opened.'

For Lowe who, like Charles Saatchi, craved favourable headlines in the magazine that everyone in the business read, it was a devastating blow. 'I know he was deeply hurt and upset,' recalled a former close colleague. 'He was already very irritated by hearing talk that it was Bell's agency. Tim didn't seek out that kind of publicity but he didn't exactly discourage it either. I think the *Campaign* piece was the point of no return for Frank.'

From that moment Bell and Lowe began to circle each other like caged cats. In 1986 Bruce Haines was offered and accepted the job of deputy managing director at the agency in an attempt to calm the waters. 'I was expected to go in and help resolve the tensions,' he said. But he became increasingly concerned about the 'politics of the agency' and reneged on the deal. When Haines told managing director David Jones of his decision, Bell came into the room, sat down and poured drinks for Haines and himself. Jones left them alone, expecting his chief executive to win over the wavering new recruit. 'I know what this is about,' said Bell. 'You're nervous about working for Frank Lowe. You know, it's far more important to be popular with me than Frank.' Haines thought that that summed up the politics of the agency. Now chairman of Leagas Delagus, he recalled, 'Frank Lowe had a reputation for being difficult to work with, but Tim Bell's idea that it was my reason for not joining was completely wrong. It was my conversation with him that reassured me I was making the right decision.'

This type of manoeuvring extended to presentations. In 1988 Bell led a successful pitch for British Rail, whom he had handled at Saatchi's, and proposed a £1.5 million corporate campaign on television. Based on a production budget of £750,000, Frank Lowe took over on the creative side and produced a superb mini-epic of an advertisement, commissioning music from Vangelis and hiring the director Hugh Hudson, both of whom had been behind the classic *Chariots of Fire*. The two-and-a-half-minute ad started with a one-verse commentary written by W.H. Auden for a 1930s British film called *Night Mail*. Two more verses were written by the agency's Paul Weinberger and the voice-over was by the actor Tom Courtenay. It was more like a short film than an advertisement and it was Frank Lowe and his team at their creative best.

When it came to presenting the finished product to British Rail, Bell was excluded. Before the meeting Lowe asked the account handler, Stephen Woodward, who was attending. 'Myself, Tim and you,' he replied, surprised to be asked. 'I don't think Tim needs to be there. Can you tell him?' replied Lowe. Bell's reaction was, 'OK, no big deal.' But, according to Woodward, 'I don't know if he was just being a gentleman.'

It was this underlying tension that propelled Bell faster towards a wider communications brief. He loved advertising but his differences with Lowe were too fundamental to be reconciled and he was, in fact, already moving away from just presenting and selling ads. At Saatchi's he had been in perpetual motion, winning and retaining clients, now he was advising his clients on how the advertisements fitted into their overall marketing strategy. He was becoming more interested in integrated communications policies, which encompassed advertising, public relations, corporate imagery and, later, political lobbying. But, as Bell later admitted, he was driving in that direction partly, if not largely, 'because Frank Lowe couldn't stand me'.[5] That was a simplification, said during an off-the-cuff private speech to the Marketing Society, and the rift was never personal. They may not have been blood brothers but were always friends. The problem was that, like Charles Saatchi before him, Lowe felt threatened by Bell. Fortunately, his chief executive's horizons were now beyond advertising. Big business awaited him.

TAKEOVER FEVER

A hostile takeover bid was one of the best arenas for a multi-faceted communications operation. By 1986, fuelled by a record rise in the stock market, merger mania had resulted in the greatest takeover spree ever. The total value of corporate takeover bids launched in the first three months of that year amounted to a staggering £20 billion. And during this period of frenetic financial activity, one recurring theme emerged: the perceived value of a company was almost as important as its real one. Share prices were increasingly determined by public image, reputation and media coverage. This was particularly so during an unwanted bid. 'Shareholders' perception is all-important – they will cast the votes,' said Gordon Reece, a PR veteran of such battles. 'If they see their company is doing well with strong, fighting management they will support it. If they perceive management as weak and vacillating, they will vote with their feet.'[6]

One of the most controversial and bitter takeovers in 1986 was Guinness's epic but successful capture of the rival drinks giant Distillers. It was driven by Ernest Saunders, the chief executive, who had helped to transform Guinness from a vulnerable one-product company with a market value of £90 million into a dynamic multi-brand outfit capitalised at £3.5 billion. Saunders, known as 'Deadly Ernest', was a marketing man with a passion for brands and not a financier, but he understood the influence of the media on stock values. Once described as 'a first-division operator who manicures every sentence before delivery', he was a consummate news manager. During Guinness's £37 million bid for Arthur Bell and Co., the Scottish whisky firm, Saunders usually devoted most of Friday evening and Saturday to briefing financial journalists and stockbroking analysts. He told them his offer was both logical and likely to succeed and was rewarded with favourable coverage in the Sunday papers. On Saturday evening, he would take the BA shuttle to Edinburgh and be in his hotel the next day to face questions from sceptical Scottish journalists, anxious about the implications for Arthur Bell of new English owners.[7]

Stage two was a £1 million advertising campaign. For this Guinness turned to Lowe Howard-Spink and Bell. At the time of the bid – in summer 1985 – advertising in takeovers was unregulated and, for a brief period, an undiluted war of words developed. Tim Bell took charge of the account and relished the challenge. It was his kind of campaign: fast-moving with plenty of crisis and controversy. For the first time, readers of the *Financial Times*, accustomed to mundane corporate advertising, were treated to brash black headlines like 'Bell's On the Rocks?' above a telling graph of the enemy's falling share price. The whisky firm responded in kind, and back and forth went the slogans.

On 23 August 1985, after a two-month campaign, Guinness secured control of Arthur Bell's whisky with a 70 per cent shareholding. It was a triumph for Saunders, as Guinness's pre-tax profits rose to £86 million, and it was Tim Bell's first experience of a major takeover. Liaising with merchant bankers, lawyers and financial advisers, he was now working to a wider communications brief. Three months later Saunders acknowledged this. In late November 1985, before his bid for Distillers, the Guinness boss was asked by John Connell, its chairman, for 'advice on PR'. 'I didn't say anything about what I had at the back of my mind,' recalled Saunders. 'I wanted to see how he was reacting. I recommended Tim Bell in London and Colin Liddell in Scotland, two advisers I had used.'[8]

When Saunders launched his £2.2 billion offensive against Distillers on 20 January 1986, he knew that he needed all the marketing artillery at his disposal. 'I have never been in a war,' he said at the time, 'but I imagine the takeover is as close as I have come to one.'[9] To deliver his firepower, he needed the best PR lieutenants. Brian Basham had run a successful campaign during the takeover of Bell's whisky, but had resigned from Guinness and was now working for the Argyll group who also thirsted for Distillers. And so, on Maurice Saatchi's recommendation, Saunders immediately hired the recently knighted Gordon Reece as a consultant on a retainer of £4,000 a month. Lowe Howard-Spink were retained for advertising, with Bell in charge of the account. For advice on lobbying the government, Guinness turned to GJW, a firm of lobbyists. With an overall communications budget of close to £15 million, Saunders began to convene meetings, with Bell and Reece ever-present.

This time, though, financial journalists were not so sympathetic to Guinness's case and pushed for a referral to the Monopolies and Mergers Commission (MMC). 'We have chosen our man [side] for this bid,' Ian Watson, city editor of the *Sunday Telegraph*, told Saunders.[10] Basham, now in the rival Argyll camp, was particularly adept at the 'Friday Night Drop' in which the Sunday newspapers were fed tasty exclusives, and the 7 a.m. delivery to the London *Evening Standard* when bleary-eyed morning reporters were often staring at white spaces on the page.

Guinness was losing the propaganda skirmishes, so Saunders decided to use advertising to bypass the hostile press and appeal direct to the shareholders and public. There followed an unprecedented £18 million campaign in just three weeks based on a strategy of saying to shareholders: here's a successful British company, international expansion is the key to prosperity. One of Lowe's most effective ads warned that the whisky business could suffer the fate of the UK motorcycle industry if it remained parochial. An advertisement even appeared in the *Sun* on either side of the page three girl.

As the Takeover Panel now monitored and regulated the advertising, there was constant pressure in the offices of Lowe Howard-Spink and Bell. 'We had to manage a situation when every day the Panel would decide at 6 p.m. on the ads we were allowed to run,' recalled a former creative co-ordinator at the agency. 'We would then have to produce artwork and get it to the newspapers within three hours or we missed the paper. Tim represented us on all the committee meetings at Guinness at the highest level. He was really in the thick of it and it pretty much took up all his time.'

At first Guinness's campaign went badly, and at 4 p.m. on 13 February 1986, their bid was referred to the MMC. Saunders was furious. That afternoon he arranged for Gordon Reece to draft a letter to the Prime Minister, which asked for an explanation of the decision, and demanded to see Geoffrey Pattie, the trade and industry minister responsible. The letter was hand delivered to 10 Downing Street and within the hour a meeting had been set for the next day with several DTI civil servants. They confirmed the referral decision. However, instead of submitting to a long inquiry, Saunders withdrew his bid and sold Guinness's whisky interests to Lonrho at a fire-sale price. This was designed to circumvent the monopoly concentration of drinks brands. He was then allowed to submit a new, revised bid for Distillers.

But Guinness was still anxious to avoid an investigation by the MMC so a discreet but heavy lobbying of the Prime Minister began to take place. Sir Jack Lyons, a management consultant for Guinness and friend of Mrs Thatcher, wrote a private letter to her, claiming that a referral of the bid to the MMC would be 'disastrous'. A week later, on 11 March 1986, Saunders attended a party at Birdcage Walk, near Buckingham Palace, to celebrate Sir Gordon Reece's recent knighthood. Tim Bell was there too and, Saunders recalled, 'It was attended by practically the entire cabinet and most of the editors of Fleet Street newspapers. I haven't worked so hard in three hours in my life. I managed to get round most of the cabinet and most of the editors. It was a wonderful opportunity to personally put the case on the basis of the vision of Britain having a great international drinks company.'[1] Ten days later the government announced that Guinness's bid would not be subject to an MMC inquiry. Incredibly, the company paid Sir Jack Lyons £3 million for his part in changing the government's mind.

Reece later acknowledged the role of outside consultants during this delicate period: 'Politics and public relations drive a hostile takeover battle until the first closing date. Then, assuming the bid has not been referred, it is largely a financial matter.'[12] But Guinness's bid for Distillers was no ordinary business deal.

The takeover was completed on 19 April 1986, with the acquisition of 50.7 per cent of the shares. One of Guinness's firm pledges was that if its bid was successful, it would relocate to Edinburgh, and Sir Thomas Risk, then governor of the Bank of Scotland, would become non-executive chairman of the new, merged group. Saunders would remain as chief executive. It was at this stage that Tim Bell replaced his advertising suit with a broader communications outfit. 'Tim had a background role when we were discussing how to put across our case regarding the Scottish company,' Saunders told me. 'He was giving advice on how to handle it in terms of presentation.'

Within two months Saunders was claiming that he was finding it difficult to persuade the Guinness board to ratify Risk's appointment. On Friday 11 July 1986, John Chiene, Guinness's stockbroker, spent an hour with Saunders and Lord Iveagh, the then chairman. The broker insisted that they fulfil their pledge to appoint a new independent and non-executive chairman but Saunders stormed out of the meeting without saying goodbye to Chiene.[13] Two days later, an article in the *Sunday Times* by Ivan Fallon stated, for the first time, that 'Risk is not wholly acceptable to the Guinness board . . . I understand there have been secret discussions as to who should replace him.' Fallon recommended that Saunders himself should assume the role of executive chairman.[14]

That immediately raised the temperature and later that evening, Sunday 13 July, Saunders convened a crisis meeting, which ran until 2 a.m. It was attended by members of the Guinness 'War Cabinet': Thomas Ward, an American lawyer, Olivier Roux, a management consultant from Bain and Co., and, most notably, Christopher Ashton Jones, a PR executive from Dewe Rogerson, and Tim Bell.[15] Ashton Jones, now retired, confirmed Bell's presence at the meeting but could not recall what was said. The next morning *The Times* gave the story more authority: 'Saunders Heads New Guinness Order'. Later that day Guinness released a statement – 'following leaks' – that confirmed Saunders's appointment as executive chairman.

The following month Bell drove to Champneys, the Hertfordshire health farm then owned by Guinness, in a brand new red Ferrari for a two-day seminar attended by Olivier Roux, Ernest Saunders and Sir Gordon Reece. By now Bell's advice was analytical, diagnostic and beyond his advertising brief. 'We used Tim for communications in a number of ways,' a former Guinness board director told me. 'When we wanted to reposition the company in marketing terms, he would assess the media reaction and set up meetings. If Ernest wanted to meet someone, it would be Tim who would fix it.'

Bell was later at pains to deny that he was a PR consultant to Guinness: 'I was there to oversee the advertising,' he said. 'We [Lowe Howard-Spink and Bell] had no public-relations companies at the time and I did not advise on public relations during the Distillers bid.'[16] This is disputed by other Guinness consultants. 'There was no question that he was used for PR as well as advertising,' said a senior source at GJW, the lobbyists. This was confirmed to a large extent by Rodney Dewe, chief executive of Dewe Rogerson and in charge of the Guinness account. 'Tim concentrated on making sure the PR line was agreed within the company,' he told me. 'He was also involved in helping to draft press releases, shareholders' letters, basically anything that was sent out. But he would leave the briefing of the financial press to others, so I suppose it depends on what you mean by PR.'

In *Nightmare*, the authorised book of the Guinness affair by Saunders's son James, Bell is described as a 'PR consultant'.[17] On reflection, Ernest Saunders is more circumspect: 'He was not our PR adviser as such. He was more involved in presentation and communication. I would say he was the account handler but he always had a PR bent. He played little role in the process of winning the bid. His real involvement was when things became rough.'

Life became very rough for Saunders at 9.30 a.m. on Monday 1 December 1986, when the DTI inspectors arrived at Guinness's headquarters at Portman Square to seize company documents. It was the beginning of their inquiry into the conduct of the Distillers takeover. The central allegation was that Saunders and three commercial cohorts had set up a network of fronts so that they could buy Distillers shares illegally. One of Saunders's first acts was to summon Gordon Reece and, according to Rodney Dewe, Tim Bell. 'I was impressed by Tim's sense of urgency,' recalled Dewe. And a senior GJW source said that both Reece and Bell had been hired for the comfort factor. 'They were both demonstrably close to the Premier and cabinet ministers so that if there was any trouble they could be brought in to fix it with their contacts.'

But as the net closed around certain Guinness executives, Bell and Reece became understandably unavailable. 'They just ran away,' recalled Saunders. The former chief executive recalls being at home in Penn, near Beaconsfield, on 9 January 1987, when he learnt that Bell was visiting a neighbour, the racing driver Paddy Hopkirk. Earlier that day Saunders had agreed to step aside on full pay while the DTI investigation continued and was depressed. He telephoned Bell and asked him to drop by. At first Bell was reluctant but then agreed. When he walked in he was inscrutable, stony-faced and, unusually for Bell, tight-lipped. He had been made fully aware of the political implications of the Guinness scandal and did not want to be associated with it. Saunders asked for his advice and help, but his former PR consultant stared at him and said, 'I'm sorry I can't help you.' Frank Lowe, however, called occasionally asking if there was anything he could do.

Saunders could be forgiven for citing an old jingle about outside advisers, lawyers and moneymen: 'Professional people have no cares/Whoever loses, they get theirs'. But the greatest public relations and advertising advice in the world was not going to save Saunders, Gerald Ronson, chairman of Heron Corporation, the stockbroker Anthony Parnes and Sir Jack Lyons. In August 1990, all four were found guilty of serious crimes in connection with the Distillers takeover, and all, except Lyons who was ill, went to jail. Lyons was fined £3 million – the fee he had received for writing that letter to the Prime Minister.

INFORM AND PERSUADE

The Guinness affair may have ended disastrously but Bell now had experience in a communications network at the highest level. Public relations was for him a natural progression: like advertising, it was paid advocacy by a third party. On 13 September 1986, just after Guinness's takeover of Distillers, Lowe Howard-Spink and Bell paid

£3.9 million for Good Relations, the then pre-eminent PR firm. Bell was at the heart of the negotiations and it was his formal entrance into corporate PR. In 1984 when he was still at Saatchi and Saatchi he had made an initial approach for Good Relations but was sceptical about the industry. 'I thought PR people were a bunch of wankers who went out to lunch a lot,' he confessed, in reference to the earlier bid. 'But this was a time when a lot of the US advertising agencies were acquiring PR arms, so it made sense for the largest British agency to acquire one.'[18] But Good Relations resisted Saatchi's charms.

The PR agency was now incorporated into a new company, Lowe Bell Communications, with Bell as chairman. 'More synergy is needed,' he said at the time. 'Companies are now placing more emphasis on PR in their communications portfolios and the business is becoming more strategic.'[19] Seven months later, on 17 April 1987, Bell became deputy chairman of the Lowe Howard-Spink group, and relinquished his position as chief executive. It was presented as a promotion, but it was actually a lateral move, away from the mainstream advertising network and into PR, corporate marketing and image-making. The transition was now complete and the 45-year-old Tim Bell had entered a brave new world.

Public relations does not have a good PR. Historically, its executives have been viewed as champagne-swilling, silver-tongued conmen, who promise and charge a huge amount but deliver little. Edward L. Bernays, one of America's greatest PR practitioners, described it more grandly as 'the science of influencing public opinion', but, as the UK PR consultant Matthew Freud quipped, 'For a while it became the science of taking people out to lunch.'[20] In the United States the most celebrated press agent was a brash New Yorker called Jim Moran. He had once contrived a bar-room brawl between a fairly well-known band-leader and a bystander. When the judge asked why they had been fighting, the band-leader replied that it was over the recipe for Pimm's cup. It turned out that Moran was on Pimm's payroll and the company had been experiencing difficulty in establishing the brand name in the public eye. The 'brawl' court case received so much publicity that Moran solved his client's problem with a single blow – so to speak.[21] For decades the image of public relations was derived from the movie *Sweet Smell of Success*, in which the seedy Sidney Falco, played by Tony Curtis, attempts to plant and sell stories to the all-powerful columnist J.J. Hunsecker, played by Burt Lancaster.

In Britain PR had became synonymous with hospitality and conspicuous consumption. Large quantities of alcohol was the communications strategy of the 1950s and early 1960s. And journalists, of course, were not unwilling recipients when a company's message was projected in this way. In those days, it wasn't a sophisticated profession: 'PR tended to be done by ex-army officers who thought they were terribly good with people,' said Tim Bell dismissively.[22]

Today the clients of PR consultants are more demanding in an increasingly competitive world. In financial PR, a more fundamental change took place in the late 1960s and early 1970s when companies became aware of the correlation between image and share price. The man who most exploited that was the late John Addey, a tough-talking Yorkshireman who had qualified as a barrister and twice fought elections as a Conservative parliamentary candidate. He first came to prominence in 1968 when acting for Rupert Murdoch during his takeover of the *News of the World*. Financial journalists were, even then, shocked to receive details of the shady business dealings of Robert Maxwell, Murdoch's great rival. Addey set up his own PR company and bestrode the City like a puppet-master, pulling strings here and releasing them there to make his industrialist clients dance to his tune. His homosexuality was also an advantage in acquiring clients, particularly some merchant banks. According to his *Times* obituary:

> Addey was an adroit practitioner of the 'hunches and lunches' school of PR, that was much in vogue at the time. He preferred to depict it as standing up to the merchant bankers, plotting takeover or defence strategies and talking up the share price while bossing the chairman around or providing a shoulder for him to cry on when he lost his nerve . . . He was the first PR consultant to dare to give his clients advice on every aspect of strategy, including whether or not they should make a particular bid.[23]

The consultant who inherited and continued that tradition was Brian Basham, who worked for John Addey Associates between 1973 and 1976. Born in 1943, the son of a south London butcher, Basham was once notorious for his party trick of biting chunks out of champagne glasses. He worked as a financial journalist at the *Daily Telegraph* and *The Times*, and then learned the PR craft at Addey's shoulder. In 1976 he set up Broad Street Associates and has been as successful as his mentor, representing, among others, Mohammed Al-Fayed, Hanson plc, Saatchi and Saatchi, Cable and Wireless, Guinness, and British Airways.

Despite his win-at-any-price style, Basham started to charge huge fees almost by accident. He had provided some corporate PR advice to a merchant banker, and although the assignment took only a few hours, he saved the client a huge amount of money. The client asked Basham: 'What are you going to charge me?'

Basham was unsure – it was the first time he had done this kind of work. 'I don't know – twenty-five', he said, thinking £2,500.

'£25,000. Done,' said the client, quick as at flash. After they had shaken hands, the client added that he would have paid £250,000 because the advice had saved him millions.

In the mid-1980s companies became almost intoxicated in their attitude to spending money during takeover bids. 'Chairmen will do anything to win, and they don't mind what they pay,' said one PR consultant. 'For a brief window of a few months, PRs can do almost anything.'[24] Fees went through the roof and Basham was able to charge retainers of £10,000 a week and nobody blinked an eyelid. Later, for some clients this increased to £50,000. Fees of £1 million a year were not unusual. In previous times, the PR consultant had waited outside the boardroom, now they were invited inside for strategy meetings. Companies saw favourable publicity as a valuable commodity and manipulating the media was now taken as seriously as advice from bankers and lawyers. A leaked memo from the PR firm Grandfield Rork Collins to an Australian law firm makes the point best: 'We have timed the announcement in order to maximise the chances of a *Sunday Telegraph* story . . . we should NOT let the manipulation of the timing of this announcement become apparent. We must continue to drive the news in all this, forcing Allen's [a rival law firm] to be reactive.'[25]

When Tim Bell became chairman of Lowe Bell Communications in September 1986, he was fully aware of the power he held. He had witnessed the effect that stories in *Campaign* had on the advertising industry. Now he was in charge of a corporate PR apparatus. 'The truth is that a strong story placed in the newspaper, picked up by everybody else will actually have more impact than an advertising campaign,' he said, ten years later at a Marketing Society lunch. He added, more casually, 'Don't write a press release when a good leak will do.'[26]

The chief PR vehicle at his disposal was the multi-purpose Good Relations plc, which had just been acquired from its founder Tony Good, the doyen of independent financial PR. But Good, who stayed on as Bell's deputy chairman, was uneasy about his new masters. He was from the old school where clients were carefully checked out before being represented: 'We never took on a client that we felt uncomfortable about in terms of talking on behalf of or to the media,' he said.

Lowe and Bell, on the other hand, as paid advocates believe that everyone has the right to have their case presented and heard, regardless of ethical considerations. In advertising, it is more of a question of *how* rather than *should* an account be handled. 'When we were taken over by Lowe Howard-Spink it hired a restaurant to welcome the whole company,' recalled Good. 'One of the presentations was about one of their most famous and successful advertisements. The presenter showed off the sales growth charts and took pride in saying that this was achieved despite the fact that the product came bottom of all performance tests. That was when I questioned whether I was doing the right thing.'

Bell had been interested initially in the work of Good Relations but that tapered off. According to Peter Bradley, a former senior executive, he adopted, quite uncharacteristically, a lofty, detached management style. During the next three years Bell visited the offices in Russell Square only twice, once at very short notice. Bradley claims his approach was to create an atmosphere of awe and mystique, a new corporate style copied from Lord Hanson whom Bell hero-worshipped.[27]

The erstwhile advertising executive had now entered the corporate stratosphere of multi-millionaires, titled tycoons and celebrated industrialists. As PR is a people business, Bell was developing his own niche of advising on a personal basis just the chairman and chief executives of major corporations rather than devising orthodox media campaigns. Briefing financial journalists was now left to underlings.

Bell is a commercial power broker and a corporate consultant rather than a conventional PR man. 'I don't come into public relations,' he said. 'I'm in communications strategy and management. Public relations is still very young, absolutely non-scientific and there isn't anyone to base it on. In fact, what I think about PR is completely unprintable, because, with a few exceptions, they're a completely amateurish bunch. There are two sides to it. One is a mechanical process, press releases and all that stuff. Then there's giving advice or consultancy. There's a lot of competition to do the former, but those who do the second are few and far between. What's missing is an ability to analyse a communications situation and develop a strategy.'[28]

While Bell's staff dirty their hands with the press statements, he sells a consultancy cocktail of media savvy, political connections, corporate gossip and personal advice to the chairman or chief executive. But it is in the human touch that Bell has always specialised. 'He has an instinctive empathy with them, perhaps because he shares so many of their anxieties and aspirations,' said a former colleague.[29] 'Tim's gift,' says a friend, 'is being simultaneously an equal to tycoons while gently and flatteringly reminding them just how important they really are. A lot of these men are less secure than you'd think. Tim tells them what to do, and how to handle their relationships with government. He'll say: "Do that and Whitehall will think such-and-such, but if you do *this* they'll like you even more."'[30] He would advise them to reserve tables for friends at the Conservative Winter Ball for an opportunity to talk informally to cabinet ministers. And the visual image is still never far from his mind – 'For Lord's sake, don't wear that godawful grey tie on *News at Ten* tonight, chairman,' he will say. 'It makes you look like a loser already.'[31]

Underlying his *modus operandi* has been an unashamed reverence for famous and successful people. 'He reminded me of an extremely powdered and pampered courtesan,' Peter Bradley told me. 'It seemed to me there was a sensual undertone to his regard for powerful people, authority and status. Whenever I was with him he was a hell of a flirt and there was something titillating about his flirtation with power. Although it was business, he always managed to make it personal and that was part of his charm and success. He could turn it on with just about anyone.' In 1986 Christine Barker, then editor of *Campaign*, witnessed this when she had lunch with Bell at L'Etoile.

They were sitting at his usual window table when he noticed Jeremy Isaacs, then chief executive of Channel 4, across the restaurant. 'You see Isaacs over there,' Bell whispered to his guest, 'He's a pinko.' He went on to fulminate against Channel 4 and its programmes. However, at the end of the lunch he walked over to the television executive's table and fawned all over him. As they walked out onto Charlotte Street, an astonished Barker blurted out, 'What a cheek! You're such a bullshit artist.'

Bell just smiled. 'Hey, girl,' he replied. 'How do you think I got where I am today?'

But Bell is more than just a sweet-talking image-maker obsessed with celebrities and media trivialities; he has survived in the corporate world because he knows how to communicate a serious, complex message in an accessible way. 'Tim is a great advocate on behalf of his clients, but his real skill is to get to the heart of the matter,' said Nick Miles, former deputy chairman of Lowe Bell Communications and now head of Financial Dynamics. 'He would say things like, "Well, that's all very well, but people won't believe that", or "It's not compelling", or "It's too complicated" or "It just ain't going to play", and then explain why. We could be sitting in three-hour meetings and suddenly he would jump in and say, "It all boils down to three things." Someone might disagree that there were in fact 109, but Tim would always insist that there were three or five, never more than that.'

Another, more frustrated, admirer said: 'You face him across the table and there he is full of charm and the joy of life. What you don't realise is that he is always pushing his view or his aim. He just never gives up. If he can't persuade you to take one course of action he will try another route. If that doesn't work, he will go for a third option. The end result is that bloody Bell always get what he wants.'[32]

HEROES

'I'm very lucky,' Bell told Nicholas Coleridge, editorial director of Condé Nast magazines over lunch in early 1989. 'You see, I've met most of my heroes, worked for some of them and some have even invited me to their houses.'[33] The industrialist Bell most admires is Lord Weinstock, managing director of GEC from 1963 until his retirement in September 1996.

Born in 1924, the son of Polish-Jewish immigrants, Arnold Weinstock's father, a master cutter with a West End tailor, died when he was four years old and his mother five years later. After the war he joined the Admiralty as a statistician, then spent seven years in finance and property development before joining Michael Sobell at Radio and Allied Industries, which took over the General Electric Company (GEC) in 1961. After a series of audacious takeovers the company became a huge manufacturing success.

Since he came to prominence in the late 1960s Weinstock has had a rollercoaster public image. At first he was regarded as the doyen of the corporate world, at ease with both Labour and Conservative governments. Then, in the late 1970s and early 1980s, he was portrayed as an austere, dour businessman sitting on top of a cash mountain but not investing long-term, and as a remote figure heading a huge industrial combine. Newspaper stories appeared about how Weinstock turned out all the lights in the office before he went home each night, and how he would not spend money on the GEC head office because he did not want to appear wasteful. By the mid-1980s he was also very powerful, having expanded GEC by several takeovers. Sections of the financial press and the City were sceptical: they tended to look for a rising share price that brought a short-term result as a symbol of prosperity, while GEC stock was stable and produce respectable long-term dividends. The result was that GEC sat uneasily in the new world of flamboyant takeovers and conglomerates and was itself vulnerable to a City-inspired bid.

Weinstock had relatively little interest in communications, corporate image or the media: he had built a successful and prosperous business and saw no need for it, although he remained close to some City editors. However, by disengaging himself from the outside world Bell argues that he unwittingly encouraged this unfavourable public image.

When Bell began advising GEC in late 1985, he believed that rebuilding the image of its chief executive would take a long time. But first he was faced with more immediate and unhappy dilemmas. The government was in the midst of the Westland crisis and for the first, and probably only, time Bell found himself working in the opposite camp to Margaret Thatcher. The issue at hand was the future ownership of the Westland helicopter company: on one side was the American option, led by Sikorsky, favoured by the Prime Minister; on the other was a European consortium led by GEC and supported by Michael Heseltine, who resigned as defence secretary over Mrs Thatcher's handling of the affair in cabinet. As GEC's advertising agency, Lowe Howard-Spink and Bell were working flat out on a campaign to woo Westland shareholders and Bell was in charge of the account. It was a gut-wrenching ordeal for him because he risked incurring the wrath of the Prime Minister. By all accounts he detached himself as much as possible from the fracas. But it was not an auspicious beginning to his relationship with GEC.

Bell found working on the GEC account an exhilarating experience. He was fascinated by the world of weapons and electronics and loved the thrill of the chase of deals often involving billions of pounds. In February 1989, he was immersed in defending GEC against a £6 billion takeover bid by Metsun, a consortium comprised largely of Plessey and US defence firms. Bell took personal charge of GEC's communications strategy, attending daily meetings with Weinstock. Meanwhile, Gordon Reece represented Plessey. As it turned out, GEC not only survived but later swallowed Plessey.

However, it was the challenge of making Lord Weinstock an idol of British industry that really turned on Bell, who believed that Weinstock's public image was a distortion of his true personality. Bell would tell journalists that, far from being a hoarder of cash, Weinstock was privately almost extravagant, spending his money on racehorses and indulging in his passion for Mozart operas. 'I think he is a great man,' said Bell, 'and I think it's important that people recognise the greatest people because they act as an inspiration to others . . . He is a fantastically charming and funny man. He does terrific jokes and finds life very funny most of the time. He's got a twinkle in his eye and a very English view of the world. He's interested in every subject and can speak about all his companies in the most intimate detail. You'd never believe one man could possibly store that much information in his head.'[34]

For almost five years Bell and his colleagues projected Weinstock and promoted his achievements, persuading, cajoling and briefing the media. Eventually, Bell claims, he transformed Weinstock's and

GEC's corporate and public images. His benchmark was an article by Ivan Fallon, then deputy editor of the *Sunday Times*, whose column often sprinkled stardust on favoured tycoons. He wrote that he withdrew his past criticisms of Lord Weinstock and now regarded him as Britain's greatest manager. 'Rubbish,' said Fallon, now editorial director of Tony O'Reilly's Argyll Group in South Africa. 'I have known Arnold Weinstock since 1967 and *always* regarded him as the best industrialist in Britain. There was a time when I criticised his negativity and caution, but I don't remember even talking to Tim about him. My relationship with Arnold Weinstock was always direct and personal. It was never via Tim.'

Other PR consultants also dispute Bell's analysis of GEC's 'transformed' public and media image. They argue that the company and its managing director have always needed repositioning in terms of their corporate profile. 'Bell may have improved it,' said one City PR adviser, 'but he certainly never changed people's minds to that kind of extent.'

Another tycoon favoured by Bell – partly because of his political connections and support for Mrs Thatcher – is Sir Jeffrey (now Lord) Sterling, chairman of P&O since 1983. 'Jeffrey is brilliant at communications,' said Bell.[35] P&O's chairman has been more astute at PR than Weinstock so Bell's relationship with him has been broader. Lord Sterling is a much more political animal and P&O has been a regular contributor to Tory Party funds, donating £1,027,500 between 1979 and 1995.

Born in 1934, Sterling, like Bell, was a grammar-school boy, educated at Reigate Grammar and then Preston Manor County School. He too preferred music to academic work, and trained as a violinist at the Guildhall School of Music. At the age of twenty-one, his career took a radical change of course when he became a clerk at the Stock Exchange. Under the tutelage of Sir Isaac Wolfson, chairman of Great Universal Stores, Sterling rose rapidly as a stockbroker. In 1969, he acquired an investment trust from Slater Walker, renamed it Sterling Guarantee Trust and set about building an investment and property empire. Despite being hit hard by the property crash of 1974, Sterling's reputation grew as a negotiator and manager, particularly when he prevented Town and Country Properties from going bankrupt. For this he received the eternal gratitude of the City as a knock-on effect in the property market had been feared.

Sterling has woven himself into the fabric of the British Establishment in business and government: in 1979 he joined the board of British Airways and P&O in 1980. In 1983, when P&O was on the receiving end of an unwelcome bid by Trafalgar House, it was Sterling was took the helm. His close political ties are amply demonstrated by his role as a special adviser between 1982 and 1990 to successive secretaries of state for trade and industry (Patrick Jenkin, Cecil Parkinson, Norman Tebbit, Leon Brittan, Paul Channon, Lord Young and Nicholas Ridley).

By 1988, despite the *Herald of Free Enterprise* disaster, P&O had grown into a £2.2 billion conglomerate, embracing property and housebuilding as well as its maritime interests. But in early February the company's 2,300 seamen went on strike after the management had announced job cuts so that £6 million per year could be saved on its ferry services from Dover, to Zeebrugge and Boulogne. It was a highly damaging dispute as P&O was forced to cancel all their sailings out of Dover over the Easter holiday period, which affected nearly 100,000 holidaymakers.

Bell was immediately summoned, ostensibly to advise on the public relations and advertising campaign to persuade the seamen to return to work. But his brief was clearly broader as he liaised closely with David Hart, his accomplice during the miners' strike. Hart had remained close to the Prime Minister and had been active during the 1987 general election. Five days after the Conservative victory, Mrs Thatcher wrote to him: 'Thank you for all your contributions which you sent me during the campaign for speeches. As you know from the newspaper headlines, these contributions were used to very good effect and I want you to know how grateful I am.'

Hart had established a reputation for himself as a fixer who commuted between the commercial and political worlds. He saw the P&O dispute as another industrial war, motivated by political forces, in which he would play a strategic role just as he had during the 1984–85 miners' strike. For his part, Bell believed Hart could help his client as it faced a commercial and public-relations crisis only months after the *Herald of Free Enterprise* sank, with the loss of hundreds of lives. On 17 March 1988, the two men had lunch at Cecconi's in Burlington Gardens, Mayfair, where they discussed the dispute. Unknown to Bell, Hart was already keen to join the fray and was already devising a strategy. But he needed Bell's agreement. He got it. 'Tim's on board,' he said afterwards to friends.

A week later, on 23 March 1988, as P&O and the National Union of Seamen met at ACAS to attempt to prevent the dispute escalating into a national ferry strike, Hart and Bell met again. This time the venue was Lowe Howard-Spink and Bell's head office in Knightsbridge and they were joined by Stephen Sherbourne, recently recruited by Lowe Bell Communications after a five-year stint as Mrs Thatcher's political secretary at 10 Downing Street. According to Hart, Bell commissioned him 'to carry out certain activities on behalf of P&O'.

The nature of these 'activities' was specified at a further meeting, at P&O's headquarters in Pall Mall, attended by Hart, Bell, Sherbourne and Sterling himself. According to a source present at the meeting, Hart proposed some 'outrageous and extremist ideas on how to smash the strike. He wanted to send in the heavy artillery.' Hart suggested going down to Dover and Felixstowe and running security checks on the pickets. He said he could arrange 'special people' to infiltrate the strikers and gather intelligence about their tactics.

Bell was uneasy about Hart's proposals. 'It might be better to adopt a more low-key approach,' he said. Sterling made little comment, and seemed preoccupied with the more immediate practical problems. Hart, however, was unperturbed about the muted response and commissioned special research on 'how to identify subversives'.

After the strike, Hart became irritated when the 'promised' fee was not forthcoming. On 22 September 1988, he wrote to Bell at his home address in Belgravia:

When you asked me to carry out certain activities on behalf of P&O, you made it clear we would receive payment in due course. At lunch the other day, however, I began to feel like the proverbial donkey that had a carrot attached to a stick, just out of reach, in front of his nose. I am just writing to let you know that this donkey does not wish to have his arse kicked. I expect a substantial sum, very soon, so that I can go on making a better Britain.

*   *   *

Bell had sidestepped Hart's more radical plans. But it was an indication of the nature of his relationship with Sterling: there was more to it than mere media management, corporate affairs and advertising. Politics played a large part.

'I'VE GOT TO GO AND SEE HER'

Tim Bell trades off his contacts and he has had plenty at the highest political level. There is no limit to the amount of business that flows from access to the political epicentre and businessmen love being close to the centre of power and when they enter Bell's Mayfair office most clients are impressed. As you walk up the stairs, there is what Bell calls his 'Downing Street Wall' – a gallery of photographs of his heroes notably: Rupert Murdoch, Lord Hanson, Sir James Goldsmith, Marmaduke Hussey and, of course, Margaret Thatcher – 'with love'.

By the mid-1980s Bell's close relationship with the Prime Minister was well known in the business world and was a distinct commercial asset. 'Everyone knew that the connection was a useful marketing tool to get new clients and Bell was brilliant at exploiting that,' said a former colleague.

On one occasion Bell visited a seasoned industrialist to pitch for a PR account. Bell asked him to outline his company and business plans so that he could evaluate what kind of PR campaign was required. The industrialist provided some basic details and rather clichéd statements about future expansion and investment plans. 'I don't usually do this, but what you've just told me is incredible,' replied Bell. 'It's absolutely fascinating and you have some amazing ideas. This is so important that I would like to talk to David Young [then trade and industry secretary] immediately.' In front of the startled industrialist, Bell picked up the phone, rang Young and said: 'David, I'm with ——— . What he's told me is so incredible that I really think the Prime Minister should know all about it immediately. Why don't we set up a meeting for him at Chequers?' The businessman smiled to himself throughout this performance. While others may have been seduced by such tricks, he wasn't, and Bell didn't get the account.

The London and Edinburgh Trust, a property company formerly

owned by John and Peter Beckwith which had donated £150,000 to Tory Party funds, was more impressed. Bell secured the account after a lunch at the Hyde Park Hotel, Knightsbridge. He turned on the charm and Lowe Bell Communications was hired for an estimated annual fee of £100,000. 'I think we got the business because the Beckwiths had little experience of corporate communications or public affairs,' recalled Peter Bradley, a former Good Relations director. At first Lowe Bell devoted their senior executives to the client and had regular meetings. According to Bradley, though: 'Basically, the sessions consisted of Tim regaling their board with endless anecdotes about Mrs Thatcher. One involved her being unable to recite a joke written by her speech-writers in which she was supposed to say "Keep Taking the Tablets". At first this material was lapped up and they were fascinated by it, because they thought they were getting the inside political track, but not much actual work was done. The meetings effectively consisted of Tim lying on their boardroom table and inviting them to tickle his tummy. By then he had been a status symbol and I guess the Beckwiths thought that such proximity to the heart of government was useful and they could afford the fee. But then they lost interest and patience with this and their attendance dropped off and the dates kept being altered . . . A lot of businessmen have a fascination for political power and Bell was the consummate performer who could take advantage of that for commercial benefit as well as being a skilled practitioner in his own right.'

Rodney Dewe, chairman of the rival City PR firm Dewe Rogerson, often heard Bell say before he left a meeting or social function: 'I've got to go and see her,' meaning the Prime Minister. On one occasion, however, Dewe and Bell were on the panel to choose the J.O. Hambro Businessman of the Year award. At 6.45 p.m., Bell suddenly announced, 'I'm sorry, I have to leave. I've got to go and see her.' This amused Lord King, chairman of the panel. After Bell left the room, King leaned over to Dewe and said, 'I happen to know the Prime Minister is not in London.' Dewe, an admirer of Bell, took a charitable view of the incident: 'He was either trying to show off and impress people or he needed to get out of the meeting and needed an excuse to get away.'

Chapter Seven

1987 – A Covert Campaign

'Ssssh about Tim. No one must know about his visit'
Mrs Thatcher to Lord Young, at Chequers, 10 May 1987,
the week before the general election campaign began

Lord Tebbit, the former Tory cabinet minister and party chairman, has a favourite saying about Mrs Thatcher and 10 Downing Street, which he repeated to me when I met him at the House of Lords in March 1996. 'As soon as a Prime Minster goes into Number 10,' he remarked, 'the windows get smaller and the longer one stays the smaller they get. It was to Margaret's credit that her windows remained large.'

One reason why she avoided becoming a prisoner of Downing Street was her cultivation of outside confidants. She favoured successful self-made industrialists like Lord Hanson, Sir Hector Laing, former chairman of United Biscuits, and Lord King. Although she saw them infrequently, Mrs Thatcher often liked a visit at 'Slipper Time' – about 10.30 p.m. after dinner, for a glass of weak whisky. Other courtiers included influential editors like Sir David English of the *Daily Mail* and Sir John Junor and Sir Nicholas Lloyd of the *Daily Express*. And on the selling and presentation of her policies, there were Tim Bell and Sir Gordon Reece. 'I like to work with people I know,' she would say.

In some ways Bell was the common link between all her 'friends'. He knew most of them and had a commercial relationship with some. 'Tim was at the heart of that loose group of informal business advisers to Mrs Thatcher,' said Stephen Woodward, a former senior executive at Lowe Howard-Spink. 'She was on the phone with great frequency

... There was always a group of people in Tim's office at the end of the day and his phone would ring all the time with businessmen, cabinet ministers or Mrs Thatcher on the other end.'

In the spring of 1986, the Prime Minister was on the telephone to Bell more than usual. Her government was in the midst of a serious political crisis. The confidence factor was draining away. Unemployment was still high and her health and education policies were increasingly unpopular. The administration had lost direction and focus and, since the New Year, had stumbled from one calamity to another. On 15 January 1986, Mrs Thatcher had even said privately that she might have to resign over the Westland affair, after it had been claimed that the leak of a selected extract of a confidential Attorney-General's letter critical of Michael Heseltine had been sanctioned by No. 10. This was followed by a major row over the proposed sale of Land Rover to the American company General Motors. Most significantly, Mrs Thatcher herself was under fire for being too extreme and losing touch with the basic aspirations of voters. Private opinion polls showed for the first time that she was referred to, even in Tory circles, as TBW (That Bloody Woman).

It was a litany of bad news and the thankless task of communicating it to the Prime Minister was left to Michael Dobbs, chief of staff at Central Office, and John Sharkey, the Saatchi executive now in charge of the Tory account. They delivered their research and conclusions to Mrs Thatcher and senior cabinet ministers at Chequers on 13 April 1986. The Prime Minister received their report in stony silence. She did not like the message, particularly the finding that she was not forward-looking. What made it worse was that she did not have a personal rapport with the messengers. She missed Tim. She did not mind receiving disturbing dispatches from *him*.

Tim Bell was not at Chequers, primarily because he had left Saatchi's. He was paid the £24,000 a year retainer for the Tory account, but that was a 'golden handcuffs' arrangement not a contract. Maurice Saatchi made it crystal clear that he did not want his former chairman anywhere near the account. 'They'd rather I went away and crawled under a stone,' recalled Bell.[1] However, there were more substantial reasons for Bell's absence.

Norman Tebbit, the new Tory Party chairman, knew about Bell's past cocaine habit. A fellow senior cabinet minister had told him about it during the 1983 election campaign and Tebbit resolved that if he became chairman he would exclude Bell. It was just too dangerous for the party of law and order and family values to be employing a former drug-user. After entering Central Office, Tebbit was even more keen to ignore Bell when he learned of Bell's conviction for 'obscenely' exposing himself. His worst fears were justified when a *Daily Mirror* journalist telephoned the Tory Party press office and asked about the conviction.

Tebbit had no personal animus towards Bell. 'Tim is a very good courtier, Maurice [Saatchi] is not quite such a good one – and I am a very bad one,' said the former chairman. 'Tim had amazing charm. That is his strength and that is why he is such a good salesman.'[2] But he decided that he could not afford the risk of allowing Bell to continue to advise the Prime Minister or be closely involved in a general election.

Mrs Thatcher, of course, was anxious for Bell to be brought back as part of the campaign team, and only learned of his criminal record when Tebbit broke the news to her. He was concerned that the *Daily Mirror* would uncover the conviction and publish the story above a photograph of Bell walking into 10 Downing Street which, he said, was clearly damaging to the party. Mrs Thatcher was shocked but clung to the hope that her favourite media adviser could still be included: 'I might have been prepared to insist,' she wrote in her memoirs, 'but this would have caused more important problems with Norman and Central Office.'[3]

She later told Tebbit that Bell's friends were unhappy about his attitude. But the party chairman was adamant. The case had been held in public session at Hampstead Magistrates' Court and Bell had pleaded guilty. Tebbit was not prepared to take the political gamble, despite the attempts of Michael Dobbs, his closest adviser, to bring Bell back into the fold.

Bell was angry at being banished into political exile and became critical of Tebbit's style of chairmanship. 'He [Tebbit] ousted me from having any connection with the party,' he said later. 'I had known him very well before, but he managed introvertly rather than extrovertly . . . Cecil [Parkinson] reached out to people, walked around the building, chatted to everybody, called them in, would stop with anybody and talk about the latest argument. Norman closed the door when he went into his office and communication was an entirely restricted process.'[4]

A telling indication of the frisson between Tebbit and Bell came with the suggestion that a communications triumvirate of Cecil Parkinson (who was then also in exile over the Sarah Keays affair), Bell and Sir Gordon Reece should meet the Prime Minister every morning at 8.50 a.m. to discuss the public presentation of government policies. Mrs Thatcher was keen on the proposal but it was stopped by Norman Tebbit, Bernard Ingham and John Wakeham, the chief whip.[5]

But Bell remained determined to be involved in the election campaign. He was helped by the differences and tension that existed between Mrs Thatcher and Tebbit. On 15 April 1986, the chairman let it be known that he was angry at not having been consulted by the Prime Minister over the decision to allow American jets to use British RAF bases on their way to bombing Libya. In Tebbit's view, she also procrastinated constantly over his desire to reallocate senior Central Office officials like Jeffrey Archer, and the appointment of a much-needed communications director. On her side, Mrs Thatcher was unhappy with Saatchi's work, which Tebbit defended, and she felt, too, that his political support for her had diminished.

What started as billows of smoke above Downing Street and Smith Square turned into a full-scale blaze: fires were stoked against Tebbit in informal discreet briefings of selected editors and political correspondents. Mrs Thatcher had become convinced that her chairman was plotting to replace her, using Central Office as a power base. This view was confirmed by outside advisers.

Suddenly, in the summer of 1986, a flurry of anti-Tebbit stories spread throughout the pro-Conservative papers. On 20 July 1986, 'Tebbit Faces Chop' was the headline above a *News of the World* story. Written by Rodney Tyler, the story stated that Tebbit 'faced the sack in a row over the party's publicity . . . The Premier is known to be unhappy about the work now being done by advertising agents Saatchi and Saatchi.' Two weeks later a full page of the *Mail on Sunday* was devoted to 'A Hero Falls From Grace – Why There's No Place Now for Norman Tebbit in the Charmed Circle at No. 10.' It continued: 'An extraordinary campaign is under way, involving and perhaps even orchestrated by the Prime Minister, to drive Norman Tebbit out of front-line politics.' The next day, Monday 4 August 1986, the *Sun*'s Trevor Kavanagh reported 'Outcast Tebbit Close to Quitting', citing as his sources 'Ministers and key Downing Street advisers'. The stories continued throughout the week, which Charles Reiss, political editor of the London *Evening Standard*, described as 'the latest stage in the series of carefully planted stories'.[6]

So who was the political arsonist lighting the anti-Tebbit fires? None of the several political correspondents I interviewed could recall and others refused to talk to me. Sources close to Tebbit argue it was either disenchanted senior Central Office officials or outsiders. The former party chairman is more circumspect: 'Looking back I realised that many of the stories must have resulted from regular press briefings by someone whose position gave him credibility with the lobby,' he said. 'Whoever it was also had a fair amount of inside knowledge . . . There was no doubt that someone was actively trying to undermine the confidence of the Prime Minister in Central Office, Saatchi's and me.'[7]

By Thursday 7 August 1986, Tebbit could no longer contain his anger about the untrue articles in the press. He marched into 10 Downing Street, clutching a file of press cuttings, and confronted Mrs Thatcher about the whispering campaign. 'Look, this is not helping,' he told her. 'Either I go or this has to stop.' The Prime Minister, who rarely read the newspapers unless they were drawn to her attention, was startled and said she did not know the source of the stories. Two days later she telephoned Tebbit from Chequers. During a twenty-minute conversation, she reassured him of her support and that there was no question of removing him. He in turn stressed his allegiance to her. That cleared the air, although it was more of a ceasefire than a truce.

'WHERE'S TIM?'

After the Summer of Discontent and a refreshing holiday in France, Norman Tebbit returned to lay plans for his party's revival. He commissioned Saatchi's to devise a new political and marketing strategy. Their research showed that the government was perceived as complacent and had run out of ideas. 'Our theme was "The Next Move Forward",' recalled John Sharkey, Saatchi's account director. 'The agency was involved in an unprecedented degree in planning and staging the conference, designing the publicity material – even drafting the outlines for the ministers' speeches.'8 The result was a highly successful conference, helped considerably by a coherent theme.

However, as thoughts turned to the election, Mrs Thatcher continued to express anxieties about the absence of Parkinson, Bell and Reece. At a meeting at 10 Downing Street, she confronted Maurice Saatchi and Jeremy Sinclair: 'Why isn't Tim involved? I understand you have him under contract.' Maurice replied that his inclusion would cause resentment among the staff as other people had been phased in to take over his role.9 'Well, I don't want to work with people I don't know,' she said. 'I want to work with people I know.'

Nevertheless, in the early months of 1987 Bell and Mrs Thatcher continued to meet socially. On 16 February, she gently, and characteristically, teased him about his weight increase. 'I'll lose weight, Prime Minister, if you had an election. The work should soon get the weight off,' he replied.

'I can't call an election just for you to slim,' she replied.10

A month later, on 17 March 1987, an appointment was made that not only changed the nature of the campaign but also provided a covert conduit for Bell to be a player. Lord Young, the employment secretary, who had no constituency commitments, offered his services to the Prime Minister. She agreed and he became a deputy chairman. Young was allotted the task of running her countrywide tours and conducting top-level briefings for Fleet Street editors. Tebbit welcomed the appointment: he trusted Young as a valued colleague. But other cabinet ministers were astonished. Nigel Lawson, chancellor of the exchequer, described it as 'unbelievably perverse': 'David [Young] had many excellent qualities. He was a genuine believer in the enterprise culture, had useful business experience and a particularly fertile mind, which was always coming up with ingenious ideas and schemes, all of which – given his business background – were practical and many of them had merit. But David was a businessman . . . without ever having stood for political office or even been a local party worker. As a result, he knew less about election campaigning and had his finger further from the public pulse than any other cabinet colleague.

'He was, however, a great believer in the power of advertising . . . He seemed to believe that it was the choice of advertising agency which would determine the outcome of the election. Margaret [Thatcher], who was always inclined to think that if a policy was unpopular it could only be because of poor presentation, had a weakness for this line of thinking.'[11]

Unknown to Tebbit, however, the idea for Lord Young to be parachuted into Smith Square with his long-time secretary had emanated from Tim Bell. Two weeks earlier, on 2 March, Young had had dinner with Howell James, his special adviser, and Bell. The ambitious cabinet minister had told them how keen he was to contribute to the campaign and Bell had suggested he offer his services to the Prime Minister.[12]

Young, who had made a fortune out of the industrial property boom of the 1960s and had never fought an election campaign, and Bell had become friends. Young was fascinated by mass marketing and the media, while Bell was impressed by the businessman's meteoric rise to the cabinet. 'Tim is extremely taken with the way Lord Young can have all that power and influence without being troubled by the electorate,' a friend said at the time.[13] In June 1985, when Young, then head of the Cabinet Office's Enterprise Unit, wanted to appoint a special adviser to act as his press officer, Bell had introduced him to Howell James.[14] One of Bell's closest friends, James was a 31-year-old affable Welshman who had worked at Capital Radio and then TV-am where, he later claimed, he had been press officer to Roland Rat. He then worked briefly at the Dorchester Hotel. But when James joined Young's Enterprise Unit in May 1985 it was not as a civil servant. He was seconded to Young and his salary was paid by Bell who, in effect, was giving thousands of pounds worth of employment services to the Cabinet Office for nothing. When asked by the *Times* what was in it for him, Bell replied, 'Nothing. You either make a commitment towards your society or you don't.'[15]

James stayed for two years, until 1987, when he was hired as corporate affairs director at the BBC. Lord Young, now trade and industry secretary, needed a new special adviser. Once again Bell 'had just the man'. This time Young met Peter Luff, who had been head of Edward Heath's private office and then a director of Good Relations a subsidiary of Lowe Howard-Spink and Bell. After entering the DTI, part of his salary continued to be paid by the agency. Luff stayed for two years and then rejoined Lowe Bell Communications as a consultant. In 1992 he was elected Conservative MP for Worcester and has been an adviser to Lowe Bell Political since 1995.

Civil servants who worked closely with Lord Young in both the Enterprise Unit and the DTI did not share Bell's view of himself as altruistic. 'It was disgraceful,' said a former official, who worked closely with both James and Luff. 'They were employees of Bell's and yet they were working at the highest level in Young's office. They had access to all the inside information of a senior cabinet minister's office, particularly commercial intelligence in the DTI. I am not saying they took advantage of it, but that's not the point. There was a conflict of interests and it was Bell currying favour with a cabinet minister. There was no mechanism for monitoring such a situation. Perhaps it was unique to Bell, I don't know.'

Young's appointment as deputy chairman was wrongly presented – deliberately – as Tebbit's idea. As the election grew closer, his responsibilities expanded, to include co-ordinating the launch of the manifesto and contributing to party political broadcasts, and he took on more of the presentation duties. This, of course, was a godsend for Tim Bell, whose efforts to contribute were continually blocked by Tebbit: he had a connection at the highest level inside Central Office. He was also assisted by Mrs Thatcher's affection and her frustration at Tebbit's objections to him. In his fascinating, if highly partial, book on the 1987 election, Rodney Tyler, a close friend of Bell, does not allude to the real reason for Tebbit's hostility. But he reports accurately that the Prime Minister did not press for Bell's inclusion because it was not 'worth the row it would cause'.[16]

Instead, the Prime Minister and Lord Young ensured that, despite the express wishes of their party chairman, Bell would be a secret adviser throughout the election campaign. Mrs Thatcher's private meetings with him began at Chequers on the evening of Saturday 9 May 1987, two days before she told the cabinet of the date for the general election. That afternoon she was polishing the contents of the manifesto with Norman Tebbit and Brian Griffiths, head of the No 10 Policy Unit. While she was thus engaged, Bell and his then fiancée Virginia were smuggled into the downstairs study and kept there until Tebbit left.

The ostensible reason for Bell's visit was a private family dinner to celebrate Denis Thatcher's seventy-second birthday. But in fact Mrs Thatcher wanted to discuss her communications strategy for the forthcoming election. According to Rodney Tyler's account of the meeting in *Campaign*:

They discussed the presentation of herself, and the tone of voice she wanted to adopt. Bell suggested she should start to drop the 'we' of the government – because it was redolent of the royal 'we' – and switch instead to the 'I' of the Prime Minister. They agreed that her instinct was right not to try to be 'cuddly' during the campaign . . . and that even though she might be attacked for being uncaring, she should remain above the fray – although never remote from it. They discussed which major set-piece TV interviews she should take part in, and when, which ministers were best on television in which circumstances, the preparation of her newspaper articles and the themes for her major speeches and election broadcasts.[17]

Among the political strategies they chatted about was an offensive against the SDP-Liberal Alliance, as advocated by Norman Tebbit. 'This is all wrong,' claimed Bell.

'Why?' she asked.

'What's wrong with what we did last time?' asked Bell. 'That gave you a 144-seat majority. What's changed? We were in government then, we are now . . . The Alliance was wobbling around the edge in 1983. It still is. Labour was in disarray. It still is. If anything, everything is better, because the economic miracle is in place and you've got the miners' strike resolved in place of the Falklands. Okay, modernise, update, freshen, but someone will have to spend a long time convincing me not to do exactly what we did before.'

'You mean we shouldn't do this?' asked the Prime Minister

'Attacking the Alliance is madness,' continued Bell. 'You would strengthen and exaggerate their position. It's like the brand leader in the supermarket attacking the small local brand. Suddenly everybody hears about it and thinks if the big guy is attacking it, it must be really good.'

'But everyone has heard of David Owen and David Steel.'

'That's not true,' claimed Bell. 'To this day, ten per cent of the population thinks that Winston Churchill is still Prime Minister.'[18]

After this pre-dinner tête-à-tête, she stressed to him the need for secrecy about his role.

The following afternoon senior cabinet ministers gathered at Chequers to discuss the election date and arrangements for the campaign. After lunch Lord Young noticed that Mrs Thatcher was on her own. He sidled up to her and asked if she had had a good meeting with Bell. The Prime Minister looked startled. 'Tim!' she whispered, turning round to see if anyone was listening. 'Come over here – shhh about Tim. No one here must know about his visit.'[19]

Mrs Thatcher was playing with fire. Not only was she risking a potentially catastrophic split with her party chairman, but she had set up what was essentially a clandestine, back-door channel of communications advice. It was a recipe for disaster.

COVERT ACTION

After the starting pistol was fired on 18 May, the Tory campaign was off to a sluggish start. One reason for this was that the tension between Downing Street and Smith Square had re-emerged. 'This led to the campaign not running as smoothly as it should,' John Sharkey, Saatchi's account director, said with characteristic understatement.

There was chaos, mainly because the task of organising the Prime Minister's personal tour had been allocated to the inexperienced Lord Young. She turned up at factories that had either closed down or were empty of workers. Visits were made to an East Midlands school on a bank holiday and to Wales during Wakes Week. Hasty replanning led to frantic travelling, which exhausted Mrs Thatcher. 'Central Office' was inevitably blamed for the mess by her entourage, although it was outside their control.[20]

On advertising, Mrs Thatcher insisted that 'it was going to be the most positive campaign ever'. But Central Office believed this was short-sighted. 'It's much more difficult for positive advertising to work in the political arena,' said Michael Dobbs. It runs contrary to the nature of the beast. It was naïve to think that the whole campaign could be positive. We planned a balanced campaign. The daily press conferences would project positive messages and the advertising would do what Saatchi's always did best – knocking hell out of the Labour party.' The agency agreed, arguing that it was difficult to write positive ads that people noticed, and that there was also a risk of sounding complacent. As insurance, Tebbit commissioned some ads that 'were controversial to such a degree that I would have used them only if the contest looked close'.[21]

However, politicians like positive advertising and Mrs Thatcher was no exception. Influenced by Bell, who argued that knocking copy demoralised her, she threw out many of Saatchi's early advertisements. He said that the Tory manifesto should be presented to counter Labour's charge that the government's policies penalised the poorest and weakest in society to the benefit of the strong and wealthy. People should also be told that they need not feel guilty about doing well. For it was only by their success, claimed Bell, that society could afford to care for the less fortunate.[22]

This conflicted with Saatchi's strategy of hammering the opposition. Relations with the agency deteriorated further when its executives discovered that the Prime Minister was simultaneously and secretly taking counsel from Bell. 'The fact that Thatcher was quite two-faced throughout the run-up to the election proved very irritating,' recalled Jeremy Sinclair, who was in charge of Saatchi's creative output.

By now, it was tacitly understood by most ministers that Bell had an unofficial role in the campaign and major promotional work was undertaken separately from Saatchi's. One example was a video about the Tory manifesto, devised and supervised by Bell and Antony Jay, one of the creators of *Yes Minister*. The film included senior cabinet members, except the Prime Minister, talking straight to camera off-the-cuff for two minutes, without an autocue, on what they would do if re-elected. When Norman Tebbit was due to appear, Bell had to scamper out through a side entrance until that part of the recording was finished. On Monday 18 May, the first day of the campaign, it was shown to Mrs Thatcher, who liked it enormously. However, it contained no direct contribution from her. 'It's very good, but it's a bit like Hamlet without the Prince,' she said. 'I'm not a glorified foreign secretary. I want to be in it.' Lord Young rang Adrian Rowbotham, the video's director. 'Sorry, guys,' he said. 'You have to film the Prime Minister.' After frantic scripting by Bell and Jay, this took place at Lord McAlpine's house in Great College Street, Westminster, at 5 p.m. that afternoon. The next day copies of the video were distributed to all 650 Conservative candidates.

*   *   *

By the end of the first week, the Tory campaign had come under attack for being 'lacklustre' and 'less than sunny', in contrast to Labour's slick, glossy launch. Although the Conservatives' 8 per cent opinion-poll lead had not been dented, siren voices began to plague the Prime Minister. That morning Lord Young grew unhappy about 'co-ordination' and expressed his anxieties over lunch with Bell and Howell James. In the evening Mrs Thatcher received a phone call from her daughter Carol who had just returned from a journalistic assignment in Jordan. She was 'horrified' by events so far: 'You'd better get your act together or start packing,' she told her mother. Later that night the Prime Minister left a message for Bell to call her. He had gone out to dinner with Nicholas Lloyd, editor of the *Daily Express*, and his wife, Eve Pollard, editor of the *Mail on Sunday*'s *You* magazine, at Harry's Bar in Mayfair. After dinner he rang her from his car outside the restaurant. He said he thought there were 'dangers in the situation, but not insuperable ones'. At 11.45 p.m. Mrs Thatcher called Young and expressed her concern. She agreed to meet him and Bell.[23]

The next day was a miserable rainy day for Mrs Thatcher, and her tour again went badly. At six thirty, when Bell and Young arrived at her upstairs flat in Downing Street, she was upset and rattled. Bell led the discussion with Stephen Sherbourne, the Prime Minister's political secretary, taking notes. He said that Hugh Hudson's party election broadcast on Neil Kinnock had been powerful and that Labour had won the first week. She snapped that Bell's analysis did not constitute 'constructive criticism'. 'It's a fact, Prime Minister. That's what's constructive about it,' replied Bell, who then calmed her down by reminding her of previous election victories.[24]

Lord Young interjected: 'Unleash Norman. He's got to go for Kinnock – we've really got to destroy this nonsensical image that Kinnock has created. You must go not against Kinnock, but against the Labour party and show what their hidden manifesto really is . . . It's really got to attack him.'

'We have to select the right people for television,' replied Mrs Thatcher. 'I can't do it by myself, I must do it with Norman because he's the chairman.'

'Use responsible people,' said Bell. 'Like David [Young], Douglas [Hurd, then home secretary]. Then you've got to have the combative people – Kenneth Baker [then education secretary] and Kenneth

Clarke [Young's deputy at Employment]. Geoffrey Howe would be one of the quiet people. We've got to concentrate on those for television, and use *only* those.'[25]

The Prime Minister agreed. It was resolved to 'unleash Norman' and attack Labour more vigorously. She would revive the theme of what she called Labour's 'Iceberg Manifesto' – one tenth visible, nine tenths hidden. By then it was 8.15 p.m. and Young left while Bell stayed until 11 p.m. The 'exile' was back on the mainland. Fortunately for him, Lord Young was good at maintaining discretion: 'It was like walking on eggshells in Central Office,' he later confided.[26]

During the second week of the campaign the 'exile' was joined by Sir Gordon Reece, despite the potential embarrassment of his consultancy to Guinness. On Thursday 28 May, Bell met Young for lunch at Mark's Club. It had been a better week for the Conservatives because Labour had lost ground over their defence policy, but they decided that a 'new issue' was required to keep the opposition on the defensive and that the Tories should avoid the 'caring issues', particularly health. They should aim instead to disrupt the debate with their own agenda.[27]

The next day Bell and Young reconvened at 5 p.m. at Lord McAlpine's house in Great College Street with Bell producing storyboards for his proposed strategy for the following week. He recommended attacking Labour for the first three or four days and then turning positive. Young agreed, and they went to 10 Downing Street. Just after 8 p.m. Mrs Thatcher arrived at the upstairs flat. Although the Tory lead had continued to hold steady, she complained bitterly about the 'problems of the campaign'. Bell presented his 'attack strategy' which focused on the 'fear issues'. This involved projecting what the Tories believed were the likely consequences of Labour's policies – strikes, secondary picketing, more crime, higher inflation and increased taxation. The weary Prime Minister accepted the premise and it was agreed that these themes should be incorporated into media interviews and ministers' speeches. The onslaught against Kinnock and Labour would continue.[28]

So far, most of Bell's suggestions had fitted in with Central Office's plans and the potential for conflict was limited. However, by Monday 1 June, Norman Tebbit had heard rumours of Bell's activities, and that morning's Tory press conference was adorned by a new graphic – a wilting red rose – that had been prepared in the offices of Lowe

Howard-Spink and Bell, not by Saatchi and Saatchi. Tebbit was irritated: not only about Bell's involvement but other advertising agencies, like Young and Rubicam, were also offering alternative strategies to the Prime Minister. Mrs Thatcher's already tense mood was aggravated by an abscessed tooth.

Lord Young was also nervous and, on Wednesday 3 June, he was rattled by two rogue opinion polls, one on *Newsnight* and the other a Gallup poll to be published in the next day's *Daily Telegraph*, which claimed that the party's lead was down to 4 per cent. At 10.15 p.m. that evening he joined Bell and Stephen Sherbourne for a meeting at Downing Street, at which Mrs Thatcher was tired and downcast. 'She was looking more upset than I could remember for a long time,' said her daughter Carol.[29] Bell tried to revive her spirits by calling for a more co-ordinated programme. 'The idea', he said, 'is to get everyone singing from the same hymn book.'[30] That comment, given the dramatic and extraordinary events of the following day, was laced with irony.

PANIC IN 10 DOWNING STREET

The person in the Conservative Party who knew most about opinion polls and political market research was Keith Britto, its mild-mannered hard-working deputy marketing director. He was a veteran of both the 1979 and 1983 elections and knew all about the dramatic ebb and flow of campaigns. As he sat at his desk in Smith Square in the early hours of Thursday 4 June 1987, he remained unperturbed. He had looked carefully at the two polls from the day before and dismissed them. *Newsnight*'s 'poll' stated that the Tories' lead was down to 2.5 per cent (a ridiculous finding, given the trend), while Gallup had been consistently at variance with the mainstream.

However, just before 10 a.m. something unusual happened. Britto began to receive a stream of telephone calls from stockbrokers and analysts in the City asking about a new Marplan poll, which had cut the party's lead to just 2 per cent. This was worrying. He immediately called the polling company, who assured him it was untrue. They had not even received the results yet as they were still conducting interviews. But the rumour spread like wildfire and inevitably reached the ears of Mrs Thatcher, cabinet ministers and their aides.

By 12.30 the stock market had dropped appreciably and panic had set in. Britto was under siege. Downing Street was on the phone every ten minutes and Lord Young every twenty minutes. 'What about this poll?' he kept asking. And yet the research was still unfinished. The truth was that the rumour was being circulated deliberately to ensure that share prices dropped and that a financial killing could be made, by buying when the market fell and selling soon afterwards. 'Someone made a huge amount of money that day,' Britto told me.

Meanwhile, at the press conference at Central Office that morning, Mrs Thatcher had blundered badly over a question on private health when she said that she had private medical insurance 'to enable me to go into hospital on the day I want, at the time I want and with the doctor I want'. The remark was, as the Prime Minister later admitted, 'insensitive, callous and uncaring' and was fully exploited by the opposition.[31] At 10.15 a.m. she had a meeting with Lord Young, William Whitelaw and Norman Tebbit, during which she ripped into Saatchi's advertising. She admitted grudgingly that the ad showing a picture of a surrendering soldier with his arms held aloft above the caption 'Labour's Defence Policy' was 'quite a good piece of work' (in fact, most observers thought it was devastatingly effective).[32] But, having taken private counsel from Bell, she now wanted positive advertising about the government's achievements. Michael Dobbs, Tebbit's chief of staff, was instructed to bring over the new work from Saatchi's to Downing Street.[33] 'It was the sort of meeting that a gentleman would prefer to forget,' Dobbs told me. 'The handbag had a lot of bricks in it, that morning.'

Over at the agency's head office in Charlotte Street the Brothers and senior executives were angry. Now that they knew about Bell's covert advice to their client, they suspected that he was undermining their creative work. 'Your agency needs to be careful,' Whitelaw warned them. 'There are other factions at work inside the party. You need to get some protection from Norman (Tebbit).'

The parallel channels of communications advice – Bell and Young v. Tebbit and Saatchi's – had always been a time-bomb, ticking away under Downing Street. Now it was about to explode. At 11 a.m. Dobbs telephoned John Sharkey, the agency's account director. 'Thatcher has thrown out the ads,' he said. 'You need to do some more.'

Sharkey went to see him at Smith Square and during their meeting Lord Young walked in and instructed Sharkey on the new "positive" advertising campaign.

Sharkey returned to Charlotte Street with an unclear brief. He called Tebbit for clarification, and received different instructions. Sharkey called back Dobbs and was given yet another version. Faced with a farce worthy of *Yes Minister*, Sharkey was in a tricky predicament. He was required to show the new ads to the Prime Minister at 5.15 p.m. that afternoon. Which line should he follow? He spoke to Maurice and Charles Saatchi because he needed one coherent direction. They agreed to keep to the broad positive theme of 'Britain is Great Again – Don't Let Labour Wreck It'.

By early afternoon the Marplan poll had still remained unfinished. People were saying that the poll would show Labour *ahead* of the Tories. As panic of seismic proportions gripped the Conservatives. Dobbs recalls hearing Tebbit quoting Rudyard Kipling, Mrs Thatcher's favourite poet :

> If you can keep your head while all about you
> Are losing theirs and blaming it on you,
> If you can trust yourself when all men doubt you
> But make allowance for their doubting too . . .

He could not remember the final words, but it was the sentiment that mattered. If you can do those things: 'You'll be a Man, my son'.[34]

Meanwhile, over at their offices in Knightsbridge, Tim Bell and Frank Lowe sat down to compose their own campaign. As he sat at his desk, Bell received a phone call from a BBC journalist inquiring about the role of the Brothers during the election. 'You don't want to deal with those people,' he replied. 'They're totally ruthless. They're like a mafia.' After working through lunch eight draft ads were completed. At 3.20 p.m. Bell went to 10 Downing Street for a meeting to discuss the next Tory election broadcast. Conveniently for him Saatchi's creative director, Jeremy Sinclair, was away in Paris and Tebbit was at Central Office, so Bell could walk through the front door rather than sneaking in behind the dustbins.

At 5 p.m., after the meeting broke up, Bell outlined his agency's ideas to Lord Young, who asked him to bring over the mock-ups. 'What will you do with it?' asked Bell.

'I'll tell you what I'll do with it,' Young blurted out. 'If she doesn't like it and if she doesn't take it, I'll resign.'[35]

The pressure was getting to Lord Young. For thirty minutes he paced backwards and forwards at Downing Street, periodically arranging for others to ring Britto about the mysterious poll. He was convinced that the advertising campaign was the turning point of the election. 'I felt we were on the point of losing it and I said so,' he recorded in his diary later that night.[36] At 5.30 p.m. Howell James arrived in a torrential downpour with sixteen boards on which was mounted the rough artwork for Bell's strategy. The adverts were based on a familiar formula: a grand positive statement about the government – 'Income tax is down to its lowest level for twenty years' – followed by a smaller negative statement. The slogan at the bottom of each draft – Life's Better With the Conservatives. Don't Let Labour Ruin It' – was the one Bell had drawn on in 1979 from his favourite political advertising campaign in 1959.

Soon afterwards Mrs Thatcher walked into No. 10 and was met in the corridor by Lord Young. She examined the ads, and said, 'Excellent, this is exactly what we need.' Then she looked questioningly at Young.

'Tim,' he said.

'Well, what do I do now?' she asked.

'Prime Minister, it's very simple,' said Young. 'I have Saatchi's waiting for me with their campaign. I'll bring them over for you to have a look at it. If you like it, we'll do it. If you don't like it, all you have to say to them is "No, I don't like it, David has got something better."'[37]

At 6.30 p.m. John Sharkey and Maurice Saatchi arrived to present their ads to the Prime Minister. As they walked across Downing Street a thunderstorm broke out. The weather seemed appropriate for what was about to happen. As they walked into the lobby they could hear the Prime Minister shouting at the hapless aide who was attempting to brief her for an interview that evening.

Young waited impatiently for Tebbit to arrive. Despite being warned by Lord McAlpine that this was the day Conservative fortunes would appear to wobble, he was still tense.

When Tebbit arrived, Young told him economical with the truth 'Norman, she's asked for some other things to be done.'

The chairman was shown the ads. 'Who did this?' he asked.

'Look at the programme,' said Young.

'No, no. Tell me who did it.'

'Tim Bell.'

'Well, that's it then, that's it,' he said, clearly irritated.

Young lost control and grabbed Tebbit by the shoulders. 'Norman, listen to me,' he shouted. 'We're about to lose this fucking election. You're going to go, I'm going to go, the whole thing is going to go. The entire election depends upon her doing fine performances for the next five days – she has to be happy. Now look at this campaign, look at it.'

'It looks very good,' replied Tebbit.

'We'll look and see what they've got from Saatchi's. If that's better, we'll use that, and if this is better, we'll use this.'

'All right,' said Tebbit, without much enthusiasm.

'It's your future, my future and all our futures, and the future of this flaming country,' Young said.[38]

When Lord Young saw Saatchi's new ads, he was dismissive: 'This is not what she wanted,' and Tebbit agreed. The two returned to Lowe and Bell's mock-ups. They summoned Maurice Saatchi to look at them. At that moment Young received the long-awaited poll result, which showed the Tories maintaining a 10 per cent lead over Labour and went to tell Tebbit and Maurice Saatchi the good news.

Meanwhile, Sharkey was waiting anxiously upstairs. After a few minutes he became restless and walked down to join them. He was greeted by the remarkable sight and sound of Young, Tebbit and Maurice Saatchi all shouting at each other: Young was complaining that Saatchi's had exceeded their brief, Tebbit was angry at Bell's involvement and Saatchi was furious at what he saw as his former colleague's betrayal. Sharkey promptly joined in the shouting match. 'I can't possibly do this,' said Saatchi, pointing to Bell's ads.

Young again lost his composure. 'Now look, Maurice,' he roared. 'How much are you worth? How much are your companies worth? Do you know how much you'll be worth this time next week if we lose the election? You'll be broke, I'll be broke, the whole country will be broke. Now forget your bloody pride. This is the programme she wants and this is the programme you're going to do.'[39]

Maurice looked at Bell's ads. 'This is the work of an amateur,' he said. 'I can't do anything with these ads. They're Tim's, aren't they?'

'Forget about that, just do something similar,' replied Young. 'It's what she wants. It's the positive upbeat message that she wants.' He agreed reluctantly, and returned to his office with Sharkey to amend their ads.

The next day the new version was approved at Central Office. As it happened, according to John Sharkey, the final ads were not substantially different from Saatchi's original drafts. For example, the headline of one had stated: 'Every Labour government since the war has put inflation up' above the body copy of 'Today Britain has the lowest inflation for twenty years'. In the new version the same words were retained but the body copy became the headline and vice versa.[40] The essence of the change was in tone and presentation, from aggressive to positive. Full-page space was then booked in every newspaper except the *Mirror* for the next week at a cost of nearly £2.5 million – the largest-ever political advertising blitz in Britain. At 7 p.m. Channel 4 *News* reported the real results of the Marplan and other polls: the Tories remained way ahead. 'Wobbly Thursday', as it became known, was over.

Experienced political campaigners looked on aghast at the events of that dramatic day. Keith Britto had kept cool while waiting for the curious Marplan poll. 'The trend was very clear throughout the campaign,' Britto reflected. 'We were going to win. We didn't need to spend that kind of money on advertising.'

Other senior Central Office personnel thought that Young and the 'exiles' had panicked. 'Yes, they did wobble,' said a former adviser to Lord Young, who was based at Smith Square during the election, 'but there was no need to wobble. Central Office was like a hysterical girls' school or a ward in an overworked and understaffed hospital. You don't run on the ward every time someone coughs and a patient gets hiccups. What happened was that these supposedly great men panicked and it didn't help that Mrs Thatcher was already highly strung and behaving like a bad-tempered headmistress.'

Bell blamed 'Wobbly Thursday' on the natural high tension of an election. 'Everything's on the line,' he later reflected. 'If you lose it, all the things you've been building over the years and for the next term are gone. It's not where you win half the argument. You are left with nothing.

'I think the tension was caused by three things. One was that private information was received which suggested that things weren't going quite as well as they might be. Whether that information turns out to be wrong is irrelevant. At the time it's another piece of information that worries you. Second, we were getting close to polling day and it gets tense when you're getting near the moment of truth. Third, in terms of presentation Labour had run a very slick and polished campaign. If every time you turn on the TV and see that campaign and then you look at your own and it's not quite under control, it makes you nervous ... The key problem with tension is that it unsettles the leader, and the person who matters most in a campaign is the one leading the troops ... It just means a few people have to gather round her, make a few encouraging noises and do a bit of work, because the Prime Minister always feels she's having to do everything herself.'[41]

Tebbit resented Bell and his accomplices as 'a cacophony of discordant and ill-co-ordinated advice'.[42] He believed they were jostling for position and claiming undeserved credit so that they could reap the political spoils of war afterwards. It was in their interests for the Tory campaign to be perceived as faltering because that created a role for them. Privately, the party chairman likened Bell and the exiles to a coterie of courtiers buzzing round the Queen each vying with the other to say 'I bring bad news from the front.'[43] By sowing the seeds of confusion and despair in her mind, they could then rescue her by charging into battle and single-handedly slaying the dragon.

Perhaps a more objective observer was Nigel Lawson. In his opinion, which he shares with Sir Bernard Ingham, most people have decided how they are going to vote before the start of the campaign. He was unusually well placed to judge the mood of the electorate in 1987 as he spent most of his time in marginal constituencies. 'It was, in fact, abundantly clear – to anyone who had any sense of what was actually happening on the ground – that there had been no change in electoral intentions at all,' he said. 'I always asked the party workers wherever I went what their canvass returns were showing. As for wobbly Thursday, they were totally mystified. There had been no wobble in *their* constituency.'[44]

A week later, when the Conservatives secured an overwhelming victory with a 101-seat majority, Tebbit and Saatchi's felt fully vindicated. 'It had rallied the faithful to an unprecedented degree,' said John Sharkey. 'Never before had a party maintained the same support from the beginning to the end of the campaign proper.'

But Bell disagreed. 'I think the last week's activity changed the atmosphere of the whole thing,' he said in 1995. 'It was a knockout blow and it set everyone up to feel self-confident and it made the Prime Minister feel good. Up until then she had just felt demoralised.'[45]

The hostility between the rival camps was underlined when Bell was not invited to the celebration party at Central Office. Instead, he watched the results on television through the early hours of Friday 12 June 1987. Later that day he went to the Stella Artois tennis tournament at the Queen's club in West Kensington where he was surprised to receive a call from 10 Downing Street. Mrs Thatcher was ringing to thank him for his 'invaluable contribution.'[46] After all, she had been Bell's client, not the Conservative Party.

FEAR AND LOATHING
AT CHARLOTTE STREET

It is no exaggeration to say that the Brothers were apoplectic with rage when they learnt the full extent of Bell's role. It was humiliating that their client, the Tory Party, was being asked by the press in mid-campaign whether Saatchi's were going to be sacked. Charles, in particular, could barely contain his rage that Bell, of all people, had interfered with his agency's carefully crafted creative work. At the height of the panic on 'Wobbly Thursday', he rang Frank Lowe to complain. 'It's total chaos. What the hell is he [Bell] doing?' asked Charles in exasperation.

'I can't do anything about him,' replied Lowe defensively.

'Well, you'll have to do something or he'll lose us the fucking election,' said Charles.

The weekend papers after the campaign compounded their misery. Instead of highlighting another advertising triumph for Saatchi and Saatchi, they were full of claims about other people's contributions and speculation that the agency would be dismissed. 'The future of Saatchi as the Tory Party's agents would now appear to be in the balance,' reported the *Observer*.

The next morning, Monday 15 June 1987, the Brothers were even more unhappy to read a *Daily Mail* story headlined 'Not Saatchi Triumph at All' with a photograph of a smiling Bell and Lowe above the caption: 'Happy to Help'. The piece appeared in Nigel Dempster's influential diary column after a telephone call from Lowe, who complained that his chief executive had not received the credit he deserved. Dempster obliged and portrayed Bell as the saviour of the campaign: 'Privately, Mrs Thatcher is congratulating Tim Bell . . . At a crisis meeting on 4 June he produced the ads which changed the fortunes of the Conservative Party.' The story concluded with Lowe saying: 'We were very happy to be of assistance at a crucial point in the campaign.'

The article enraged Tebbit and the Saatchis. They believed they had thought out and implemented a clear strategy, which had succeeded against many expectations. In the agency's view, Bell had meddled unnecessarily and was now trying to claim the plaudits. That Monday morning Charles Saatchi was attaching obscenities to any mention of Bell's name.

To quote a favourite Maurice saying, it was time to 'hit back and hit hard'. That afternoon Brian Basham, the agency's PR consultant, was summoned to plan a counter-campaign. Despite his allegiance to Labour, Basham had taken on the account because the row was hitting Saatchi's share price. For him it was a commercial situation and he was defending his client. But he was also intrigued to see how the Tory campaign was run from the inside.

When Basham arrived at Charlotte Street, he found agency executives spitting blood over Bell. Some wanted to expose his criminal conviction from 1977 and disclose documentary evidence of his former use of cocaine. But they changed their minds, largely because of strong public and private support from Norman Tebbit.

Following up the *Daily Mail* piece, Channel 4 *News* asked Tebbit for an interview about the 'campaign strategy'. A wily political operator, Tebbit believed their agenda was really Tim Bell. Just before 7 p.m. Basham arrived for a meeting with Charles Saatchi, who told him what was happening. They sat down to watch the interview. There was no mention of Bell, but Tebbit vigorously defended Saatchis, claiming that the election result vindicated the agency. At 7.50 p.m. Charles turned to Basham and said: 'I should get a call from Norman at any moment.' Sure enough, Tebbit rang through and the loudspeaker was turned on. 'How did it go?' asked Saatchi.

'I fixed his motor,' said Tebbit bluntly.

'What do you mean?'

'I got there fifteen minutes early and called the producer over. I said to him, "You've got me here pretending that you want to talk about the campaign when you really want to talk about Tim Bell. I am happy to talk about Bell. But if you ask me, I shall say that the Conservative Party could not possibly employ someone with a criminal record who was a former drug user." They never asked me a word about Bell.' With that he put down the phone.

Saatchi and Basham roared with laughter. But Charles's amusement lasted barely an hour. At 9.30 p.m. BBC's *Panorama* broadcast a film on the election, which claimed that on 'Wobbly Thursday' Mrs Thatcher 'had effectively dispensed with Saatchi and Saatchi and handed her campaign over to advisers from another agency'. The Brothers were incensed.

The next day a statement was released describing the report as part of a 'campaign of disinformation' from rival agencies, and a libel writ was issued against the BBC. Central Office confirmed that Saatchi's was 'at no time fired, nor did the question of firing arise'.[47]

By the following afternoon, Wednesday 17 June, the row had turned into a full-scale feud between the agencies. Accusations were exchanged. Each side was leaking against each other but the pressure was now on Lowe Howard-Spink and Bell. At one point rumours that the chairman and chief executive had fallen out and that the press were to publish stories about Bell's secret past sent their share price crashing by 62p – £12 million off the value of the company. Lowe himself was fed up: 'I regret ever writing those ads now,' he said. 'I never should have got the agency involved.'[48]

Bell made no public comment but privately he accused the Saatchis of hijacking his ads on 'Wobbly Thursday' and presenting them as their own. He was sufficiently angry to consult Peter Carter-Ruck, the libel lawyer, about the possibility of suing Saatchi's for their claim about a 'disinformation campaign'.[49]

Meanwhile, the re-elected Prime Minister was also seething about the public rift. When Sir Gordon Reece telephoned her on the Wednesday she told him: 'It really is unseemly. I've just won an election by a hundred seats, and all anyone can talk about is which advertising agency wrote which ad in the campaign. You know the Saatchis, Tim and Frank Lowe. Can't you stop it?' Sir Gordon did his best but to no avail. Finally, the industrialist Lord Hanson intervened. It is usually said of him that he loved 'Mrs Thatcher, free enterprise and the United States – in no particular order'. As he watched the row escalate, he felt it was damaging the first two of his passions. He also knew that he had the commercial leverage to negotiate a peace settlement: he owned the Imperial Group, the huge cigarette company, which were major clients of Saatchi and Saatchi, while Lowe Howard-Spink and Bell also held several Hanson accounts.[50]

On Thursday 18 June, Hanson and Lowe met to discuss the acrimony, which showed no signs of subsiding. Lowe was keen for conciliation as it was hurting his share price and told Hanson that he could silence Bell. But the Brothers did not want peace talks: they wanted victory, preferably with casualties and the spilling of blood. As Maurice liked to say: 'It's not enough for us to win. The other side must be seen to lose.' But Hanson knew that the Saatchis valued his business. While Lowe was in his office he arranged a conference telephone call to Maurice and Charles. Hanson said he thought the war should end, if only to refocus attention on the Prime Minister's election triumph. The Brothers were reluctant, but did not want to antagonise a major client. They agreed to a truce, but only on condition that Bell's name did not appear on the joint statement. 'They really seemed to hate him,' said Lowe, who was equally exasperated with Bell.[51]

Later that day a press release was issued under the heading 'All Smiles at Lowe and Saatchi'. Both sides, it stated, wanted to 'end the rift, between them: 'Frank Lowe wants to congratulate the Saatchis on their great success with the Tory election campaign and the Saatchis want to thank Frank Lowe for his valuable contribution during the campaign.' Acute observers noticed the omission of Bell's name: 'Both Charles and Frank refused to allow Bell to be mentioned,' said Brian Basham, who wrote the statement.

However, three weeks later, Bell had the last word. On 12 July 1987, the *Sunday Times* published the first of two extracts from the book *Campaign* by Rodney Tyler, who had been hired twice as a consultant by Bell since he had left Saatchi's in February 1986. 'I received one small payment and one larger one', said Tyler, who now works at Lowe Bell Communications. 'The last time I worked for him [Bell] was in January 1987.'[52] The book – christened by Tebbit 'For Whom the Bell Told' – threatened to reopen the wounds of the warring advertising factions: it portrayed Bell and Lord Young as gallant knights saving their queen from the barbarian hordes while her official courtiers lacked a battle plan, leaving her exposed to potential defeat.

This partial portrayal of their advertising campaign was one of several reasons why Saatchi's resigned three months later from the Conservative Party account. Heavy criticism of their work reflected badly on the agency and had produced an element of weariness. When Tebbit left Central Office they lost one of their strongest defenders.

In his letter to Mrs Thatcher on 21 October 1987 Maurice Saatchi stated other factors. He told her that his company was widening its range of activities to include direct satellite broadcasting and financial services, and as both these areas were heavily regulated by the government, there were potential areas of conflict with the Tory Party account. 'We are conscious that this might open the company, public authorities and ministers to misrepresentation,' wrote Maurice, and it was therefore 'with great sadness' that he was ending their formal relationship. In her reply Mrs Thatcher shared his regret and thanked the agency for presenting her policies 'skilfully and effectively', which she would never forget.

It was the end of an era for Saatchi and Saatchi. The Tory Party account had helped make them the biggest agency in the world – always their treasured dream. Tim Bell's relationship with the Brothers had now deteriorated to such an extent that they refused to talk to each other, let alone meet, and it would be another two years before they exchanged a civil word. But Bell's direct line to 10 Downing Street remained intact – indeed prospered – and his commercial career flourished. For the next two years he reaped the financial rewards and became more settled in his personal life, but selling the Prime Minister would become increasingly difficult.

Chapter Eight

Personal Coronation,
Political Abdication

'We don't want any trickery from you PR chaps. We're dealing
with MPs, and they're a rather sophisticated electorate'
Peter Morrison, parliamentary private secretary
to Mrs Thatcher, talking to Tim Bell and
Sir Gordon Reece, during the 1990 campaign
for the Conservative Party leadership

Tim Bell's reputation as chief courtier at Queen Margaret's Palace
was enhanced by the 1987 general election. Despite the vitriolic
war of words with the Brothers, it was perceived that he had played a
decisive role in the latter part of the campaign. His relationship with
the Prime Minister was stronger than ever and, unlike the traumatic
aftermath of 1983, he was content and settled in his personal life.

In the spring of 1987 Bell had bought a large Regency house on
Gerald Road, in the heart of Belgravia and a mere 150 yards from
Michael Howard, now home secretary. 'Enoch Powell is round the
corner,' he said proudly, 'and we back on to Sir Noël Coward's old
house.'[1] Virginia, helped by the interior designer Janet Shand-Kydd,[2]
decorated their new home lavishly in a sumptuous baroque style
dominated by purple, green and Chinese yellow, and furnished it
with marble-topped tables, Aubusson rugs and velvet sofas. The
couple also rented a weekend cottage close to Petworth House,
West Sussex, where they bought several acres of land surrounding
a nineteenth-century farmhouse.

Bell was now a wealthy man, although he later disputed that

description. 'I'm not rich, I'm well off,' he contended. 'Rich people have more money than they can ever spend. Well-off people have enough to live well without borrowing.'³ He had walked away from Saatchi's with a net dividend of £2.5 million, but Bell has never been primarily motivated by the accumulation of cash: 'Coming as I do from the middle classes, I didn't know what to do with it. So I spent it,' he said. 'People like me aren't meant to have capital, we have to earn our living.'⁴

Most of the money went on the Belgravia house, but a substantial amount was spent on an indulgent lifestyle. By the spring of 1988, he was part of the Thatcherite jet-set, earning £335,000 a year. He would be chauffeur-driven to lunch at Harry's Bar or Mark's Club and dine at Cecconi's or the Savoy Grill. He would fly by Concorde with Louis Vuitton bags, wearing the finest French or Italian suits. He joined the Vanderbilt, Harbour, and Bath and Racquets Clubs; which were also useful places to meet clients. In the summer, he and Virginia would rent a house in Tuscany, and spend winters in Australia and Palm Beach. At weekends, the couple drove to Sussex or jetted off to the French Riviera to stay at hotels like the Hôtel du Cap, on the Cap d'Antibes or Bel-Air Cap Ferrat at St Jean Cap Ferrat. 'I like and enjoy that kind of lifestyle,' he later remarked. 'I have worked very hard all my life and have earned a great deal of money. I am sure I have been overpaid time and time again. There's no logic to why I earned very large sums of money at Saatchi's other than I did. I can't produce a justification of why that's right other than I did buy the shares, I took the risk and I made the money and that's how the system works.'⁵

In July 1988, Bell and Virginia were married. Once she had returned to England in early 1984, it was clear to friends that the relationship was permanent. She and Bell became engaged in early 1985: 'We plan to marry in the autumn,' he said, in April of that year.⁶ But he was still married to his first wife, Sue, and so six months later the divorce went through. However, the wedding seemed no nearer and friends assumed that Bell was procrastinating. 'No', remarked Virginia. 'It was just that time went on and I never organised it. I didn't think it was necessary. We lived as though we were married and it never bothered me, because I didn't in any way feel insecure. At times it was *Tim* who would get a bit worried. Then I woke up one morning and said: "Perhaps we'd better get married as we're going away on this holiday." "Right," he shouted, and he was on the telephone before he was dressed.'[7]

On 11 July 1988, after a brief early-morning civil ceremony at Marylebone Register Office, the couple caught a midday flight to Nice. On landing at the Côte d'Azur, they flew by helicopter to Monte Carlo and boarded a friend's yacht at Cap d'Ail. A full religious service took place, on board, where the marriage was blessed by the Queen's chaplain. The best man was Sir Gordon Reece and Virginia's matron-of-honour was Lady English, wife of Sir David.

There followed a glittering reception, with the crew in white uniforms, masses of flowers and the orchestra from Monte Carlo's Hôtel de Paris, which came on board for dinner. Messages of congratulation were read out, including one from Mrs Thatcher. Tim and Virginia honeymooned on the yacht, cruising the Mediterranean with the Englishes. 'David is the perfect editor and a great friend,' said Bell later, 'powerful, definitive, strong and a great tail-twister.'[8]

Bell had always wanted children and, four months later, on 11 November 1988, Virginia gave birth to a daughter. 'The birth took place at the Portland Hospital, where the Duchess of York had her baby,' said Virginia. 'I quite understand why she liked it so much. They did look after me very well.'[9] The baby was named Daisy, the Victorian diminutive of Margaret. When asked if her child was named after Mrs Thatcher, she laughed: 'It wasn't in *my* mind, God knows what was in Tim's mind. I just loved the name and it suits her. I'm sure that the Prime Minister does not think "Daisy" is a very serious name, but I pointed out to her that if Daisy wants to be prime minister she can always change it.'[10]

In April 1991, a son and heir arrived. Named Harry, his godmother is Eve Pollard, former editor of the *Sunday Express*. Bell was soon considering his boy's future: 'I'd like him to become very rich early in life so that he can look after me,' he said, half jokingly. 'But I'm not sure I'd like him to go into advertising.'[11]

It is often the case that men who became fathers relatively late in life are doting and devoted parents and Tim Bell, forty-seven when Daisy was born, is no exception. He telephones home three or four times a day and is often back at the house to tuck his offspring into bed before going out with Virginia or returning to the office. 'When the nanny says she must put Daisy to bed, I can't bear it,' he said. 'I'm a terrible influence.'[12]

Marriage and children have mellowed him. Before, he was in perpetual motion. Now his fascination with power and influence was tempered with a desire for domestic and personal stability. 'I am not bored with being home yet – though who's to say what will happen?' said Virginia, a year after Daisy's birth. 'I must say Tim gets a bit nervous whenever anybody mentions me going back to work.'[13] A sign of his search for contentment was his attendance at Sunday services at St Michael's Church in Chester Square, Belgravia. Daisy was christened there – Sir David Frost and Sir David English feature among her five godparents – and the family were regular participants for a while at the evangelical Church of England services. Bell also had several private conversations with the vicar David Prior, some of a confessional nature. He is renowned for his inspirational preaching and for ministering to the spiritual needs of some of London's most powerful businessmen. Before his marriage Bell had been, by his own account, 'obsessed with having a successful career', now his life was more settled and secure.[14]

Soon after returning from his honeymoon in the South of France, Bell turned his mind to the future shape of his career. His growing interest in developing an integrated communications consultancy was progressing well and by the spring of 1989, Lowe Bell Communications – comprising Good Relations, GR Design, NML Presentations, Lowe Bell Financial and political lobbyists GJW – contributed 9 per cent of pre-tax profits to the Lowe group profits. New accounts included the Burton Group's Sir Ralph Halpern, the Australian brewery businessman Alan Bond, and Gerald Ratner. For a variety of reasons all three came unstuck, but then they were profit-makers for the holding company. In July 1989, the Lowe Bell Financial net caught its biggest fish yet when it was hired by the Hoylake consortium, led by Sir James Goldsmith and Jacob Rothschild, in its takeover bid for the tobacco giant BAT.

As the fees for corporate PR rocketed, Bell realised that at last he could run his own independent operation. At first he was nervous but was strongly encouraged by Piers Pottinger, an enthusiastic fellow director. After nine months of protracted and complex negotiations, he agreed to buy out Lowe Bell Communications from the holding company, Lowe Howard-Spink and Bell plc, which was renamed the Lowe Group. Bell's new outfit included four of the five PR and design firms, GJW remaining under the Lowe corporate umbrella. The deal – signed on 6 September 1989 – was worth £7.6 million. It was financed by a loan of £4 million from the National Westminster Bank plus another £1 million of working capital. The Lowe Group provided a £1.5 million loan on a subordinated basis while also paying a further £1 million for a 24.5 per cent stake in Bell's new holding company, Chime Communications. The other shareholders were Bell (30 per cent), Piers Pottinger (20 per cent), Hambros-Magan, the merchant bank which advised the management team (10 per cent) and, most intriguingly, the Barclay brothers who subscribed £600,000 for a 15 per cent stake through their company Ellerman Investments Ltd.[15]

The Barclay brothers are among Europe's most mysterious and secretive businessmen. Based in Monte Carlo, they had made a fortune in property, shipping and casinos. Now worth an estimated £500 million, their business interests are ultimately controlled by BI Ltd, a Bermuda-registered company. They have also ventured into newspapers and own the *European* and the *Scotsman*. They are obsessively private and have bought their own island, Brecqhou, near Sark in the Channel Islands. 'Privacy is a valuable commodity,' David Barclay once said in a rare interview. 'There is no incentive for us to talk about our business affairs.'[16] They are represented by Bell, who is a personal friend of David Barclay. 'They are marvellous, just the kind of shareholders many companies would like to have,' said Piers Pottinger, the new deputy chairman of Lowe Bell Communications. 'They are courteous, helpful and kind when they need to be.'[17]

Bell's departure from Lowe was cordial: both men realised that their differences were irreconcilable. 'Tim and Frank were difficult to contain in the same unit. They had very different styles,' Tony Good, deputy chairman of Lowe Bell Communications between 1986 and 1989, told me. 'Just as the Brothers helped him in advertising, so Frank consciously or sub-consciously pushed Tim towards PR.' Despite the previous tension, it was a relatively smooth transition. 'Nobody could be more pleased than I that things have worked out so well,' Lowe wrote to his former deputy chairman. 'And nobody could have greater hope for a successful partnership and a continuing friendship.' Bell commented that he would use 'whatever it takes' to make Lowe Bell Communications the best outfit in the business.[18] It was certainly a sweet financial deal, with Lowe retaining a large slice of the new company and Bell remaining a director of Lowe Group plc, plus owning 200,000 share options.

Now based in Hertford Street, Mayfair, Bell set about restructuring his company. His managing director and closest colleague was, and is, Piers Pottinger. Born in 1954 and educated at Winchester, his father, George, had been a senior Scottish Office civil servant, who had been jailed for five years in 1974 over his corrupt relationship with the architect John Poulson. Pottinger is close to Bell, who maintains they have a strong partnership. 'We talk every day, every weekend and discuss everything,' he said. But there is little doubt as to who is the boss. When Amanda Hall of *PR Week* arrived to interview Pottinger for a major feature, originally at Bell's suggestion, he panicked. 'You'll have to talk to Tim. You'll have to talk to Tim,' he blurted out repeatedly, in a way that Hall thought 'reminiscent of the frantic behaviour of the White Rabbit in *Alice in Wonderland*'.[19] Still, Pottinger's presence has coincided with a steady growth in the company, and he appears to complement his chairman in style and substance: he controls the City and financial clients while Bell handles the corporate accounts.

The smartest recruit was Stephen Sherbourne: who later became head of Lowe Bell Consultants and then Lowe Bell Political. As Mrs Thatcher's political secretary at 10 Downing Street from 1983 until 1988, he was ideally placed to handle Westminster and Whitehall. He is highly regarded by his fellow professionals as a political lobbyist. Another notable appointment was Arthur Brittenden, who joined Lowe Bell as a senior consultant in 1988, after seven years as director of corporate relations at News International and on the board of Times Newspapers.

Lowe Bell Communications has certainly been a commercial success: by 1995 total operating fee income had risen to £18.6 million – up from £12.2 million in 1990 – with a turnover of £27,509,000. The company represents 457 clients. Bell's long-treasured dream of an integrated communications network has also been realised: the company is structured for most needs – City (Lowe Bell Financial), public affairs (Lowe Bell Political), corporate (Good Relations and Lowe Bell Consultants), advertising (First Financial) and design (Smithfield). And Bell himself is supremely confident of his approach. When asked by *PR Week* what he knew about public relations, given that he had been in advertising almost all his working life, he replied: 'I don't understand this separation between PR and advertising. To my mind, all communications requires strategy and management. There are several ways of executing that strategy. One is through advertising, another is through PR . . . The account manager of an ad agency does exactly what we do, except that because advertising is what he does for a living, he always recommends an advertising solution to a communications problem. And PR agencies will always recommend a PR solution. We don't. Sometimes we recommend advertising, sometimes PR, sometimes we recommend doing nothing, doing an in-house sales promotion – anything.'[20]

The consensus in the communications industry is that Lowe Bell's strength is the acquisition of new business, using their chairman's network of contacts and presentation skills. A glance at their client list shows how much they have depended on his cultivation of Conservative-supporting industrialists: News International, BSkyB, HarperCollins (Rupert Murdoch); Hanson plc (Lord Hanson); Cable and Wireless (Lord Young); Carlton Communications (Michael Green); British Airways (Lord King); and P & O (Lord Sterling). Another reason for the company's success is that almost every client is left with the strong impression that their business is being handled exclusively by Tim Bell himself.

THE PRIVATISATION OF PR

After the 1989 management buy-out, one of Lowe Bell's first – and certainly most intriguing – new clients was the secretary of state for energy, John Wakeham, who had recently taken over from Cecil Parkinson.

By this time government expenditure on advertising and marketing had increased dramatically from £20 million in 1979 to at least £100 million a decade later. This was largely because ministers, particularly the trade and industry secretary Lord Young, believed that many civil servants were not sympathetic to the radical elements of Thatcherism. Instead of relying on what they saw as the sluggish enthusiasm of officials to promote government policy, they preferred to appeal directly to the public. Hence the use of committed, highly paid private PR consultants and advertising agencies.

No one was more committed than Tim Bell, and when it came to electricity privatisation he was at the front of the queue pitching for business. From the beginning, it was a difficult and controversial sell-off and Cecil Parkinson, the energy secretary, had been unhappy with the early advertising slogans – 'If it fails, we all fail' – which he thought too threatening. He called in Bell, an old friend, as a marketing adviser.[21]

Initially, Lowe Bell Communications was hired to promote the regional electricity distribution companies, while Valin Pollen International represented National Power and PowerGen. However, the privatisation did not progress well and Parkinson was replaced by John Wakeham, who was also close to Bell. One of Wakeham's first moves was to review his department's external PR consultants. He decided that the promotion of electricity privatisation should be handled by one agency and so Lowe Bell, Dewe Rogerson and Valin Pollen were invited to pitch for the contract. Dewe Rogerson, who were privatisation specialists, were hired 'to provide marketing and PR advice to both the Department of Energy and the electricity supply industry'.[22]

Despite losing the £2 million account, Lowe Bell was given a contract 'as a special marketing and PR adviser' to Wakeham. This commission was unusual in that other cabinet ministers, such as Nicholas Ridley, had privatised industries without needing extra image-makers. Details of Bell's retainer were a closely guarded secret. The minister refused to disclose information about it, citing 'commercial confidentiality'.[23] Until I pointed it out to him, Sir Bernard Ingham was not aware of this contract, even though as head of the government's information service, he should have been informed of it. 'I could have better understood the employment of Lowe Bell had Dewe Rogerson not been engaged to represent both the electricity supply industry and the Department of Energy'. Sir Bernard told me. 'Presumably, John Wakeham wished to have his own independent advice. In which case, this raises the question as to why Dewe Rogerson were appointed in a dual role. In my view, that is a very interesting question. But I cannot answer it because I have no idea what the reason might have been.'

Officially, Bell was to advise the energy secretary on 'an overall strategy' for his department and electricity privatisation. The contract was 'totally confidential' and solely with Wakeham. Its contents were

RUNNING THE AGENCY. Outside Saatchi's office in Charlotte Street in May 1982. As chairman and managing director, Bell was at the peak of his powers, but the following year would be traumatic and tempestuous as his relationship with Maurice and Charles rapidly deteriorated

TIM BELL THE TIME IS NIGH!

PROOF THAT ADVERTISING WORKS!

Bell in characteristic pose in his office. A copy of *The Fourth Protocol* by Frederick Forsyth lies on his desk

A POSTER BEYOND THE PALE. This Saatchi and Saatchi advertisement attacking Michael Foot, leader of the Labour Party during the 1983 general election campaign, was never published. Senior Conservative figures vetoed it as too personal and believed it would be counter-productive

AS A PENSIONER HE'D BE BETTER OFF VOTING CONSERVATIVE.

As a pensioner in 1979 Michael Foot would have received £31.20 a week.

Now, under the Conservatives, he would receive £52.55 a week.

An increase of 68 per cent, way above any rise in prices over that period.

Under the Conservatives he would have received a Christmas bonus every

year. A pleasant change after the cold Labour winters of '75 and '76.

As a pensioner he's better off voting Conservative.

Let's hope this time he puts his cross in the Conservative box.

It won't make him Prime Minister. But that's just as well for everybody.

Tim finally married his
Australian girlfriend, Virginia
Hornbrook, in 1988. After a
registry wedding in
Marylebone, the couple flew
to Monaco where they
boarded a yacht to celebrate
with a handful of close
friends. From left to right: Sir
David English, editor of the
Daily Mail, Sir Gordon Reece,
Virginia, Tim, Lady English

Sir David English looks on
approvingly during the
ceremony aboard a yacht
owned by the Barclay
Brothers, the property tycoons
who later became a
shareholder in Lowe Bell
Communications (David
Barclay is behind Bell to
the left)

LOOKING AFTER MARK. Just before Mark Thatcher's stag party at the Stafford Hotel in 1987. Bell advised the Prime Minister's son on public relations 'as a friend' not as a client

A FRAGILE PARTNERSHIP. All smiles but Bell's four years working with Frank Lowe, the talented but temperamental advertising executive, was marred by constant rows and tension

STARS OF THE '80s. Greeting the film star Joan Collins whom he greatly admires. In 1989 Bell paid tribute to her on TV, comparing her to Mrs Thatcher and describing her performance as Alexis in *Dynasty* as 'Cleopatra in a contemporary setting'

MELLORGATE. This photo-opportunity only prolonged the agony for Cabinet Minister David Mellor who consulted Bell over press revelations about his affair with the actress Antonia De Sancha

BA'S SPIN SURGEON. With Lord King at a special dinner for the former chairman of British Airways at the Savoy Hotel on 6 September 1994. The previous year Bell was hired by BA to manage the crisis after revelations of 'dirty tricks' by the airline against their rival Virgin

REUNITED. At the first anniversary party of M and C Saatchi in June 1996, Bell poses happily with Maurice. It was a remarkable reunion. In the late 1980s, Bell fell out so badly with the Saatchi brothers that they refused to speak to each other

kept even from officials and special advisors. Every morning at 8.30 a.m. from Monday to Thursday, Bell had a private meeting over breakfast with Wakeham in his ministerial office at Thames House, Palace Street. Civil servants, aides and secretaries were not allowed to attend these tête-à-têtes, which lasted 30–45 minutes. The only other participant was Sir Gordon Reece, who often accompanied Bell, offering pearls of PR wisdom in between puffs of his Havana cigars. But he was not under a retainer.

One tangible aspect of the deal was Bell's membership of the panel that selected the advertising agency to promote electricity privatisation. In late April 1990, he arrived at the Saatchi and Saatchi offices to hear their pitch for the account. It was the first time he had set foot there since he had left five years previously. Paul Cowan, a Saatchi account executive, recalls seeing Bell leaning over the desk talking intently to the delighted receptionist. 'It was like a flashback and, to mix metaphors, as though the cobwebs had been blown away,' he said.

The £20 million contract went to Wight Rutherford Collins and Scott (WRCS), whose chairman, Robin Wight, was an informal adviser on advertising to the Conservative Party.[24]

In parliament, Wakeham would not answer specific questions about Bell's consultancy, except to say: 'To gain proper value for the assets, advice is needed on their value and how to market them. The Labour government used advisers for similar reasons when they were in power.'[25]

Lowe Bell continued to benefit from the electricity flotation, which generated total fees of £150 million for private advisers – stockbrokers, bankers, PR consultants, property valuers, advertising agencies and accountants. After the privatisation they were hired by East Midlands Electricity, National Power and PowerGen. And the Department of Energy. It was a prosperous start for the new agency and an indication of the benefits to business of political connections at the highest level. Tim Bell had come a long way from what he had once called 'silly little suburbia' and was now as captain of his own corporate ship, in control of his own destiny.[26] He no longer needed a Charles Saatchi or a Frank Lowe to please and serve, and could indulge himself with the people he liked most, clients who often doubled as friends. 'I love people with influence,' he later said, 'and I spend a lot of time talking to a lot of very influential, powerful and famous people. I can't think of anything better. It's like being a glorified gossip columnist who sits here all day gossiping about the news.'[27]

However, as Bell set out to conquer the communications world and enter a bright new commercial era, his most famous client – the Conservative Party plc and its chief executive Margaret Thatcher – were about to enter a dark and dangerous period.

THE YEAR OF LIVING DANGEROUSLY

Nineteen eighty-nine should have been a year of celebration for the Conservative government. It was the tenth anniversary of their period in office and the opposition showed no real signs of overturning a 101-seat majority at the next election. But there were ominous signs. Mrs Thatcher was viewed as increasingly authoritarian and remote, over-concentrating political power at No.10. Despite Bell's earlier advice, she was developing regal tendencies, notably when she announced: 'We have become a grandmother.' On policy, Europe was causing dissent and division among MPs and ministers, and in the country the poll tax was almost universally unpopular.

In the early months of 1989 it had been the activities of Tory-controlled Westminster City Council that caused most concern at Central Office. They were facing an avalanche of criticism over their sale of cemeteries for 15 pence to property speculators, who then sold the land for millions. Lady Porter, the wealthy council leader, who was anxious about the political and public-relations fall-out of the issue, invited outside consultants for discreet discussions. 'One could hardly say that Tim Bell was a regular adviser on a private basis to any of the members,' said William Phillips, former managing director of the council, 'but he came along, as a good consultant would, in the hope of getting some business out of giving his thoughts.'[28]

In early February, Lady Porter was sufficiently concerned to hire Lowe Bell Communications at her own expense. 'I am there to protect her backside,' acknowledged Alan Kilkenny, a senior Lowe Bell director. 'There's a need to promote her achievements, such as the council's environment, anti-litter and dog-fouling campaigns.

But everything has been clouded by the cemeteries issue.' Lady Porter refused to disclose the fee. 'Look,' she said curtly. 'I am sharpening up. A lot of my friends and supporters have said it is a disgrace what is going on.'[29] Lowe Bell took on the account although their parent company, Good Relations, was run by Paul Dimoldenberg and Peter Bradley, who were leaders of Westminster Council's opposition Labour group.

One of their first tasks was to produce, design and print a report called *The Westminster Initiative*. This was a propaganda document, which formed part of a campaign known as the 'Westminster Project'. Lowe Bell was paid by an organisation called Friends of the City of Westminster whose 'office' was at Sharles and Co., an accountancy firm based in Mayfair. The group had been set up to fund the Westminster Project, which had been launched at a House of Commons cocktail party attended by Mrs Thatcher, Tory MPs and sympathetic businessmen. They were told that unless funds were raised the Conservatives could lose control of the council.

Lowe Bell were retained by Lady Porter and commissioned for a more specific project designed to preserve the Tory group in power: to lobby the government to reduce their community charge, or poll tax as it was popularly known. The account, run by the Prime Minister's former political secretary Stephen Sherbourne, was worth a basic fee of £30,000, paid 'from private sources'.

On Friday 27 May 1989, Sherbourne met Barry Legg, then a Westminster city councillor and later Conservative MP for Milton Keynes, to discuss the assignment. Legg wanted a poll-tax reduction of £100. In a letter after the meeting, Sherbourne said that this would mean a reduction from £413 down to £238, after the safety net was eliminated. They also discussed what constituted 'success' in terms of a success-fee in the contract. Sherbourne suggested that this should be calculated on the basis of a 'sliding scale'. He concluded: 'While you are right to want to achieve a reduction [of the poll tax] of this kind, it is fairly ambitious. I therefore propose that a success-fee, on top of the basic £30,000 fee, should take the form of a sliding scale and that it should be £30,000, in the event of achieving £238.'[30]

Lowe Bell's request for a 100 per cent increase of their fee was not well received by Lady Porter and the contract was switched to GJW, the political lobbyists who helped reduce the council's poll tax to £195.

*   *   *

While Lowe Bell was trying to help Mrs Thatcher's favourite council with its chief political burden, the Prime Minister had her own pressing problems. Her ratings in the opinion polls as a leader had slumped and there was strong criticism in the press of her performance. Her increasingly Presidential style was isolating her from the aspirations of ordinary voters which, until then, she had never allowed to happen.

In these circumstances her tenth anniversary party as Prime Minister was a relatively muted occasion. She invited ten of her closest confidants, who had been with her since May 1979. An indication of her growing detachment was that at first she did not notice the absence of Sir Gordon Reece, one of her dearest friends. 'Where's Gordon?' she suddenly asked Tim Bell.

'He's in the London Clinic', he replied. 'He's just had an operation.'

Mrs Thatcher asked him to get Sir Gordon on the phone, so Bell called the hospital. After being put through, Reece answered with a weak, croaky 'Hellooo.'

'Gordon, how are you feeling?'

'I'm feeling dreadful.'

'I've got Margaret for you on the line,' said Bell.

'Oh, right, fine, good, put her on,' Reece replied, suddenly sprightly, his voice improving by the second.[31]

Despite the effect Mrs Thatcher still had on people, Bell believed she should have considered resigning after ten years in office. After all, she had earlier promised to do so and, in his view, she was 'on the crest of a wave' and at the top of her career. She could have abdicated in a blaze of glory. 'I certainly thought it was worthy of consideration,' he said later.[32] Although this was said in hindsight, it seems that the idea had been discussed.

Soon after Sir Gordon Reece left hospital, he and Bell went to Chequers for dinner with the Prime Minister and her husband. During the meal Denis broached the subject of his wife's retirement. 'I thought that we'd been there too long,' Denis explained later. 'The thought of another election really appalled me – and the possibility of losing, too.' Mrs Thatcher was somewhat annoyed. According to former Tory party chairman Kenneth Baker, she had no intention of stepping down. She enjoyed the power and influence of being

Prime Minister too much, and was fearful that Michael Heseltine would succeed her.[33]

After dinner, Mrs Thatcher went upstairs to work on her red boxes. Bell, Sir Gordon and Denis then had a 'very relaxed evening' – a euphemism for the consumption of a large amount of alcohol. Denis came back to the point of contention. 'You know, I really think she should go,' he told them. 'She should go now while she's ahead and, Gordon, I think you're the man to tell her. She'll never listen to me and she'll never listen to Tim, he's too young. But she'll listen to you. She trusts you and you've been close to her for ever.'

'But, Denis, I can't do that', replied Sir Gordon.

'Why not?' asked Denis.

'Well, because I love her.'

'Steady on, man, she's my wife, you know,' said Denis, rather taken aback.[34]

The first test of Mrs Thatcher's decision to remain in 10 Downing Street came with the European Parliament elections on 15 June 1989. As Saatchi's had resigned the Tory account and Norman Tebbit was no longer party chairman, there were no obstacles to Bell's involvement and he was allowed a free hand in the party's advertising strategy. In any case, he had vetted and more or less appointed the Tories' new director of communications, Brendan Bruce, who had been recommended by Lord Young and interviewed personally by the Prime Minister. Bruce, a 37-year-old advertising executive at D'Arcy Masius Benton and Bowles, was – in sharp contrast to Bell – a non-smoking, teetotal bachelor, almost unknown in Conservative Party circles. Also, the advertising agency chosen for the European campaign, Allen Brady and Marsh, was a wholly-owned subsidiary of Lowe Howard-Spink, which made Bell the account handler. It was just like the old days again.

The Tory campaign was hampered from the beginning by two major factors: division and apathy. The government and the party were largely Euro-sceptic while Conservative MEPs, of course, were avid EC supporters, most Tory activists were hostile to Brussels and Strasbourg. They were not convinced that the European Parliament should even exist and were not inclined, therefore, to go to the ballot box. It was a recipe for confusion and chaos.

Bell and Bruce were well aware of the split and a brief was drawn up for Allen Brady and Marsh to produce advertisements which would galvanise Conservative supporters by warning them of the dangers of Labour winning the election by default. The result was a poster bearing the slogan 'Don't Let Labour In Through the Back Door', which was also incorporated into Mrs Thatcher's speeches. It was attacked for implying that the opposition had a chance of winning and Labour mocked it, declaring that they were happy to enter through the front door.

Another anti-apathy advertisement – 'Stay At Home on June 15th and You'll Live on a Diet of Brussels' – attracted even more severe criticism. Cabinet ministers like chancellor Nigel Lawson privately thought it 'crude', 'bad politics' and 'ubiquitous'. 'One of the great strengths of the Thatcher government,' he later wrote, 'had been you knew where it stood. This clarity had considerable appeal. But over Europe, the public was totally confused.'[35] Other Conservative commentators argued that although the poster may have earned plaudits from other advertising executives, it had little impact on the voters. 'They tried to be too clever,' said Harvey Thomas, former director of presentations and campaigns at Tory Central Office. 'The essence of good campaigning is to present the party well, as it really is, not to put on a performance and try to impress the electorate by putting on a show. We tried to win the argument not the people.'

The 'Diet of Brussels' poster was personally approved by the Prime Minister, but lambasted by Sir Leon Brittan, President of the European Commission, and former trade and industry secretary. He described it as 'quite extraordinarily negative, damaging and confusing' and said it gave a 'very bad impression'.[36] Brendan Bruce was frustrated by the 'negative' charge, as he had commissioned positive advertisements as part of a 'balanced' communications strategy, which were never used. Allen Brady and Marsh had drawn up a series of 'pro-Europe' posters, notably one that stated: 'Britain our Home. Europe our Future'. These were presented by Bell at 10 Downing Street but vetoed by Mrs Thatcher.[37]

Far from encouraging people to vote, the £400,000 advertising campaign failed to enthuse them. 'In my view, a good poster is one which makes its meaning absolutely clear as you go past it at forty miles per hour in car,' said Norman Tebbit. 'Diet of Brussels' is quite funny as a platform joke but not as a poster. It was an injunction to Tory voters to stay at home.'[38]

Already handicapped by a divided party, the incoherent advertising messages contributed to a disastrous election result. The Conservatives lost 13 of their 45 seats in the European Parliament and their share of the vote slumped to 34 per cent. The inquest was brutal. Adjectives were thrown like poisoned arrows – 'chaotic' and 'monumental folly' were some of the more polite ones – and Bell was at the centre of the controversy. Tebbit, who lamented the loss of Saatchi's, described the poster campaign as 'the worst election advertising in living memory'.[39] Bell defended it: 'I think the campaign was accurate to the strategy,' he said, while Central Office played down his role, describing him as a 'consultant'.[40] As for Mrs Thatcher, when asked if she accepted any responsibility for the disaster, she replied: 'No, no, no. Not at all.'[41]

Despite the Prime Minister's public complacency, she realised privately that support for her government was wilting. In these circumstances, according to Nigel Lawson, her tendency was to blame deficient presentation rather than accept that her policies could be flawed and the aftermath of the European election débâcle was no exception. Four weeks later, on 26 July 1989, she appointed Kenneth Baker as the new Tory chairman. Like Lord Young, he was an ardent believer in political advertising and enjoyed the propaganda war. He admired Bell and asked him to play an even more active role in the party's communications approach.

Working closely together, Bell, Brendan Bruce and Baker decided not to retain an advertising agency full-time. Instead, an informal, *ad hoc* committee of sympathetic advertising executives, copywriters, art directors and media buyers was established, co-ordinated by Bruce and Bell, who had the power to commission and brief such experts for specific tasks. The idea was similar to Labour's Shadow Communications Agency of volunteers, except that the Tory consultants would be paid. A closer model was the 'Tuesday Team' of outside media advisers who helped elect Ronald Reagan US President in 1980.

This new structure gave Bell more influence in the party than ever before. He was entering his most authoritative period as the government's media fixer and strategist and had a power base in both Downing Street and Central Office. Mrs Thatcher remained intensely loyal to him, and Bruce, while being a capable advertising man, was a political novice and depended on Bell for guidance. 'He was consulted on everything,' recalled a former Tory adviser.

One of his first consultations was over the growing rift between Nigel Lawson and Mrs Thatcher. This was ostensibly about Sir Alan Walters, her economic adviser, who persistently and publicly argued that the government should not join the exchange rate mechanism, despite Lawson's committed and stated policy to do so under the right conditions. The Prime Minister continued to back Sir Alan throughout the late summer of 1989, and the schism deepened between her and her chancellor.

From Tim Bell's standpoint, however, their falling-out was as much about a power struggle and style of government as it was about macro-economic policy. Mrs Thatcher's relationship with Lawson had been excellent, until just after the tax-cutting budget of 1988. At that point, in her eyes, he was a great chancellor and she often described him as 'unassailable'. 'In my view,' Bell said, 'all of this went to his head and he started to try and control the economy without reference to the First Lord of the Treasury, the Prime Minister, which I thought was unfortunate.' Bell claimed later to have had first-hand knowledge of decisions taken in No. 11 Downing Street that were never referred to No. 10. 'She got very cross about it,' he said. 'Her instinct was to battle with Lawson and some of the rows were legendary and you could hear them, apparently, between the walls of No. 10 and No. 11.'[42]

Bell, of course, took Mrs Thatcher's side and so did her supporters in Fleet Street. On 10 October 1989, the first day of that year's Tory Party conference in Blackpool, the *Daily Mail* devoted the whole of its front page to an astonishing attack on Lawson. Under the banner headline 'This Bankrupt Chancellor', and accompanied by a large, unflattering cartoon, the article accused Lawson of being 'a fanatical exponent of slow death' and 'betraying himself, his party, his Prime Minister and the British people'. There was no byline except 'Comment', which implies that it was sanctioned and almost certainly written by the editor Sir David English, an unquestioning admirer of Mrs Thatcher. That morning the Prime Minister telephoned Lawson to tell him that she had been 'horrified' by the article, but the damage was done. The chancellor was under siege by the media throughout the conference with journalists yelling at him: 'When are you going to resign, Mr Lawson?'[43]

The pressure intensified with Sir Alan Walters' continued criticism of the chancellor's and the government's policy on the exchange rate mechanism while remaining an adviser at No. 10. Two weeks after the *Daily Mail* onslaught, Lawson's patience ran out. In his view, the Prime Minister had pledged allegiance to her part-time, America-based economic adviser over her chancellor. After she refused to sack Sir Alan and was only moderately supportive of Lawson in the Commons, he resigned.

The chancellor's shock departure produced turmoil in the party. A hasty reshuffle ensued and John Major took over at the Treasury. Stunned Tory backbenchers muttered that all this was damaging to the Prime Minister's position and served only to fuel criticism of her 'autocratic' style of government. At the heart of the mayhem was Tim Bell, sitting in his Mayfair office, chain-smoking Piccadilly cigarettes and fielding telephone calls from ministers and Central Office asking for advice. He was calling the shots. 'Yes, I think Kenneth [Baker, then party chairman] should go to the south-east,' he told Brendan Bruce, 'but make sure he's ready to come back at a moment's notice.' After discussing other ministers, he said, 'And get John Major to talk to the *Financial Times*. They went completely over the top this morning.' (The paper's editorial had backed Lawson, arguing, accurately as it turned out, that 'the behaviour of the Prime Minister which drove him from office may be the beginning of the end for her too'). Typically, Bell was keen on spinning a positive agenda: 'I think the word today is confidence,' he said, before taking another puff of his cigarette.

When Kenneth Baker telephoned, Bell was in an evangelical Thatcherite mood. 'You can't threaten the Prime Minister and get away with it,' he reflected, as lunch-time approached. 'His [Lawson's] resignation is tantamount to high treason.'

Bell had not appeared surprised at Lawson's resignation. He told a colleague that morning that Lawson and Geoffrey Howe – then foreign secretary – had threatened to resign the previous year over the ERM just before the Madrid Summit. As this was publicly disclosed only much later by the former chancellor, Bell clearly had inside information.

As 1990 dawned Mrs Thatcher faced other acts of rebellion by once-loyal subjects and courtiers. In the country the poll tax continued to cause resentment, while in the party Europe remained a source of division and friction. Kenneth Baker realised it was no longer feasible 'to go on reacting tactically to the various crises, putting out the blaze here or there like some political fire brigade.'[44] And so in January 1990, he held a seminar at Hever Castle in Kent to formulate an election-winning strategy. He brought with him the full Central Office campaign team, as well as Brian Griffiths, head of the Downing Street Policy Unit, and David Willetts, director of the Centre for Policy Studies. It was a measure of his continuing influence that Bell also attended, along with his colleague Stephen Sherbourne.

The other significant figure present was Dick Wirthlin, the American pollster who had been a key adviser to President Reagan and was now a consultant to Central Office. His method of polling – with which Bell was in sympathy for it had been on this basis that he had planned the strategy of the 1979 election campaign – was to identify key emotions and values rather than issues to determine how people vote. Wirthlin argued that the British people were motivated by 'hope' and looking for 'a sense of security'. Private polling research had shown, though, that these aspirations were being undermined by the poll tax and high mortgage rates.

Bell's presentation demonstrated how this disillusionment was reflected in the media. He pointed out that editors and journalists were also middle-class voters and, consequently, their coverage was increasingly critical. This was intensified by competition for sales among newspapers, which meant they were more likely to 'seek out crisis and controversy'. However, most editors believed the Tories would still win the next election.[45]

A sure sign that this was unlikely to happen under Mrs Thatcher's leadership occurred two months later, on 22 March 1990, when the Conservatives lost a by-election in Mid-Staffordshire, despite having had a majority of over 19,000. It was a catastrophe for the party and almost solely due to the poll tax. 'I was deeply worried,' recalled Mrs Thatcher. 'The political atmosphere was becoming grim. All my instincts told me that we could not continue as we were.'[46] But when Baker, Bell and Sir Gordon Reece had dinner with her at Chequers two days later, she would not accept that the policy needed a complete face-lift.

That weekend marked the only occasion when Bell ventured into the policy area. Together with Stephen Sherbourne and Sir Gordon Reece, he compiled a paper on the poll tax and argued that it could destroy Mrs Thatcher. He pulled no punches about the extent of its unpopularity: 'People are getting bills for £1500 and they've never had a bill that big in the whole of their lives and they blame it on you, Prime Minister,' said Bell.

'Well, they can pay it off in easy payments,' snapped Mrs Thatcher, naïvely.

He argued that she was in grave danger of losing her natural supporters. 'You're a dragon-slayer and all of a sudden you've invented a dragon,' he told her. 'A dragon with intense fire and huge teeth, and you appear to be the dragon's promoter instead of its slayer.' Bell concluded that she would need to spend about £3 billion to make the poll tax acceptable to the nation and another £1.5 million to promote the policy.[47]

The Prime Minister agreed to a fundamental review. But, according to her party chairman, she was 'unwilling to concede' that such vast sums would need to be spent to convince the country.[48] Instead, she blamed 'irresponsible local authorities' whose 'over-spending' was driving up the level of the poll tax,[49] a tactic that was used two months later in the local election campaigns. The high-risk strategy was to defend the community charge in principle and blame the figures on 'extravagant' Labour authorities.

Funds were obtained for an advertising campaign, and Bell and Brendan Bruce worked together on a communications plan under the theme of 'Conservative Councils Cost You Less'. They agreed on three main points: first, that the principle of the poll tax might be accepted, because everyone should contribute financially towards local government; second, that the real problem was the amount people were being asked to pay; third, that if they could persuade people that the tax was high only under Labour councils, then they could use one of their favourite themes – 'Labour Costs You More'.

It was time for some spin-doctoring. Bruce persuaded the media that if the Tories held on to Westminster and Wandsworth – where the community charge was low – that would be considered a 'victory', irrespective of Labour gains elsewhere. Then the advertising campaign hammered away at opposition-controlled councils.

But, the attempt to sell the poll tax was not bought by the voters: Labour won the election nationally. And although Bruce convinced the media that the Tories had won because they had retained control of Westminster and Wandsworth, he later admitted that they had lost. This bizarre interpretation was peddled on the day after the results had come in with a photograph of Kenneth Baker's beaming face beneath the *Sun*'s front-page headline: 'Kinnock Poll Axed'. 'The final act of the spin patrol,' recalled Bruce, 'was to book a table for myself, Kenneth Baker and Central Office staff for lunch on the terrace of the Commons where the political correspondents congregate in summer. We celebrated our victory in grand style and, by the end of the lunch, most of the reporters from the Sunday papers had wandered over for a chat.'[50]

The whole operation was, of course, a mirage and a deception. But these were desperate days for the Conservatives. Mrs Thatcher stubbornly refused to reform the poll tax, let alone abolish it. Hence, the government remained unpopular and their policies in other spheres – crime, education and health – did not help matters.

Once again the Party decided that the way in which the message was being transmitted – rather than the message itself – was the problem. In the spring of 1990, Kenneth Baker hosted an informal dinner at Mark's Club in Mayfair, attended by four senior advertising and PR executives – Tim Bell, John Banks from Young and Rubicam, Robin Wight from WRCS and Sir Gordon Reece – to analyse the government's travails. Presentation not policy needed attention, they decided, believing that many of the government's policies were so radical that they were vulnerable to misinterpretation.

The performance of cabinet ministers was studied and it was agreed that three in particular were not projecting their policies well: David Waddington, the home secretary, was deemed too hard-line and had not handled the Strangeways prison riot adeptly; John MacGregor, at Education, was embroiled in controversy over his reform of the national curriculum; and Kenneth Clarke, the health secretary, had looked and sounded like a bar-room bully during the ambulance dispute despite his compassionate credentials.[51]

The solution, suggested Sir Gordon Reece, was to allocate a 'special communications adviser' to each beleaguered minister in order to sharpen up his act. Baker agreed immediately and, by the end of the week, had assigned Tim Bell to David Waddington, John Banks to Kenneth Clarke and Robin Wight to John MacGregor. The idea was for these consultants, or 'minders' as they became known, to provide informal analysis of PR and advertising campaigns from a party political standpoint. Their terms of reference were to identify the minister's audience and how, where and when policy should be communicated. The assignment would be reviewed after three months. They would be unpaid, apart from out-of-pocket expenses.[52]

The choice of Kenneth Clarke for this sort of treatment was more than a little bizarre. For the unpretentious health secretary to accept advice from an image consultant was, as his biographer Malcolm Balen stated, 'as likely as Dracula renouncing his nocturnal habits and offering to become an NHS blood donor'.[53] Clarke was cheerfully impervious to the entreaties of the advertising world and it did not take Banks long to realise that he had accepted Mission Impossible. 'Pointless,' recalled the advertising executive. 'You can say, "Look, you shouldn't wear suede with grey, and really the beer belly isn't on, and you'll have to put the cigars out because it's the NHS." His view would be, "I'm sorry, take me for what I am."'[54] However, it was not a completely lost cause. Clarke was interested in commissioning research into the NHS: 'He wanted to know what people actually thought of the NHS and the reforms he was proposing,' recalled Banks, whose agency conducted polls and gave the material to Clarke.

Bell and Wight had already done some preliminary work on their ministers when on 29 April 1990 their new role was disclosed in the *Independent on Sunday*. Senior departmental press officers were furious and telephoned Bernard Ingham, head of the Government Information Service (GIS), to express their concern. He, too, was angry, because the appointments had been made without consulting the directors of information in the three relevant ministries.

The next morning Ingham telephoned Kenneth Baker at Central Office and told him his scheme 'was seen as a grave reflection on the competence of the GIS – indeed as an insult to it'. He added that it would be 'damaging to its morale' unless there was proper consultation and clarification. 'It is absolutely essential,' he said, 'that ministers and Bell, Banks and Wight handled the GIS with kid gloves, given the circumstances of their appointment.' Baker regretted the publicity, as no official appointment had been made, and added, rather naïvely, that he was sorry that the GIS felt the idea reflected poorly on them. 'That had not been the intention,' he said. He agreed to make clear that the three PR minders were party appointments and not a comment on the press officers in the education, home and health departments.[55]

That afternoon Ingham wrote a memorandum detailing his conversation with the Tory chairman and sent it to all heads of information in Whitehall. Within days the document was leaked and its full contents appeared on the front page of the following week's *Mail on Sunday*. The minders idea was promptly aborted.

As he looks back on the episode, Bernard Ingham's anger has not subsided. 'The whole thing was stupid nonsense,' he told me. 'It would not have helped ministers in any way. If I achieved anything during my eleven years in 10 Downing Street, it was to stop the rise of the spin-doctors. Bell was like an embryonic Mandelson. It's important to keep them in place and I had to kill off that gimmick. In any case Ken Clarke didn't need that kind of advice and it was insulting to the ministers. You couldn't have outsiders running around Whitehall after them. The idea was absurd so I smothered it before it was born.'

ABDICATION OR PALACE COUP?

The cabinet minister who really needed unexpurgated and brutally realistic advice in the summer of 1990 was the one sitting in 10 Downing Street. 'Her great strength was that she knew exactly what ordinary folk were thinking and feeling, and what mattered to them', said Bell. 'But at the end she did not have the faintest idea.'[56] She had become the Prisoner of Downing Street.

There is some dispute about why this occurred. Some say that eleven years as Prime Minister had instilled in her excessive self-confidence, almost a sense of indestructibility. She had confronted political crises before and believed she could overcome them again. She also seemed detached from Westminster, touring the globe as a grand international stateswoman dealing with epic events like the Gulf War and the end of the Cold War. By comparison local government finance paled in significance.

Others, like Bell, argue that her immediate advisers in 10 Downing

Street were either not telling her what was going on or did not know themselves. 'I think she was being kept away from what was happening,' said Bell. 'Close friends found it more difficult to get in to see her. She was guarded much more and the security had become tighter. It was difficult to get through to her, compared to earlier years. She was busy all the time, never had a minute to see anybody . . . Terrible things went on. Our [telephone] calls were monitored and then a civil servant would go in to see her and say: "He's wrong. That isn't what happened." The purpose of monitoring [at No.10] is that if you say you'll do something, they write it down in their book. It's not about saying what he said was wrong. They lied to her, they would all create this illusion.'[57]

Whatever the explanation, her understanding of political realities was fast deteriorating. On Saturday 14 October 1990, Mrs Thatcher celebrated her sixty-fifth birthday with a dinner party at Chequers attended by her closest friends: Jeffrey and Mary Archer, John and Alison Wakeham, Tim and Virginia Bell, Gordon Reece and Kenneth Baker. She was tired and almost dropped off to sleep during the dinner. Baker gave her a print of Lord Salisbury rolling up his sleeves, saying: 'What a good team we've got, there's a lot of work to do.' He then delivered a typically optimistic speech, pledging undying support and loyalty to the bitter end.[58]

The party was subdued as many guests were thinking about one man: Michael Heseltine. Bell viewed him, ironically given his own personality, as a highly emotional man who for many years had campaigned covertly against Mrs Thatcher. It was no secret that Heseltine was preparing to challenge for the leadership and just needed the right moment.

Political events were moving in his direction. Four days after the Chequers dinner, the Tories saw a 16,900 majority overturned into a Liberal victory at the Eastbourne by-election. It was another calamitous result but still Heseltine waited.

His opportunity came on 13 November 1990. Geoffrey Howe, the once ultra-loyal Leader of the Commons and deputy Prime Minister, delivered a devastating resignation speech, which Mrs Thatcher later described bitterly as 'a final act of bile and treachery'.[59] Howe concluded dramatically: 'I have done what I believe to be right for my party and my country. The time has come for others to consider their response to the tragic conflict of loyalty with which I have myself wrestled for perhaps too long.' During the speech Kenneth Baker sat next to Mrs Thatcher. 'I never thought he would do that,' she remarked to Baker as they rose to leave.[60] That was a measure of her lack of political sensitivity. But it was the signal Heseltine needed and the next day he declared his candidature. The race was on.

Bell had not been as surprised as others by Howe's remarkable attack, which he heard on his car radio. He knew the former chancellor and foreign secretary reasonably well and was aware that the Prime Minister had treated him carelessly over the years. In Howe there had been a slow-burning fuse of resentment, which had now exploded.

Although he was no parliamentarian, Bell also knew that the contest between Mrs Thatcher and Heseltine would be closer than her supporters were predicting. It did not take a genius to grasp that many backbenchers were disillusioned and would vote for the candidate who could best preserve marginal seats. Bell and Gordon Reece set about their opponent. On Thursday 15 November, Bell telephoned Peter Morrison, Mrs Thatcher's parliamentary private secretary. 'Could I have a word with the PM?' he asked.

'She's rather busy just at the moment, Tim,' replied Morrison. 'But I'm running the campaign this end. Can I help?'

'Well, something rather exciting's come up. I can't reveal my sources, as they say, but I've got hold of a copy of Heseltine's draft manifesto. I can bring it straight round.'

'Oh, I think we know more or less the approach he's going to take.'

'Yeah, but I'm talking specifics – the Gulf, Europe, Cabinet, the poll tax.'

'The thing is we're pretty well up to our eyes here as it is.'

'Look, Peter, I'm here with Gordon [Reece] in his office. We're both keen to help.'

'I honestly don't think you should put yourselves out, Tim. This isn't quite your line of country, you know. It's not a media battle. We don't want any trickery from you PR chaps. We're dealing with MPs, and they're a rather sophisticated sort of electorate.'[61]

Morrison ended the conversation and Bell put down the phone in disbelief. The Prime Minister's PPS epitomised the complacent, almost comatose attitude that was endangering her position.

Two days later Bell and Reece drove to Chequers for a weekend summit. When they arrived Mrs Thatcher was giving an interview to Simon Jenkins, then editor of *The Times*. As they walked in the garden with Morrison, Bell was seething. 'What the hell is going on, Peter?' he said. 'I'm supposed to be her media adviser, and I have to find out by accident she's giving interviews. This was supposed to be a low-key campaign. No TV, no exclusives. I thought we agreed on that.'

'It's only *The Times* and *Telegraph*,' said Morrison, trying to soothe him. 'They're on our side.'

'God Almighty, she could be saying anything in there,' said Reece.

As they continued their stroll, Bell became increasingly anxious. 'I have to tell you, we're not happy with the way things are going, Peter,' he said. 'We're acting as if the twin pillars of Thatcherism are still in place. They're not. The economy's in the shit and our tax-cutting PM's poll tax has just put up the bills for seven out of ten people in this country.'

'The backbenchers are running scared,' said Reece. 'She should be talking to them, not flying off to summit conferences. That stuff is fine for general elections – it gets her air-time and makes her look confident. But right now her place is in the House. She should be showing them she cares.'

Morrison would only smile, tap his canvass list and assure them that he had enough pledges from MPs to ensure victory – even accounting for the lie factor. But Bell and Reece were not convinced. Bell had talked with Kenneth Baker earlier in the week and their analysis of Mrs Thatcher's standing made them distinctly uneasy. 'They're politicians, aren't they?' Bell said to his friend. 'They're probably all lying.'[62]

The dinner was also attended by the Wakehams, the Bakers, Lord McAlpine, John Whittingdale, the Prime Minister's political secretary, and her campaign team of Michael Neubert and Gerry Neale and their wives. After dinner the wives were escorted by Denis Thatcher to another room and a discussion took place. The atmosphere reeked of complacency. Strangely, those present felt it had been designed that way so that it was almost impossible for a proper debate to take place. 'I've done a trawl and I think you'll have a majority of forty,' Morrison told Mrs Thatcher. 'Make an allowance for the fact that perhaps fifteen of them are just telling me that [i.e. lying] and you'll have a comfortable majority. It won't be comfortable, but it'll be all right.'

'Where have we heard all that before?' said the Prime Minister, turning towards Reece.

'Ted Heath in 1975,' he replied. 'The fact is that people tell stories to representatives of party leaders because they don't want to block themselves out of future promotions.'

'Yes, exactly,' she said.[63]

Reece, Bell and Baker remained sceptical of Morrison's assessment. His mistake was to underestimate what Mrs Thatcher called 'the lie factor'.[64] But the whips were adamant. 'No, no, these are the results,' one said.

Then Morrison made his immortal comment: 'Well, unless they're lying to me.'

After the meeting Reece stayed behind to try to persuade the Prime Minister to stay in London rather than attend the summit in Paris. 'A few telephone calls from you personally tomorrow could swing the day, because if you lose you're not going to lose by many,' he told her perceptively.

'Gordon, if I pull out now [from going to Paris],' she replied, 'MPs will say that I'm running scared and think I'm going to lose. That would be even worse. No, the decision is made.'[65]

When the result was declared at 6.30 p.m. on Tuesday 20 November, Bell and Reece were in the Prime Minister's room at the Commons along with John Wakeham, David Waddington, Lord McAlpine and her campaign team. Reece had prepared champagne. But the cork remained in the bottle. Mrs Thatcher was four votes short of the required majority, which meant that if just two MPs had voted for her she would have won. But she swiftly declared herself a candidate for the second ballot: 'I fight on, I fight to win.'

Early the next morning Bell and Reece went to Central Office for a meeting with Kenneth Baker and his advisers. They decided that Mrs Thatcher should not make any more personal attacks on Heseltine as it would be counter-productive and should instead concentrate on lobbying backbenchers. But the most important part of the strategy was to enlist the active and enthusiastic support of John Major, the chancellor, and Douglas Hurd, the foreign secretary.

Bell and Reece retired to a private room at Mark's Club for lunch. A hastily improvised Thatcher defence summit took place: they were joined by Lord McAlpine, Sir David English, editor of the *Daily Mail*, and Conrad Black, proprietor of the *Daily* and *Sunday Telegraphs*. All five believed she could remain Prime Minister. At 1.15 p.m. Reece placed a call to Mrs Thatcher in the cabinet room of No.10.

'What shall I do?' she asked. 'I think they want me to go.'

'Don't be ridiculous,' replied Reece. 'You must fight on. We're all agreed.' He turned to the group who shouted, like a Greek chorus, 'Fight on.'

After Reece put down the phone he said, 'It's very important that those who proposed and seconded her should speak out strongly.' He again took the initiative and telephoned John Major, who was at home in Huntingdon convalescing after an operation on a wisdom tooth. Both Reece and English urged him to return to London immediately and appear on television expressing his strong support for the Prime Minister. Major neither opposed nor endorsed the idea. 'I'll have to think about it,' he said, after a long pause.[66]

Later that day Mrs Thatcher saw each of her cabinet colleagues separately to discuss whether she should resign or enter the second ballot. Bell believed this was a fatal mistake. He considered the cabinet to be a collective group, not a set of individuals. A canvass of each minister would almost inevitably produce a divided result. 'She should have addressed them *en masse*,' he said. 'I'm sure that quite a lot of them would not have dared to say what they really thought. There's not a great deal of courage among them.'[67]

Bell's worst fears were realised. A majority of the Cabinet opposed her entering the second ballot. By late evening Mrs Thatcher had made up her mind. At 11.15 p.m. she telephoned Bell, who was having dinner with friends. 'I've decided to go. Can you come and see me?' she said, and hung up. Bell had taken the call in the dining room where the other guests were seated. He tried to compose himself but tears rolled down his cheeks. For a few moments he stood with his back to the party, listening to the dialling tone and wondering how to keep the news private – two journalists were at the table. He called over his wife and explained what had happened.[68]

Before he went to Downing Street, Bell drove to Belsize Park to collect Reece, who was having dinner with Sir Nicholas Lloyd, editor of the *Daily Express*, and his wife Eve Pollard, then editor of the Sunday paper. As he drove the short distance Bell wept uncontrollably and when he arrived at the Lloyds' house his face was streaked with tears. But he could not disclose the dramatic news – if he had it would have been banner headlines the next morning before the official announcement.

Bell and Reece made their way to Downing Street where they sat with Mrs Thatcher until 2 a.m. while she worked on her resignation speech. As they gathered Bell witnessed Andrew Turnbull, her principal private secretary, telephoning the news almost nonchalantly to people who needed to be informed in advance. One was the Governor of the Bank of England: 'I thought you ought to know for the markets that the Prime Minister will be resigning at 7.30 tomorrow morning,' he said. 'If you would keep it to yourself until then.' Bell was appalled. The civil-service machine was already taking over, he thought. 'It really was "The King is dead, long live the King",' he said later.[69]

Bell had correctly judged the gravity of the crisis facing Mrs Thatcher in 1990. But it is debatable whether he could have changed what was perhaps an inevitable course of events. After all, Bell himself argues that she was dethroned by a palace *coup* rather than a self-enforced abdication. 'I believe she was brought down,' he said. 'I don't believe she brought herself down. I think if you look at the subtleties and nuances of the way that people said things and how they behaved, including John Major and Douglas Hurd, these things were all going to undermine her position. There was very little show of total loyalty and determination to keep her as Prime Minister . . . They did sign the proposal and seconding forms because that was their sense of duty and responsibility, but there was no sense of passion about it.'[70]

Bell's last day in Downing Street was spent with Mrs Thatcher, watching the result of the subsequent election between Major and Heseltine on television. Old friends like Gordon Reece and John Wakeham were also there. After it was announced, Mrs Thatcher walked through the connecting doors to No. 11 Downing Street and embraced Major. 'The future is secure,' she told him. The new Prime Minister then went outside to address the nation in front of the cameras. Mrs Thatcher wanted to accompany him but Bell dissuaded her, arguing that it would add currency to the idea that she would be a back-seat driver to the new Prime Minister. Instead, she watched from the window, just visible to the cameras.

*   *   *

Mrs Thatcher's departure from Downing Street was as traumatic and upsetting for Tim Bell as it was for her. He had identified himself so closely with her that for him, too, it was the end of an era. His only consolation was the knighthood he received from her in her resignation honours list.

Bell was ecstatic as it was exactly the type of recognition he thrived on – visible and prestigious. But his pleasure was tinged with sadness. 'I am delighted and disappointed at the same time,' he said, after receiving the honour from the Queen at Buckingham Palace. 'I am sad because Mrs Thatcher had to resign for me to get it.'[71] One reason why he loved his knighthood so much was that it placed him in a relatively small group of people. 'Having a title is lovely,' he said. 'If anyone tells you it isn't, they're lying. You get nice seats in planes and restaurants and people are deferential.'[72]

Bell celebrated his knighthood with a party at the Savoy Hotel but three months later at Ascot, Alan Bishop, a senior executive at Saatchi's witnessed a poignant moment. It was a bright summer's day and he went out on the balcony to survey the scene. A few minutes later he was joined by Bell, who greeted him in full regalia with 'Royal Enclosure' on his lapel. 'Hi, Tim,' replied Bishop, 'or should I say "Sir Timothy"?' Bell smiled and looked out quietly across the racecourse, clearly reflecting on the past. Finally, he said, 'It's a funny old world.' Mrs Thatcher had used the same words in her last cabinet meeting. It really was the end of an era. But for Tim Bell a new one was just beginning.

Chapter Nine

You Can Trust Me,
I'm a Spin Doctor

'I would rather be called a spin doctor than a hidden persuader.
Actually I rather like the term. After all, doctors are qualified
professionals, and putting the right spin on things is exactly
what we do'

Tim Bell, *PR Week*, 13 October 1995

Despite Mrs Thatcher's abrupt exit from 10 Downing Street, Bell continued to advise her. The shock of losing her job had left her disorientated, and one of her priorities was to find a new house. The Thatchers had sold 19 Flood Street and had moved into a neo-Georgian house in Hambledon Place, Dulwich, but they hated living there as it was so far from Westminster. 'A widow's house,' as Denis aptly described it, and it was certainly unsuitable for a woman cut off in her prime.[1] After selling the property, they lived in an apartment in Belgravia's Eaton Square, lent to them by Kathleen Ford, widow of Henry Ford II, and looked around for a new home. Unfortunately, their son Mark appointed himself their estate agent. His suggestions were not astute: he came up with a property, valued at £7 million, in Tite Street, Chelsea.

Bell was aware of the problem. He also knew that the Barclay brothers, shareholders in Lowe Bell Communications, owned two desirable properties in Chester Square, Belgravia, just across the street from his own home in Gerald Road. Bell thought that one, a five-storeyed terraced house at No. 73, was appropriate, and asked David Barclay whether he would sell. He agreed and offered it to the Thatchers for £700,000. When Mark was informed he reacted petulantly. 'He told Tim that he wasn't going to have a couple of businessmen just walk in and buy up his mother like that,' said a Thatcher family friend. 'He implied that the Barclays were not fit to open the door of her Daimler. He was pretty offensive.'[2]

After Mark's intervention, the property was sold to another buyer. But Bell was convinced that this was the ideal home for the Thatchers. A few weeks later as Mrs Thatcher was being driven through Belgravia, he arranged for her to be shown the exterior. She liked it and, despite her son's objections, asked the Barclay brothers if anything could be done. They persuaded the new inhabitant of No. 73 to sell them back the house; and purchase another Barclay-owned property across the square. The Thatchers were then able to buy No.73 for the original price on a ten-year lease. According to a source directly involved in the transaction, it was paid for by the Thatcher Foundation, not by the former Prime Minister.

Bell kept the faith as Thatcher's salesman by acting as PR spokesperson and trustee of the UK branch of the Foundation, and Lowe Bell Communications compiled and produced the 13-page glossy brochure that launched it. He also seconded two Lowe Bell account executives – Abel Hadden and Elizabeth Buchanan, a former special adviser to Cecil Parkinson – to handle press inquiries for Mrs Thatcher, notably over her controversial consultancy with the US tobacco corporation Philip Morris Inc.

It was Bell's almost symbiotic relationship with Mrs Thatcher and her regime that resulted in a distinctly detached association with John Major and his new administration. Bell was seen as Thatcher's chief lieutenant and so it was Sir Gordon Reece, not Bell, who had been Major's media adviser in his contest with Heseltine for the party leadership. He had attended the early-morning meetings of Major's campaign team with Norman Lamont, David Mellor and Richard Ryder at 11 Downing Street. And it was Reece who swung the support of the *Daily Mail* to Major by personally lobbying Sir David English.

The bitter leadership battle had split Central Office into two camps. Normally staff would have remained neutral. But the then party chairman, Kenneth Baker, was in the Thatcher tent, while others supported Heseltine. The new chairman, Chris Patten, was anxious to unite the party, which meant accommodating Heseltine and his supporters. Since this was a political prerequisite it would have been impossible to use Bell because he had been such an active and fervent Thatcher operative.

There was no calculated decision to keep Bell out, but the need for unity was all important and he was now on the outside track. His isolation increased when Brendan Bruce, the party's communications director, was replaced by Shaun Woodward, a 32-year-old former BBC television producer. When Woodward started work on 18 February 1991, his priority was to appoint a new full-time advertising agency and he consulted Peter Gummer, chairman of the PR firm Shandwick, and brother of cabinet minister John, to oversee the choice. Although they were not on the short-list and had been quietly courting the Labour party, Saatchi's stepped in with a typically assertive display of interest. 'Saatchi's got on because they were ravenous,' recalled Woodward. 'If you had a meeting with Bill Muirhead [the account director], you couldn't get rid of him. If you gave him a list of impossible conditions, he made them possible.'[3]

Saatchi's were rehired in March 1991 and Maurice Saatchi was again a presence at Smith Square, which made it even more difficult to utilise Bell. Although Bell was now talking to Charles Saatchi, his rift with the Brothers had not completely healed. However, Woodward, who had never fought an election campaign, consulted Bell discreetly and informally over breakfast or lunch about once a month. He liked and respected the veteran campaigner and found his advice perceptive and pragmatic. Although Bell was kept at a distance from the sound of gunfire, he was useful in one respect: the Major regime was anxious to placate Mrs Thatcher and keep her informed and Bell was the perfect conduit.

However, it soon transpired that Bell was not, after all, out of the political loop. On Sunday 17 March 1991, two days before Norman Lamont's first budget, Bell was at his country cottage when he received an urgent call from the chancellor's private office. 'The chancellor would like to see you immediately,' he was told.

'Well, could we not talk on the phone?' asked Bell.

'No, he must see you,' said the aide.

That Sunday evening Bell drove back to London and walked into Lamont's private office. 'Ah, Tim, I only have one question for you,' said the chancellor. 'Do you think I should wear these glasses or these when I make my budget speech?'

But Bell still felt frustrated at the withering away of the interlocking network between Tory publicity advisers and sympathetic editors that he had carefully built up during the Thatcher years. In establishing close relationships with editors like Sir David English of the *Daily Mail* and Sir Nicholas Lloyd of the *Daily Express*, and proprietors like Rupert Murdoch, Bell had laised between Mrs Thatcher and friendly newspapers. These links had been particularly useful during elections and at crisis times. The deal was that while these newspapers remained compliant and supportive, they would receive exclusive stories and information.

Under John Major, this well-oiled machine became rusty, which partly explains his poor press. The one occasion on which he used this alternative channel of communication it backfired badly. In the autumn of 1991, the Prime Minister wanted to disclose that there would not be an election that November. Instead of making an official announcement, however, he asked John Wakeham, who had the ministerial responsibility for 'co-ordinating the presentation of government policies', to 'put the word out'. It was decided that he would notify the five newspapers considered the 'most reliable' and loyal to the party: *The Times*, *Daily Telegraph*, *Daily Mail*, *Daily Express* and the *Sun*.[4]

Wakeham chose his moment carefully. The five political editors were called at 9.30 a.m. on Monday 6 October 1991, the first day of that year's Labour conference, and were given the story exclusively and non-attributably by the minister himself. But the leak itself leaked, and the back-door way in which the news had been sneaked out became the story. Bell was furious that he had not been consulted. He thought it idiotic of Wakeham, an old friend, to have briefed five newspapers and ignored television and radio. If the government was anxious to have disclosed the information without leaving their fingerprints, said Bell, then 'one newspaper should have been tipped off exclusively and once the story appeared, it should not have been denied'.[5]

Bell hated being excluded from the action and became increasingly critical. A week later, during the Tory conference, he talked to two experienced political editors, Don McIntyre of the *Independent* and David Wastell of the *Sunday Telegraph*, and lashed out at the party's PR operation. 'They're useless,' said Bell bitterly. 'They couldn't piss in a pot.' At dinner parties he barely concealed his contempt for Major's administration and compared it unfavourably to the Thatcher days, which hardened opinion against him. And yet, curiously, untrue press stories would occasionally appear like 'Sir Tim Brought In From the Cold' (*Mail on Sunday*), which stated, unsourced, that Bell 'has been brought back to play a vital role in Major's election campaign'.[6]

As the general election campaign got under way in March 1992, Bell was barely a member of the supporting cast. He offered advice on raising the temperature of the campaign and suggested ways to improve Major's circular roadshow, such as packing the audience with people of a similar type – nurses, immigrants, women, the elderly. But Central Office rejected them. 'Many of Tim's ideas are first-rate,' said a friend, 'but they won't consider them. He's out of favour and that's that.'[7] A Tory election planner said, 'Tim's too high profile, he attracts too much attention. That was OK under Mrs Thatcher. Because John Major is a more retiring person, Bell is not suitable.'[8] The truth was more political: the campaign door was closed to Bell because he was an unreconstructed Thatcherite, and Peter Gummer from Shandwick had taken his place.

The only occasion on which Bell got through the door occurred during the second week of the campaign. The opportunity arose because the party chairman, Chris Patten, was fighting a rearguard action in his Bath constituency – a tight marginal. He needed to spend a lot of time there and every morning at 10 a.m. after the press conference he flew by helicopter to Bath. By the time he returned to London it was late afternoon or early evening. In his absence John Wakeham acted as stand-in chairman at Central Office and was present if any key decisions needed to be taken. He was not fighting a parliamentary seat as he was about to be elevated to the House of Lords.

In Patten's absence, Wakeham summoned his old friends Sir Tim Bell and Sir Gordon Reece for advice on news management. Their influence was limited because of resistance from the Central Office machine. However, unknown to the media, Bell had a stronger connection in 10 Downing Street: Stephen Sherbourne, managing director of Lowe Bell Consultants, had been seconded there full-time to help organise media events and contribute to Major's speeches. It was through Sherbourne, who virtually lived at 10 Downing Street during the election, that Bell directed his critique and ideas.

Nevertheless, he was still at arm's length. As the campaign grew tense, Bell became agitated. He was convinced that the Tories had gone to the country too early and should have waited another two months when the budget tax cuts would appear in voters' pockets.[9] He poured it all out over lunch on Friday 3 April 1992, less than a week before the final poll, to Eleonor Goodman, political correspondent of Channel 4 News. Sitting at a nearby table were Bill Muirhead, the Saatchi's director who was running the Conservative account alongside Jeremy Sinclair, and Ivan Fallon, deputy editor of the *Sunday Times* and author of a favourable book on the Saatchis. It had been agreed with Central Office that during the campaign the agency would brief trustworthy journalists. They could not fail to hear Bell taking pot-shots at the Tory campaign.

Muirhead was in a confident mood that afternoon: he believed that Labour had made a serious tactical error in announcing details of their likely taxation levels in the shadow budget. Despite widespread criticism of the Tory campaign, he had maintained that Saatchis' advertising – 'Labour's Double Whammy – More Taxes, Higher Prices' and 'Five Years' Hard Labour – Taxes Up, Mortgages Up' – could prove decisive. But Bell thought that the agency had badly miscalculated. As he left the restaurant, he walked over to Muirhead's table and launched a savage if cogent attack on Saatchi's advertising. 'You've totally fucked it up,' Bell said. 'You've lost the election. Every ad you've done is wrong. The tax ads aren't working, and it's the wrong issue. Nobody is interested in tax. The whole strategy is flawed and it's going to be a disaster.' Muirhead was speechless and shaken at his former colleague's diatribe. Eventually, he muttered, 'I think you're wrong.' But Bell's outburst shook his confidence although private polling had indicated that their 'Labour's Tax Bombshell' slogans were making an impact.

On election night itself Bell attached his colours firmly to the mast of the *ancien régime* by attending a party at Lord McAlpine's house. It was an occasion for the Thatcherite faithful like Nicholas Ridley and Sir Gordon Reece, from which Bell moved on to a feast at the Savoy Hotel hosted by Conrad Black, proprietor of the Telegraph Group, and attended by Mrs Thatcher.[10]

Major's victory meant that Bell needed to redefine his role as a broker and networker between the worlds of politics, media and business. He was no longer influential with, or even had access to, the Prime Minister. It was barely sixteen months since he had been plotting against Michael Heseltine, the new trade and industry secretary and one of Major's most senior cabinet ministers. It would be some time before diehard Thatcherites were brought back into the fold. But Bell's hunger to be at the centre of the action was now being fed by a combination of his growing reputation and his large number of friends, contacts and clients.

'PEOPLE WITH PROBLEMS'

In 1994 Tim Bell outlined what services his company could provide. 'One third of the accounts are straight-forward launches, offering opportunities,' he said. 'One third is basically communication, keeping the name alive. Only the other third is what one might call people with problems.'[11]

Bell spent the early 1990s increasingly on the latter – crisis management. This was born out of the old PR adage – which applies equally to lawyers – that from every crisis an opportunity arises. He has always held the view that he is a professional advocate and communicator and that the background of the client is irrelevant. He believes that everyone has a right to be heard and was happy to represent Owen Oyston, the flamboyant millionaire businessman, who was a strong and active Labour Party supporter and virulent opponent of Mrs Thatcher. In 1989 Oyston was being investigated by the *Sunday Times*, who planned to publish untrue allegations about his commercial affairs. The timing could not have been worse as the tycoon was then negotiating with investment banks to finance a takeover bid. It was certainly a crisis and he hired Bell for a fee of £20,000 to use his influence with the paper: News International was one of Bell's clients. But it was to no avail and the story was published. Oyston sued for libel and won a total of £1 million in costs and damages.

In dealing with the media, a crisis for a potential client usually starts with the prospect of a story that will reveal damaging information about them. Then the story is published or broadcast and suddenly, there is enormous and unprecedented pressure on the prospective client because of the seriousness of the disclosures: the phone rings every five minutes; journalists and television cameras are camped outside their house, some of whom stay all night; their neighbours and family are being interviewed; they can't sleep. What do they do?

Unless the story is completely untrue, it's time for damage limitation. According to Bell, if an outside consultant is hired, the other side immediately thinks again: 'The first thing they're going to say is, "My God, they've taken on some PR advisers,"' he said. 'If it's me, because of my relationship with Mrs Thatcher, then I end up with a high profile as well . . . So you get into a high-profile situation and the point about this is that all criticism can be made worse by what you do next. The actual reason for nearly all crises is not what caused the damage in the first place but how you respond to it afterwards.'[12]

Bell is well suited to dealing with such situations for he is an optimist. When potential clients approach him in a panic, his instinct is to see light where there is dark or jewels where there is dust. 'I'm only interested in being positive about things,' he said. 'If something goes wrong and people tell me what's happened, instead of saying, "whose fault is it? Find the guilty person," I say, "What shall we do about it?" I look for silver linings and clouds and all those nauseating things that people like me do. That's why I've been successful at this, because what's the point in advising somebody by saying, "God, it's awful, this looks hopeless"? Anybody who is beset with problems wants somebody to walk through their door and say, "OK, there is a way out."'[13]

That escape is achieved through analysing and understanding the crisis and knowing how the story is going to run. There are various options: the client can adopt a low profile, hope the story will fizzle out and slowly build up a new perception of themselves with a medium-term strategy; they can come clean, thereby disarming the accusers; they can launch a spin offensive, which means persuading journalists round to the client's interpretation of events. More significantly, it involves exerting power in an attempt to prevent further damaging disclosures or produce more favourable coverage. In many ways, Bell is not an orthodox PR consultant or press agent: he is a dealer in information. He establishes close relationships with journalists and editors as a way of ensuring that his client's message is conveyed to his liking. He is Mephistopheles to the reporter's Faust. Favours are offered and received: if the story about the client is spiked, the journalist is handed an even better exclusive about someone else. If the article is published, future co-operation is withdrawn.

Spin-doctoring is largely concerned with the art of persuasive conversation and this is Bell's speciality. He will happily spend hours on the telephone trying to spin or kill a story. 'If he was found leaning over a dead body with a smoking gun in his hand, he would talk his way out of it,' Ron Leagas told me. His style is matey, familiar, informal, and he has that uncanny ability to draw in listeners, making them feel special. He is also the arch exponent of flattery: 'You and I have had our differences, Stewart [Steven]', he once told the former editor of the *Mail on Sunday*, 'but may I just say what a brilliant editor you've been.'

A favourite tactic, also adopted by Sir Gordon Reece, is to make friends with influential journalists and then confide amazing inside revelations and anecdotes, but strictly off-the-record. This draws the journalist into his inner sanctum but if the confidence is broken, he or she is sent into exile.

However, Bell does not trust the media. He is not beyond relaying misleading information and withholding relevant accurate material. When asked whether he had ever told a lie, he replied with disarming honesty: 'Yes, of course.' He paused. 'Let's say I've sometimes handled things badly when I've been rung at 5.30 p.m. for a comment. I've also been economical with the truth in the sense of not giving more information about a client than I need to.'[14]

His attitude towards journalists is ambivalent. In the 1970s he was often in Fleet Street pubs drinking and gossiping with reporters. He still enjoys their company and the buzz of newspapers – the speed and constant activity appeals to him. 'If I hadn't got into advertising, I would liked to have been an editor of a national paper,' he told one editor. 'I love journalism and journalists,' he said. 'The British press is still the best in the world.'[15] Yet he shared Mrs Thatcher's penchant for 'one of us' cliques. Stewart Steven, editor of the *Mail on Sunday* from 1982 until 1992, was outside that inner circle. He was not even a Tory, let alone a Thatcherite, and his paper flirted heavily with the SDP. This was insufferable for senior Tories and they asked Lord Rothermere to dismiss him because the *Mail on Sunday* was not cheerleading the Thatcherite cause. 'The Conservative Party want me to sack you,' Lord Rothermere told his editor. 'You know, of course, that makes it absolutely impossible for me to do so.'

Bell was not involved in that operation, but he shuns journalists who hold a different view of the world or who take an independent approach. Fellow PR consultants have been shocked to hear him describe some reporters as 'bastards' and 'communists'. He also has a standard line about invasion of privacy and what he calls unwarranted intrusion into people's personal lives. 'The people who prey on the kiss-and-tell are the newspapers,' he said in 1996, 'and I think they ought to stare their consciences in the eye and think about it.'[16]

When it comes to moments of potential and real crisis for his clients all these factors have influenced his decision-making. And eventually Bell's judgement was called into question – even by his closest friends.

SPREADING THE HANSON GOSPEL

One of the framed photographs ever-present on the 'Downing Street Wall' of Bell's office has been of Lord Hanson, the industrialist who has made a fortune out of acquisitions and mergers. Along with Baroness Thatcher, Rupert Murdoch, Lord Thorneycroft, Lord Weinstock and Charles Saatchi, Hanson is one of Bell's heroes.[17] The Yorkshire-born millionaire is exactly the type of self-made tycoon Bell loves to advise, as in the 1980s he was at the heart of the interface between the Conservative government and big business. Hanson plc donated £1,052,000 to the Conservative Party between 1981 and 1995 and Hanson himself was Mrs Thatcher's favourite tycoon as an unflinching advocate of uncompromising monetarism. He supported and funded (£175,000 between 1981 and 1995) the Centre for Policy Studies (CPS), the right-wing think tank, which was the intellectual inspiration for Thatcherism and which gave Hanson access to fellow disciples – notably Bell, who has been a director of the CPS since 1991.

However, it is in the commercial arena where Hanson and Bell have worked most closely together. This originates from Bell's Lowe Howard-Spink period when he oversaw the television advertisements promoting Hanson's corporate invasion of the United States. Frank Lowe and his chief executive were always keen to embark on any kind of work for Hanson and were delighted when a subsidiary of Hanson plc hired Good Relations, their PR arm, for a specific project.

A senior Good Relations director, Peter Bradley, had set up, with Bell's encouragement, a special planning and development division, whose role was to advise clients on local government procedures and public relations when seeking planning permission for major schemes. Hanson consulted the unit because he had bought land south of Peterborough and wanted to build a township. According to Bradley, it was not a pleasant experience: 'Working for Hanson was a nightmare. They had a premediated – and unnecessarily in my view – aggressive management approach. Their policy towards consultants was to be as gratuitously difficult and demanding as possible. They persecuted my staff, undermining their confidence by creating unnecessary crises. It was a policy of intimidation and a lot of it was management posturing, showing off.

'During a cricket tour of Ireland I received a very urgent phone call from Michael O'Shea [Hanson's public affairs director] demanding that I attend an emergency meeting the day I got back. That, of course, ruined my holiday. And, of course, when I attended the meeting it was not urgent at all. The truth was that Hanson management was deliberately short-staffed and so they had to work like hell and they would take it out on the consultants. They were also totally in awe of Hanson himself, it was pathetic. Most of them had a photograph of Hanson on their desk and when he came into their office they would always stand up to attention. He [Hanson] would swan around the office like a headmaster and I used to be in meetings when he put his head around the door just so people could stand up.'

However, most of Bell's work for Hanson focused on corporate takeovers. On 6 December 1985, the conglomerate launched a £2 billion bid for the Imperial Group, the giant food and tobacco corporation. It was an audacious operation, given that just four days earlier Imperial had announced an agreed merger with United Biscuits. The monopoly implications were obvious and Hanson, working closely with Bell, orchestrated a PR offensive to counter adverse comment. More significantly, and again assisted by Bell, he lobbied the government against a reference to the Monopolies and Mergers Commission (MMC). Among those targeted were well-placed MPs like Michael Portillo, then a rising star of the Tory right wing and a consultant to Hanson's close friend Lord

King, Sir Jeffrey Sterling, chairman of P&O and then a special adviser to the DTI, Brian Hayes, then permanent secretary at the DTI, Paul Channon, the secretary of state, and Michael Howard, the corporate affairs minister.[18] This subterranean political activity seemed to produce a result: Hanson's bid for Imperial was allowed to proceed unhindered by the MMC, even though United Biscuits' merger plan was referred to them. Labour MPs immediately alleged that Hanson's lobbying, close links with the Tory Party and recent 'helpful' intervention in the Westland affair had secured favourable treatment. Channon replied that the decision was based 'strictly on the merits of the individual cases'.[19]

An even more controversial episode was Hanson's purchase of a 2.8 per cent stake in ICI in May 1991, which was viewed as a pre-emptive strike for a later hostile bid. Hanson assembled a small but high-powered team of advisers, including Tim Bell, who combined his PR brief with political lobbying, Rodney Dewe, who was responsible for the institutional side, and Brian Basham, the expert City PR streetfighter, who knew instinctively how to mix it if required.

Basham was employed, largely because he had given Hanson a rough ride during the takeover of the Imperial Group. The day before Hanson's raid on ICI's shares, Basham bumped into Sir Gordon White (now Lord White), Hanson's business partner, in Harry's Bar, Mayfair. 'The next time we go for something I want you on the inside of the tent pissing out,' White told him – using the time-honoured tactic of hiring someone purely to prevent him working for the enemy. The next day Basham was told that Hanson had just bought a slice of ICI. He immediately sent a fax to White's flat in Knightsbridge. It contained only three words: 'Je suis ici.' At 7.45 p.m. that evening a fax arrived in Basham's office from Lord Hanson: 'No, you're not. Call me in the morning.'

In the ICI skirmish, Hanson over-estimated the level of his political clout, especially after Mrs Thatcher's departure from 10 Downing Street. He also believed that the battle would be fought by the usual rules in which sharp criticism is aimed at the underlying companies and accounts, rather than at the individuals who ran them. Basham was immediately doubtful that ICI would adopt this strategy. He knew Alan Parker, head of ICI's PR campaign, extremely well – he had trained him in the 1980s – and was able to predict, accurately, that ICI would take an aggressive stance. He therefore wanted to go on the offensive and suggested taking a close look at ICI, notably their environment record, alleged cartels and entertainment facilities for senior executives. 'If we're going to defend ourselves,' he told his client, 'we have to meet fire with fire.' Although White was tempted by the strategy, Hanson refused to authorise it.

Instead, Hanson chaired daily early-morning meetings at the company head office in Hanover Place, Mayfair. On one side of the boardroom table sat Lord Hanson, his son Robert and his nephew Chris Collins, who were in charge of the ICI campaign, Lord White and Martin Taylor, deputy chairman in charge of communications. On the other side were Tim Bell, Brian Basham and Roddy Dewe. It was clear from an early encounter that Bell and Basham were jostling for position. The previous day Robert Peston of the *Financial Times* had written a critical piece about Hanson. Basham advocated opening lines of communication with such journalists but Bell was dismissive: 'Oh, well, of course, Brian does like these pinkos because he's on the wrong side of the blanket himself.'

'I'm sure you're not saying I'm illegitimate, Tim,' replied Basham. 'You must mean that I'm left-of-centre and a member of the Labour Party.'

'Well, they might be a lot more use than your burnt-out lot,' said Lord Hanson, turning to Bell.

Basham saw these sessions as a waste of time, mere talking shops during which little was resolved. Bell would often start by saying, 'I would just like to make three points', and Basham would pipe up, 'Counting.' After the fifth point, he would mutter, 'Five,' but Bell would ramble on for another twenty minutes. 'His basic premise,' said Basham, 'was: "Don't talk to the press. They're all pinkos and can't be trusted."' Roddy Dewe has a similar recollection: 'There was a lot of tension and not much achieved during those meetings,' he said. 'Tim believed that the facts should be left to speak for themselves but I must say he was very skilful in drafting documents.'

In Basham's experienced view, this minimalist approach was inadequate when a client is under attack. 'You cannot influence the media unless you talk to them,' he told the Hanson camp. 'The media is a fact of life. It's part of the environment in which we live and work. It's your job as corporate executives to manage all aspects of the business and that includes your relationship with the press.'

But Hanson was doubtful. For thirty years he had run his company almost under cover, only talking to favoured journalists in the financial press. It was the 'one of us' school of PR – only talk to those you know and trust. He rationed his PR output, rarely talked off-the cuff and saw no reason to change his ways.

However, he was now being slaughtered in the propaganda war. ICI's PR army, marshalled by Alan Parker of Brunswick and co-ordinated by the accountants, was scoring repeated direct hits. The issue was no longer the merits of a potential bid but the latest revelation about Sir Gordon White's lifestyle and the company's capacity to avoid paying corporation tax. ICI were spending an estimated £220,000 a week in fees to advisers – including bankers, investigators and PR consultants – and it showed. All the trade unions, many Tory MPs and most newspapers strongly supported ICI. Also there were constant leaks from inside the Hanson camp. Their PR consultants were under suspicion, but Basham retorted by nicknaming the mole 'HP' because the stories were often attributed to a 'City source'.

Despite his lofty disdain for orthodox PR, Hanson had a short fuse when the image of his company was besmirched in the full gaze of the British Establishment. He was unaccustomed to receiving such a hostile press from Conservative newspapers, and throughout the summer his irritation grew as his laid-back PR strategy ensured that his company was constantly on the defensive. The *Observer* was his chief tormenter: Melvyn Marckus, the City editor, and Michael Gillard produced a damaging story almost weekly.

Lord Hanson, Tim Bell and Martin Taylor tried to recover lost ground by briefing City editors over lunch. Their line was that Hanson's investment was friendly not hostile. They wanted to co-operate with ICI, not swallow it. But it was too little too late and Lord Hanson became increasingly agitated. 'It was greatly frustrating for him,' said Roddy Dewe. 'He had been promised a lot and not much had been delivered.'

The climax of Hanson's disillusionment occurred on Monday 26 August 1991, when he was on holiday in Palm Springs, California. Early that morning he had received by fax a *Mail on Sunday* editorial headlined 'Is Hanson such a good gamble?' It criticised his company for unsuccessful investments in private jets, horse-racing and bloodstock. He reached for his portable word-processor and wrote an angry letter to his chief PR consultant, Tim Bell:

Dear Tim,

Since we reduced the direct approach (from us) to editors et al, we have had lots of advice from you, most of which seems to address how best we should keep the institutional investors correctly informed on Hanson. I think you're missing the point.

At that time we left you to spread the Hanson gospel to the media and politics, without involving us directly. What you had to offer us was based on 'who you know' and that you would be serving us best by influencing them indirectly but constantly. We've left that to you while we've been working, as agreed, directly on the institutions.

We're disappointed with the press recently, exemplified by this article. Libellous, in our opinion, but a clear puff from Alan Parker who shows himself to be running circles around us. Alan Parker to advise ICI on financial matters? He can't even advise his own father on how to submit a national radio bid . . . What kind of clown is he? How about exposing *his* expertise for a change. Come on, chaps, let's do *something*. He spends his client's money trying to discredit *us*.

Can't you dispel all this garbage in advance? Who is Lawrence Lever [city editor of *Mail on Sunday*] anyway? I've never heard of him, but by now all the media should have the *true* story and realise that they shouldn't be able to get away with blatant puffs like this? And your own loving relationships? Apart from Jeff Randall and Ivan Fallon [city editor and deputy editor of the *Sunday Times* respectively] and John Jay [city editor of the *Sunday Telegraph*] – who contact us direct – everyone else seems to have drifted against Hanson and comment is deteriorating. This letter is intended to show our unhappiness.

It's not for us to tell you how to do your job, but it is up to me to judge the results. Let's take just one thing. Parker and Co have managed to imprint in the media's mind the 'Lord White Lifestyle' lie, to the degree that even you partly believe it, judging from what I hear from you about our dispelling it. Shouldn't you be addressing this – and the minor bloodstock deal – day, night and holidays too? After all this time, Parker's still making plenty out of it.

I think we're entitled to better results. Weekly strategy meetings are a waste of time. We've put our faith in your ability to *sell* Hanson to your contacts. You know what a great story there is out there, but it's not getting through. You *know* what we need but I begin to have my doubts. Each time I raise them, back comes a message: 'May we get together to discuss . . .' You know your story sufficiently well by now to sell it for us.

You're in the communications business so I hope you don't mind this frank communication from me. I know you'll understand that we're entitled to look for some positive results and to let you know when we don't see them.

Sincerely, James.

The letter, headed 'personal and confidential', was faxed to Bell, who read it the same day. A copy was then sent to Tony Carlisle at Dewe Rogerson 'for information'. Hanson sent a different letter, which contained similar sentiments, to Brian Basham. That afternoon Basham faxed his reply: 'Dear James, I have shredded your memo. Unless you begin to address your PR problems seriously you're going to lose the battle. Yours Brian.'

But that was not the end of the matter. Seven weeks later a copy of Hanson's letter to Bell was leaked to the *Observer*, which published it.[20] This was highly embarrassing to Bell. Essentially, Hanson's message to his 'pre-eminent adviser', as Bell was described by deputy chairman Martin Taylor,[21] was: you are not delivering the goods and having more meetings is not going to solve the problem. Privately, Bell was furious and felt betrayed and humiliated. How could journalists he had helped on so many occasions turn on him in this way, he complained, in between a volley of expletives. Publicly he put a brave face on it: 'I can't believe serious newspapers would wish to fill their columns with private correspondence,' he said. 'Obviously my colleagues in the PR industry have not given them any good stories this week.'[22]

Hanson admitted that the leak 'caused considerable embarrassment'. He wrote to the Press Complaints Commission, claiming that publication of the document was a 'flagrant breach' of his right to privacy and confidentiality. But the press, usually so pro-Hanson, was unimpressed. Two days later, on 15 October 1991, the *Financial Times* proclaimed: 'Institutional investors said yesterday that Hanson must change its own managerial style and take account of criticisms over its corporate governance instead of simply blaming its public relations advisers for not getting its message across.'

That made his lordship even more angry. By then he had started to accept Basham's advice on being more accessible to the media and had granted an interview to the *Economist*. But it was too late. Hanson was staring a rare corporate defeat in the face. From that moment it was like Napoleon's retreat from Moscow – cold, lengthy, and with many conspicuous casualties. 'Hanson's people will tell you that they should have bought a 15 per cent stake or nothing,' Brian Basham reflected. 'What they should have done was hit ICI hard from the word go, and I have no doubt they would have won. It [the ICI investment] was a brilliant and perceptive idea, but it was executed too tentatively.'

Bell confronted the décâcle in typically flamboyant fashion. Five days after the leak of the letter, he celebrated his fiftieth birthday by throwing a huge party for 200 guests at the Dorchester Hotel. Among them were some familiar faces – former Tory chairmen Cecil Parkinson and Kenneth Baker, energy secretary John Wakeham, British Airways chairman Lord King, Sir David English and Sir Nicholas Lloyd. The disclosure of Hanson's displeasure may not have been his best birthday present, but his standing in the Establishment appeared to be undiminished.

A year later Bell was advising Hanson on the takeover bid for Rank Hovis McDougall. This time the PR machine was more low-key. When questioned about Bell's role, a Hanson spokesperson replied, 'Oh, we can't talk about how he works,' in what a journalist likened to 'the strangled voice of a butler being questioned about his master's underwear'. The press officer was then asked about the chairman's current view of Bell: 'I think I must confirm that Lord Hanson has the highest regard for Sir Tim Bell,' he said worriedly.[23]

By December 1993, Hanson plc and Bell appeared to have learned the lessons of their calamitious ICI campaign and the company became more open with financial journalists and City analysts. For the first time a press briefing was held on the day of its annual financial results. Selling the Hanson gospel became a lot easier and in 1995 Lowe Bell advised on the de-merger of its US industries.

THE CABINET MINISTER, THE ACTRESS AND THE PHOTO OPPORTUNITY

In any crisis – personal, professional or political – a multi-millionaire tycoon such as Lord Hanson has vast resources and personnel at his disposal. But most people feel almost helpless. This even applies to some cabinet ministers. They wield enormous power until they are facing potential catastrophe and then a feeling of isolation set in. They cannot use their civil servants or government facilities. The party is often wary because of the political damage the scandal or problem may cause. Apart from personal friends, a politician is almost alone. In July 1992, one such secretary of state was David Mellor, the Tory MP for Putney.

His predicament could be traced back to an evening three months earlier, during the general election campaign. In a lively French restaurant called Le Gourmet on the Kings Road, Chelsea, Paul Halloran, a close friend of Mellor and then *Private Eye*'s chief investigative reporter, was having dinner with Antonia de Sancha, a stunning six-foot 31-year-old Spanish actress. Later that night, as they sat drinking, Mellor arrived in a chauffeur-driven Jaguar lent to him by Elliot Bernerd. Halloran introduced his dinner companion.

Forty-three year-old Mellor was on the crest of a wave: he had just been made national heritage secretary, which encompassed the arts, media, heritage and sports policy, and was receiving rave reviews for his performance. Close to John Major, he was destined for higher things. A complex man, he is intellectually bright and self-confident and yet unsure and insecure in his personal life. He is, perhaps, best summed up by Matthew Parris, the former Conservative MP and *Times* columnist, who knew him well when they were backbenchers: 'Arrogant, rude, capable, ambitious, entertaining, quick-minded, sharp-tongued, liberal in his thinking and brutal in debate, Mellor was a man of steady and humane judgement in public affairs, yet often unbelievable insensitivity and self-defeating impatience in personal and political relationships. He both impressed and infuriated, often at the same time.'[24]

For some women, his personality – supplemented by the power, prestige and celebrity status of a cabinet minister – is an appealing cocktail. For de Sancha, an aspiring but struggling actress, his deep love for and knowledge of the arts was an extra attraction. He was no oil painting, but he was good company. She was intrigued. And Mellor was mesmerised by this exotic, lively, if moody, actress. She was not like the repressed, stuffy women he usually met at social functions and, although he was married with two sons, it was not long before they embarked on a passionate affair.

For several weeks Mellor went out with de Sancha and visited her in her flat in Finborough Road, west London. But she confided in her landlord, Nick Philp, and friends about the relationship. Philp realised this was a lucrative tabloid story and arranged for de Sancha's telephone and flat to be bugged. Once he secured hard evidence, Philp went to the *News of the World* to sell the tapes and everything he knew about the affair.

He dealt with the news desk and deputy editor Paul Connew, who was excited by the story. The Conservatives had always portrayed themselves as the party of the family and this was a classic tale of sex and hypocrisy in high places. After obtaining their own evidence, Connew and his colleagues were keen to proceed. But Patsy Chapman, then editor of the *News of the World*, was uneasy. She was a member of the Press Complaints Commission and was concerned that publication would result in privacy legislation. Even more pertinent, Mellor was heritage secretary and had recently warned the tabloids that they were 'drinking in the last chance saloon'. Chapman spiked the story, but left open an opportunity: 'The only way I'll run it', she told her executives, 'is if you can get an admission from Mellor.'

Meanwhile, Philp had taken his tapes to the *People*, who began to make their own recordings in de Sancha's flat. By the second week of July 1992, the *News of the World* could see the story slipping away. Connew decided to take up his editor's challenge and attempt to extract a confession from Mellor. He rang Mellor several times, but when his calls were not returned he telephoned Tim Bell, knowing that he could get access to Mellor. 'Look, Tim,' he said, 'we know about this story of Mellor having an affair. We know it's true and it's going to come out, whatever happens. We're not going to buy these tapes but someone else will. What Mellor can do is get in a first strike by coming clean with us and emerge with some dignity. It will still be embarrassing, but it will limit the damage and he can show he took the initiative and addressed the issue before he was actually exposed.' It was a classic tabloid ploy to spoil a rival's scoop.

Bell played it cool. 'I understand where you're coming from,' he replied. 'I'll put it to him and come back to you.' Late that night Bell rang the minister at his home in Putney. Mellor was surprised to receive the call – after all, the two had little in common politically. Bell was a devoted Thatcher apostle while Mellor had made little secret of his hostility to the former Prime Minister. But Bell was not going to refuse the chance to advise a cabinet minister, particularly one so close to John Major. He did not ask the minister whether the allegation was true. He was a messenger not an arbiter. But he told Mellor what the *News of the World* was claiming: that Mellor planned to leave his wife for an unemployed actress and that tapes existed which would expose their affair in some depth.

Mellor was shocked but kept calm as he listened to Bell, occasionally muttering, 'Rubbish', voicing amazement that anyone could record such conversations. But he was sceptical and suspicious of Connew's offer and did not believe that the paper could substantiate the allegation. Bell read this as a denial and two days later he called Connew. 'David Mellor says that he knows de Sancha,' he told the journalist, 'but he has no plans to leave his wife and he says if you've got the story, why not run with it? He thinks you're bluffing and you don't have it.'

But Connew could not show his hand because of his editor's opposition to publishing the story. Paul Halloran disputes to this day that Connew had the story: 'He never had it,' he said dismissively. 'The *Screws* were trying to con Mellor.' The cabinet minister agreed. On Friday 10 July, Mellor met Halloran in Soho Square to discuss the crisis. He took the view that if the *News of the World* could not crack it, nobody else could.

Nine days later, on Sunday 19 July, he was proved horribly wrong. The *People* splashed graphic details of his illicit relationship over several pages. Mellor immediately offered his resignation to the Prime Minister, pointing out a possible conflict of interest as it had been he who had commissioned the Calcutt Inquiry into privacy and the press. But Major turned him down and reassured him of his full support. Mellor soldiered on and appealed for the privacy of his family to be protected. But the story showed no signs of abating: de Sancha's less than illustrious acting career was revealed, notably a bizarre role as a one-legged prostitute who had sex with a pizza delivery man in a soft-porn film called *The Pieman*.

On the evening of Wednesday 22 July, Mellor took counsel from an old political friend, Richard Ryder, the government chief whip, who told him to say and do nothing. But, as he was driven home late that night, Mellor was horrified to read in the early editions of the papers that his father-in-law, Professor Edward Hall, had denounced him: 'If he'll cheat on our girl, he'll cheat on the nation.' Even worse, one news report alleged, wrongly, that Mellor had denied his in-laws access to his two sons.

When he arrived home he brooded on what to do. Although Major had pledged support, his father-in-law's comment was damaging and gave the press justification for pursuing the story. He decided he needed someone from the outside to keep him informed. At 3 a.m. he telephoned Bell and asked for his help and advice. This was a situation that Bell loved: a cabinet minister in trouble, isolated and under siege by the media. He thrived on being the spider at the centre of the web.

Mellor told Bell he was going down to see his in-laws later the following day. He was thinking of posing with them for photographers as a way of demonstrating family solidarity and countering the story that he had banned them from seeing his children. 'He asked me what I thought of his idea,' recalled Bell. 'I said it sounds fine. But I didn't offer any advice. I just said yes.'[25]

But Bell did more than that. He helped arrange the picture opportunity. At just after noon, despite having been advised not to do so by his departmental officials, Mellor, his wife, two sons and in-laws stood smiling for the cameras. It was a serious error on two counts. The reunion looked stilted and resulted in a litany of mocking headlines like 'The Mellors Play At Happy Families . . . Or is it Charades?'. Also, he had just appealed for privacy, so posing willingly with his family hardly helped his cause.

Despite the photo-call blunder, Bell went into action. His mission was to try to save Mellor's political career. 'If I can get Mellor through this, I will make him the first Tory minister in history to survive a sex scandal,' he said privately.[26] For the next forty-eight hours Bell rarely left the phone. His strategy was to attack the methods used by the press to get the story rather than to deal with the substance of the story itself. 'We cannot have the cabinet decided by the tabloids,' he told a friend. In a stream of calls to cabinet ministers and Fleet Street editors, he attempted to rebuild Mellor's image. He briefed journalists about the 'brother and sister' nature of the minister's marriage, while dangling the elusive prize of an 'exclusive interview' with Mellor. But more rather than fewer headlines were the result.

For Mellor, the PR consultant was like an unauthorised news service, subcontracted out from government. He was happy to spend hours on the telephone keeping the minister informed of the latest developments, and to that extent he was a useful sounding board for Mellor. But his strategic advice was inept and inappropriate: in not confronting the allegation directly with a press conference (as Paddy Ashdown did), Mellor left Fleet Street with the impression that he had something to hide, which encouraged them to pursue further revelations.

Sure enough these arrived six weeks later, on 7 September 1992, when the *Sun* began the serialisation of Antonia de Sancha's version of the affair. No details were spared. False but entertaining stories of the cabinet minister making love to her in a Chelsea football strip, reciting Shakespeare in the nude and sucking her toes appeared, complete with photographs of the mattress where the couple had frolicked. Mellor was fast becoming a laughing stock and Bell had lost control of the media agenda. Suddenly de Sancha was all over the television and radio, angry that her former lover had done nothing to help her. Bell, who had telephoned Mellor in Scotland to warn him about the *Sun*'s 'revelations', tried to hit back. 'These stories are trying to damn David Mellor by innuendo and implication but they are going to fail,' he said. 'He is not going to resign. He is going to stay put.'[27]

Mellor survived, largely because the Prime Minister and Tory MPs did not consider his extra-marital affair a resigning matter. However, the tale then took a further twist. The following week, on 14 September, a libel court hearing produced more damaging publicity. Mona Bauwens, whose father was the chairman of the PLO finance committee, was suing the *People* for implying she was a 'social outcast and leper' in an article headlined 'Top Tory and his pal from the PLO'. During the hearings it emerged that the Mellor family had been the beneficiary of a $20,000 four-week holiday at her villa in Marbella, which had started on the day before Iraq invaded Kuwait. As the PLO was almost alone internationally in supporting Saddam Hussein's actions, the press unleashed another torrent of critical comment, accusing Mellor of being 'politically insensitive' and committing an 'enormous error of judgement'.

On 22 September the hold trial ended with a split jury. There were immediate calls for Mellor's resignation, largely because he had not declared the holiday in the Register of Members' Interests. The minister again took Bell's counsel. The following evening Bell accompanied Mellor to the studios of ITN and the BBC where he hoped to salvage his reputation. 'Undoubtedly I behaved foolishly,' Mellor acknowledged on *Newsnight*, 'and I have never made any secret of that – but I think that to a lot of people in this day and age it was not a resigning matter.' He also defended his acceptance of the free holiday as within ministerial guidelines. (Privately, however, Mellor had been concerned about its implications. 'What about my free holiday? How is that going to look?' he had asked Halloran and Bauwens at a meeting earlier that year.)

Echoing Bell's view, he declared, 'It cannot even be an argument for a cabinet member to lose his position because four or five editors decide that come hell or high water they are going to stick me on the front page with any kind of distortions they choose. That is really the question. Who decides who is to be a member of the British cabinet? The Prime Minister or the editor of the *Daily Mail*?'

Although Mellor had showed some humility, Tory backbenchers had lost patience and clamoured for his resignation. The next morning he had breakfast with Bell and Elliott Bernerd, the wealthy property developer who had lent Mellor his Mayfair flat, and told them he might still survive. But the political tide was turning. By mid-morning, after consulting Sir Marcus Fox, chairman of the 1922 Tory backbench committee, Mellor realised the game was up, rang the Prime Minister and offered to quit. This time his resignation was accepted.

Bell's reputation was severely damaged by this affair. He was mercilessly mocked by fellow PR operators and journalists. Jokes circulated that being rescued by Bell was tantamount to airlifting passengers from the *Titanic* and placing them on the *Hindenburg*. To his credit, he accepted some of the blame: 'Some of the things people have criticised were my ideas, some were not,' he said. 'To the extent that my objective in advising him was to help him keep his job, I failed.'[28]

Had Mellor made peace with his in-laws and adopted the Paddy Ashdown approach – admission, contrition and regret – the story would have been killed off. Cosy off-the-record telephone briefings had zero impact and blaming the press was a worse mistake. Their methods were dubious and, yes, there had been serious fabrications. But the story essentially was true. Mellor had an adulterous affair with Antonia de Sancha. There was little point in trying to deny it or to pretend that everyone was happy with the situation. By the time that the more serious allegations about Mona Bauwens' hospitality were aired, Mellor's reputation was in tatters. So, it was said, was Bell's judgement.

CLEANING UP THE WORLD'S FAVOURITE AIRLINE

Four months after David Mellor's resignation, Bell was parachuted into another crisis situation. This time he was asked to rescue an old friend: Lord King and British Airways. BA was under heavy attack by Virgin Airlines and the media for what they called 'dirty tricks', mainly hacking into the rival carrier's computerised reservations system and impersonating Virgin personnel to poach passengers. This had shattered BA's carefully nurtured image, created by Saatchi and Saatchi, as the 'world's favourite airline' and was inflicting considerable commercial damage.

At first BA loftily dismissed the allegations. But when the evidence mounted and Virgin sued for defamation and compensation, the issue spiralled out of control. In early December 1992, the BA board met to discuss their strategy. Lord King, Charles Price, the former US ambassador to the UK, and Sir Gordon White, Lord Hanson's business partner, argued forcefully that BA should fight the case and defend the corporation's reputation in the courts But it was a minority view and the board voted to apologise to Virgin in the High Court and pay them damages of £610,000, in the hope of ending the damaging publicity.

As David Burnside, then director of public affairs, strongly sided with the minority position, his position became untenable and he resigned. Sir Colin Marshall, the chief executive, and Lord King decided to recruit a replacement from the outside. King had always been keen on assertive PR and advertising: 'Companies that habitually treat the media with disdain are apt to learn too late that when the enemy is at the gates they need all the well-informed friends they can get,' he had once said.[29]

In early January 1993, Lowe Bell Communications was hired by the BA board to 'limit and correct' the harm done by the dirty tricks fiasco. The three-month contract was worth £90,000. 'We've been hired to handle everything to do with the relationship between Virgin and BA, not the firm's normal activities,' said Bell, who took personal charge of the account. 'BA does not have to explain itself to the media – employees, regulators and shareholders, yes, but not to the media. However, it does need to have a relationship with the media.'[30]

On 22 January, Bell met Lord King at BA's head office. As a first step towards repairing the corporate wreckage, he suggested that the chairman should issue a personal apology along the lines of, 'Sorry for the brouhaha'. No, insisted the lawyers. The word 'brouhaha' might trivialise the apology already given in court. King must sound penitent.[31]

Bell was briefed to reduce the temperature of the row and his preliminary analysis was that this would be a damage-limitation operation. BA should open a dialogue with Virgin, apologise to Richard Branson for the 'regrettable incidents' and not respond further to media allegations. That was the way to weather what was becoming almost a hurricane. Once cordial relations had been restored, BA could return to restoring its corporate reputation.

Unfortunately, this strategy had an inauspicious start when it was decided that Lord King should retire as executive chairman six months early. On 5 February 1993, he attended his final board meeting. But instead of a celebration of twelve years' devoted service to the airline, the occasion was a public-relations catastrophe and personal humiliation for King. For some reason he was allowed to conduct his press conference on the steps of Enserch House, BA's corporate HQ, where he was surrounded by a throng of journalists and camera crews. As the nation watched an exhausted King flounder and stutter while reporters bombarded him with questions, a half-smiling Tim Bell was clearly visible in the shadows standing behind him. Inevitably, the public agenda was the 'dirty tricks' row. 'If you want to make what is a very happy, proper occasion for the board into something else, then go ahead,' King snapped. An ITN reporter asked what was on everyone's mind. Was his early retirement related to the 'dirty tricks' affair? 'No, madam, no,' shouted the chairman furiously, jabbing his finger at the journalist. 'No, no, no.' Then Bell ushered him back into Enserch House. 'It was a total disaster,' said one former senior BA press officer.

For Bell to allow his client to be thrown to the wolves in such a fashion was clearly a major error, and he realised that the laid-back style of PR, which had so irritated Lord Hanson, was not sufficient. It was time for some spin-doctoring. Late on Saturday 13 February, Bell hit the phones when Chris Blackhurst of the *Independent on Sunday* was preparing a story on Lord King's new salary of £220,000 a year plus substantial perks as the honorary president of BA. 'Why didn't you call me?' he shouted. 'You seem to think it's open season on BA. It isn't. It stops with this story.'[32]

But it didn't. Journalists uncovered evidence that BA were still engaged in some of the dubious practices *after* their apology in the High Court. ITN had tracked down two travel agents who testified that they were still receiving unsolicited calls from BA staff seeking to switch Virgin passengers to BA flights. 'The BA representative always offers an upgrade to business class if I switch my tickets from Virgin to BA,' said Romel Manalo of British Imports Travel in California. 'When the BA callers realise I'm the agent not the customer, they get really embarrassed and slam the phone down . . . I'm totally baffled as to how BA can access the information about Virgin passengers that I put into my computer.'[33] A professor in Los Angeles also described on camera how BA had recently tried to poach him from Virgin, and Richard Branson weighed in, saying: 'I find it amazing that only a month after admitting it in court, they are at it again.'

This was damning material and, as ITN prepared to transmit their special report on 22 February, Bell decided to go on the offensive. Time was tight as Martyn Gregory, the producer who had pioneered most of the investigative work on the story, worked on the film in the ITN editing room with the reporter, Paul Davies. Suddenly Bell rang through and Gregory took the call. Bell was desperate for information: 'We have a right to know who the professor is,' he said. 'Otherwise how can we check whether this is true or not?' Gregory, knowing that Bell's likely motivation was to try to turn the professor, offered BA the opportunity to view the material before transmission. But he refused to divulge the name of his source. Bell became angry. 'Have you any idea how much corporate damage this report could do to BA?' he said. But Gregory stood his ground.

Then Paul Davies, an experienced award-winning reporter, received a call from Bell. 'He was very forthright and seemed to be under pressure to either stop or impede the story in some way,' recalled Davies. 'He said that I had earned a high reputation and it would be dented by this irresponsible story. He also suggested that Martyn [Gregory] was not an objective journalist on this story.'

Undeterred, BA's hired hand rang Dame Sue Tinson, an associate ITN editor, honoured by Mrs Thatcher and a well-known Conservative Party supporter. A few minutes later she appeared in the cutting room asking about the item. 'What is the basis for this story?' she enquired. After being told, she replied, 'Well, you've clearly got the evidence. Let's run with it.' Still Bell did not give up. In a flurry of calls from his car phone and home, he tried unsuccessfully to contact Stewart Purvis, ITN's editor-in-chief, in a final bid to stop the story being broadcast. His efforts were in vain and it was the lead item in that night's *News at Ten*.[34]

The next day Bell rang again and tried to admonish Gregory. 'You made a mistake in last night's story,' he said, with more than a hint of glee in his voice. 'Had you told me your sources we could have traded information. I could have told you that the BA board had issued a worldwide directive on 22 January to halt the poaching of Virgin passengers, so your story was out of date.' Gregory replied that his source had been approached by BA on 25 January, which made the story even worse because they were breaking their own rules. Later when BA was asked to produce the directive, they were unable to do so. Bell then told journalists that BA were going to sue ITN and *News at Ten* for libel but, after some initial threats, they did not proceed.

Bell's new aggressive PR approach had been motivated by the pressure exerted on him to deliver by BA but also because he knew that ITN broadcast to millions and the impact of a story was so great. His next opportunity came on 28 April 1993, when Gregory produced a *World In Action* investigation, which revealed new evidence about BA's covert commercial activities. Documents showed that Sir Colin Marshall, the chief executive, had personally authorised a payment to Kroll Associates, a firm of corporate private investigators, to investigate Air Europe, another rival airline to BA. The programme was backed up by an interview with Brian Basham, BA's former PR consultant, who had first-hand knowledge of their activities. BA declined *World In Action*'s invitation to be interviewed.

The next day a journalist rang Bell to ask about the programme. 'It was extremely one-sided,' he replied. 'They didn't start with a clean sheet of paper. I didn't like the reporters they were using. The evidence of Basham was fatuous. He is a fatuous person. We will ignore the programme. We won't sue them . . . BA is not interested in *World In Action*. It has delivered abuse time after time at many targets. You've just got to ignore it. Sir Colin [Marshall] will advise Alex Bernstein [chairman of Granada TV] of the inaccuracies.'

Bell may have appeared magisterially aloof but his colleagues at Lowe Bell were not quite as assured. When BBC television news prepared an item about the new allegations, its business correspondent, Peter Morgan, spent much of the day arguing and sparring with Terry Collis, the highly strung Lowe Bell executive in charge of the BA account. BA and Lowe Bell were now clearly exasperated that the story would not go away and leave them alone.

Partly because of the jostling with Lowe Bell, Morgan's piece missed the lunchtime bulletin but was shown on the *Six O'Clock News*. Within minutes Collis was on the phone and, according to Morgan, 'screamed abuse for close to five minutes' about the item. 'There was absolutely nothing new in this,' he shouted. 'It was outrageous that Sir Colin [Marshall] should be branded in this way and roped into the story. He had nothing to do with it.' When Morgan pointed out that Sir Colin's signature was on the BA payment document to Kroll Associates, Collis replied impatiently: 'You can't expect the chief executive to check every document that comes across his desk.'

The BBC journalist was shocked by Collis's hysterical tone. 'It was an extraordinary tirade. He was close to tears with fury,' he told me. 'I've never had a call like it, before or since, and I've dealt with a lot of PR people. It was without doubt the most hostile verbal assault in my career. It was just so unprofessional.'

But the Lowe Bell onslaught was not over. For the next two hours Morgan was frantically busy, re-cutting his story for the *Nine o'Clock News*. He received another telephone call. The person at the other end was angry, and without identifying himself clearly he shouted: 'It was the most despicable piece of journalism I have ever seen and my client will be taking legal action and what's more—'

Morgan interrupted, 'I don't know who you are, but I've been talking to a man called Collis and—'

'This is Terry Collis,' exploded the irate caller, so loudly that Morgan had to hold the phone away from his ear. Collis was nothing if not persistent: at 8.40 p.m., he telephoned the editor of the *Nine O'Clock News* and complained about the BA item. Suddenly, Morgan's report was dropped from the bulletin. BBC management later said that this last-minute decision was taken for 'purely editorial reasons'.

Journalists who have covered the BA v. Virgin affair, notably Martyn Gregory, argue that such 'negative PR' tactics had some impact: 'They have bullied the broadcasters into not covering the dirty-tricks story in as much depth and even at all, particularly at the BBC which, of course, was one of Bell's clients,' said Gregory.

Peter Morgan agrees: 'I think the Lowe Bell executives were under pressure to deliver and this filtered down the company. I believe they win clients by pitching that they are the premier A team and can deliver what other PR agencies cannot. So when the stakes are high and the media coverage is critical of their clients, they become much more aggressive and intimidatory.'

Apart from Lord King's impromptu press conference, Bell's crisis management plan for BA was much shrewder than the Mellor and Hanson operations. He successfully took the heat out of the story by a three-pronged strategy: first, he advised BA executives against granting interviews as they might try to defend their corner, which could result in damaging admissions and more stories in the press; second, he correctly identified and exploited the weak underbelly of the major broadcasting companies – its editorial management; third, he told journalists: 'You know this story is the subject of legal action.' This put them off the scent. What Bell declined to mention, however, was that the 'legal action' in question was an anti-trust suit in the USA. Consequently, no sub-judice or contempt issues were relevant to the British media. As Bell said in 1994: 'I've been economical with the truth, in the sense of not giving more information about a client than I need to.'[35]

Five months later, in September 1993, Bell and Virgin crossed swords again. This followed Branson's celebrated and much-reported lunch with Guy Snowden, chairman of GTech who own a large slice of Camelot. The topic of conversation was their rival bids for the lucrative national lottery franchise, and its controversial contents are now the subject of a hotly contested libel action.

After the lunch Branson received a phone call from Tim Bell. He was immediately suspicious and asked his press officer, Will Whitehorn, to bear witness by listening to the conversation on the speaker phone. Bell was to the point: he said he acted for GTech and was following up on the lunch. According to Branson and Whitehorn, Bell said that he had heard that the meeting had not gone well. 'Are you going to be saying anything about it?' asked Bell, who was clearly trying to pour cold water over a burning bush. But Branson was not impressed. 'What's the point?' he replied. 'I'm going to bid for the lottery.'

This account of the conversation was strongly disputed by Jem Miller, the Lowe Bell account director. He accepted that Bell had called Branson at Snowden's request. But the purpose of the call had been to inform Branson that his approach to GTech to join Snowden's non-profit-making consortium would be put to the Camelot board. This was rejected. The following year Camelot were awarded the lottery contract and Bell continues to act for GTech.

'I WANT THE BBC TO FAIL'

At the height of the controversy surrounding BA's attempts to limit the damage caused by the dirty-tricks allegations, a story broke that threatened to cause equally serious harm to another British institution: the BBC. On 7 March 1993, the *Independent on Sunday* revealed that John Birt, the Corporation's director-general since 1987, was paid through a private company and offset most of his personal expenditure against tax. This time Bell was not summoned. Lowe Bell Communications was already under contract to the BBC.

The relationship can be traced to the heady late summer of 1985. The BBC was fighting a propaganda war on several fronts – controversial programmes, alleged bias, the value for money of the licence fee and the apparent arrogance and remoteness of its management. Broadcasting was increasingly high profile and the Corporation showed little sign of promoting itself in a coherent way. Even worse was its relationship with the then occupant at 10 Downing Street. 'Mrs Thatcher was not really interested in Channel 4, she was more concerned with marginalising the BBC,' said Bell later.[36]

As a pre-emptive strike Alasdair Milne, then director-general, approached Bell, then at Lowe Howard-Spink, after being introduced to him by Antony Jay, co-author of *Yes Minister*. 'We were experiencing political flak of a big order following the *Real Lives* affair' [a documentary in which a Sinn Fein and a Loyalist supporter were both interviewed equally at length], recalled Milne. 'The future of the licence fee was also in dispute. Bell thought the Corporation ought to be privatised like anything else. He clearly had not thought it through.' The director-general had to explain to Bell that selling off the BBC was not like floating the electricity industry on the Stock Exchange because the BBC has no source of income.

Milne found Bell 'charming, aggressive, right wing and very confident'.[37] But the Prime Minister's media adviser was unimpressed by Milne's argument and said privately that the BBC's very existence was 'an anomaly' in an age of consumer choice and privatisation. During the *Real Lives* row he was seen in his office shouting, 'Fucking BBC terrorists,' at the newscaster reading the six o'clock news.[38]

Despite Bell's views, in September 1985 Lowe Howard-Spink was hired as the BBC's first-ever advertising agency. It was decided that this was the most effective way of communicating directly with licence payers that they were getting value for money. What was incredible about the appointment was that, barely four weeks before his agency was awarded the account, Bell had made his private views public. 'I want the BBC to fail,' he told *Media Week* magazine, 'because I don't want that system to work. It only works now because it has a monopoly.'[39]

Based on a budget of £500,000, Lowe Howard-Spink produced a highly successful advertising campaign. Frank Lowe had the inspired idea of hiring John Cleese. The former *Monty Python* star appeared leaning on the bar in a pub and saying to the barman, 'Do you know . . .' and describing the variety and excellence of BBC programmes. The advertisement was broadcast only on BBC2 and directed by Alan Parker, the director of *Midnight Express*, who made the commercial for a case of claret.

After this effective start, the agency was paid a retainer of £75,000 a year plus production costs. Some viewers were unclear about the purpose of the campaign, but Michael Grade, then managing director of BBC Television and a populist at heart, was a keen advocate.

After about eighteen months, the BBC believed that the campaign had served its purpose, but they retained Bell as a communications consultant with a wider brief for marketing the Corporation. In January 1987, his role was boosted with the appointment of Michael Checkland, a management accountant, as the new director-general. Checkland, like Bell, believed that the BBC should be run and promoted as a business. Four weeks later, all the senior management assembled for a private weekend seminar at Ettington Park country hotel, near Stratford-upon-Avon, to discuss future policy and direction. Bell also attended and delivered a strong attack on what he called the 'old guard'. The BBC's problems, he declared, were just like those of any other nationalised industry: it was 'producer driven'. The corporation needed to perceive the public not as viewers but as customers, and licence payers as shareholders. The Corporation needed to be marketed like any other company. That meant advertising and public relations which, Bell said, had transformed the perception of other public-sector institutions like British Rail where passengers were now called customers.[40]

Most of the executives applauded the sentiments of Bell's presentation. One of the few who rejected and resented his approach was Brian Wenham, managing director of radio, who thought corporate branding was 'essentially a confidence trick'. The BBC did not have an 'image problem' with the viewers, he argued. Its success depended on whether they liked the programmes. But he was in a minority. When Checkland rose to speak he expressed much the same views as Bell, calling the BBC 'a billion-pound business'. He talked as though he was a chief executive of a multinational corporation.[41]

It was, of course, just the type of language the Prime Minister wanted to hear. Seven months later, in September 1987, that political connection was cemented with the appointment of Howell James as director of corporate affairs on a salary of £60,000 a year, which strengthened Bell's power base immeasurably. James, who had been special adviser to Cabinet Minister Lord Young, was one of his closest friends. By this time Lowe Bell Communications was up and running and a new consultancy contract was negotiated with

James, worth £125,000 a year, for a full range of advice, including PR, internal advertising, political lobbying, marketing and on-air trailers of programmes. Everything except outside advertising.

Bell's strategy, outlined in periodic presentations to the board of management was to rebrand the BBC in a corporate image. He argued that the Corporation needed to be marketed in a different way – not just on television, but as a whole. 'We need to position the BBC as a brand-leader in the market-place and provide customer services,' he told executives. This involved spending more money on marketing, Bell said, at a two-day seminar in March 1988 at Lydiard Park. Checkland did not appear to be too sure as to what all this impressive language meant in real terms. 'I think what we are actually talking about is making sure that the consumers of our programmes know precisely what we are offering,' he said.[42]

Clearly, the most important campaign was to persuade the government to agree to the licence fee as recommended by the BBC. In the past the government had viewed the Corporation as a nationalised industry that should do pretty much as it was told. Bell argued that the BBC should influence the government and reposition itself in the broadcasting industry, that it could only survive and prosper if it conveyed the message that the BBC was well managed, had quality product and was value for money. Indeed, just like any other private company competing in the market-place. He himself came up with a new marketing slogan: 'The BBC – Broadcasting At Its Best'. He also suggested that the BBC stage a televisual version of a private sector annual general meeting. Entitled *See For Yourself*, this was to be a three-hour telethon designed to show that the Corporation was no longer run by the 'old guard', but was in the safe hands of modern media professionals with the wishes of the viewers at heart. It was to be presented by Stuart Young, the BBC chairman at the time the project was agreed.[43]

Another Lowe Bell idea was 'corporate hospitality'. This, of course, was nothing new to most other corporations, but it was to the BBC. It was part of a strategy to lobby MPs, ministers, civil servants, journalists, businessmen and anyone of influence. Drinks parties and receptions were to be organised by the BBC – not by Lowe Bell – and they would have hospitality tents or receptions at Wimbledon, Goodwood races and at Lords. Bell would advise on the mix of guests and who should or should not be invited.

In September 1992, Howell James left the BBC to rejoin Lord Young, who was now chairman of Cable and Wireless. His departure was a body blow for Bell. The new corporate affairs director, Pamela Taylor, was a tough, hard-working meritocrat, who for the previous five years had been director of public affairs at the British Medical Association. She disapproved of Bell and thought his work overrated and overpriced and one of her first tasks was to look at Lowe Bell's contract. It had recently been renegotiated by James but there was nothing in the file about the discussions. When she read the new deal she was stunned to see that there were no performance indicators or aims and objectives. She was also startled at the size of the fee. Lowe Bell was paid on a retainer basis every three months and when their first invoice came in Taylor thought it 'exorbitant' and 'more than I expected'. Their total annual fee amounted to some £350,000.

Taylor decided to renegotiate the contract with Bell, who agreed to the changes in aims and objectives. But they were never authorised and incorporated. A few days later Taylor was talking to Marmaduke Hussey, who had become BBC chairman. 'I understand you want to renegotiate the contract with Tim Bell,' he said, with a hint of warning. She was surprised by this remark as she had not told anyone. 'I'm sure you won't want to be involved in the details, chairman,' she replied. 'I'm sure you wouldn't want to know how much money we're paying them.' But Bell had clearly been talking to the top brass. John Birt, the director-general, also raised the question of the PR contract unprompted by Taylor. 'We must be very careful with people like Bell,' said Birt. 'He still has a lot of influence and it's better to have him on the inside than on the outside.' Taylor asked him for his thoughts on Bell's role but he changed the subject.

Taylor believes that Bell was kept on the payroll because of the combined 'fear and comfort factor'. With his inside knowledge of the BBC he could be dangerous if he left. If he stayed he provided reassurance with his political connections. But Taylor claims this rationale was a myth, and although Bell himself was always available and accessible to her, she believed Lowe Bell's performance did not warrant their fee. 'I did not value their advice and I inherited some staff who I felt were too cosy with them,' she reflected. 'I needed to know from my staff how much they used or depended on Lowe Bell . . . For the top management he [Bell] was like an insurance policy. I think the view was that he knew everyone, so if we buy him we get access to all his contacts, but for strategic advice, he was hopeless. There were a lot of meetings but very little was achieved.'

However, another former BBC public-affairs executive, Brian Clifford, disagrees. 'Lowe Bell were very useful,' he said. 'They gave the BBC a new confidence. We became more open and direct with the media and began to challenge accepted wisdoms. It was a huge confidence-booster.' Clifford recalls Bell concluding one of his presentations: '"Remember one thing," he told the gathering. "You're very good at what you do."' It was classic Bell, giving his client the feel-good factor.

Bell's critics in the BBC argue that much of his advice merely stated the obvious: the Corporation did not need to spend £350,000 a year of licence-payers' money to tell them what they already knew. But that missed the point about the well-connected consultant with any client. As Bell was an influential outsider with a powerful reputation and demonstrably close to the Prime Minister, the BBC governors took him seriously and treated his analysis as if it was profound.

In the midst of deciding what to do about Lowe Bell, Pamela Taylor's attention was diverted by a more serious problem. In March 1993, the disclosure about John Birt's tax avoidance device hit the news stands and there was pandemonium inside and outside the BBC. People took different views, but nobody disputed that the director-general's position was under threat.

Taylor was quickly aware of the gravity of the situation and one of her first decisions was to keep Bell out because she believed that his high profile would only increase the tension. 'This story is going to run,' she told him. 'I don't want you involved in any way. It would not be appropriate.'

Bell agreed. 'Sure, I understand,' he said.

Birt retained support among senior politicians and some media commentators but the reaction among many, if not most, BBC employees was of outrage and uproar. The director-general was already unpopular with a large number of them because of what they saw as his introduction of excessive bureaucracy and centralization of power. The revelation that he was not even committed to the Corporation as a member of staff made it even worse. Even some of the governors were shocked and disapproved.

Taylor realised that the real battle for public opinion was inside not outside the BBC, and suggested that Birt should address staff meetings and write internal letters. Some would walk out, she admitted, but at least he was confronting the issue directly and honestly. When she told Bell about her strategy, he agreed: 'Yeah, he should tell them to bugger off. Here's a chance to show them he's a real man.' Taylor laughed but privately she was horrified and thought his words crass and inappropriate. 'I don't know whether Tim Bell was trying to be helpful or not,' she recalled.

It then transpired that Birt had a long-standing lunch engagement with Bell. Knowing of Taylor's opposition to their consultant's involvement, the director-general mentioned it to her. 'I've got this lunch with Tim,' he told her. 'Do you think I should go?'

'Sure, why not? That's fine,' she replied.

By the end of the first week after the story broke, Taylor was anxious that no new revelations were published. She could then arrange for the board of management to support Birt publicly to counter the calls for his resignation. But her strategy was shattered by a call from Richard Brooks, then media editor of the *Observer*, who said: 'I understand Tim Bell is now on the case.'

Taylor denied it but was worried. Then Birt rang. 'I understand Bell's involved,' she said.

'That's not true, I can assure you,' he replied.

'Well, how come he's been talking to editors and trying to cut deals on your behalf?'

Birt sighed deeply. 'I know nothing about it,' he said.

But, that is exactly what Bell had been doing. Chris Blackhurst, the *Independent on Sunday* journalist who broke the tax story, had also heard that Bell was acting for Birt. On the morning of Saturday 13 March 1993, he telephoned Bell to ask him about his activities. At first Bell denied any involvement but when the reporter persisted, he admitted having been busy in the past forty-eight hours on Birt's behalf. 'You could say I've been marshalling support,' he said.[44]

Bell acknowledged that Birt may have been unwise to have remained on a freelance contract. But many journalists and media executives had a similar arrangement. 'What were people getting so excited about?' he asked Blackhurst rhetorically. Then came the spin. 'The real story', he continued, was the way Birt had been 'set up' by the BBC 'old guard'. They had lost the debate about Birt's policies and were using the tax affair as a way of toppling him.

Blackhurst was not impressed by this line and interrupted: 'Is there any chance of having a word with John Birt?' Bell offered a deal: if the *Independent on Sunday* agreed not to run another editorial calling for the director-general's resignation, he would get an interview. Otherwise, no dice. There was no point in Blackhurst's trying to contact the governors, he added, 'they had been put-under a three-line whip not to talk.'

At that point Bell was interrupted by another call. It was none other than David Mellor, who was taking a fervently pro-Birt line. After talking to him, Bell came back on the line. He warned Blackhurst that every Sunday newspaper, except the *Observer*, would be pro-John Birt tomorrow and opposed to his resignation.[45]

However, the *Independent on Sunday* still wanted an interview with Birt so Blackhurst transferred the call to his editor, Ian Jack, who had not yet written that week's editorial. Jack repeated the interview request to Bell. 'If you were to write a leader saying that Birt should stay as director-general, then an interview might be possible,' replied Bell. 'But if the leader said Birt should resign then there is no chance of an interview.'

Jack was shocked by these words, which he considered tantamount to blackmail: 'That kind of deal is not possible,' he replied. 'He (Bell) was very confident' Jack told me. 'It's possible he may have had success with that tactic before. It was a kind of "who dares wins" approach to PR. I have never had that kind of approach before, but that could be because we were a struggling liberal newspaper and outside the Savoy Grill power-lunch circuit during which such arrangements are made.'

Bell's prediction about the hardening of support for Birt in the Sunday papers proved accurate. But the press was also full of stories about Bell's role, which infuriated the BBC public-affairs office. 'This guy's doing his own publicity,' said one executive.

Taylor spoke to Bell. 'What do you think you're doing?' she asked.

'It doesn't look good, does it?' he replied, half ruefully, half apologetically.

'So why have you got involved?'

'Well, because John [Birt] asked me to,' he replied.

Taylor was angry because it was a diversion from her agenda. From her viewpoint, Bell's activities were disruptive and only prolonged the agony rather than providing a cure. She told him to get off the case but continued to receive calls from journalists about him. Her staff wanted to take action against Bell, but she decided against it.

Publicly, Bell denied acting for Birt. When Alastair Campbell, then a *Today* columnist and now press secretary to Tony Blair, attacked his rival for being 'associated with lost causes', Bell reacted with barely concealed anger. 'How riddled with envy you are,' he wrote to Campbell the next day. 'I bet you sleep badly. Not only that, but I told your reporter that I had not been called in to advise John Birt. So you can't even write the truth. Ho hum.'[46]

Eventually, Taylor's strategy paid off. As only the board of management and governors could dismiss Birt, she had focused her attention on keeping them informed. In her judgement, they were the crucial audience to be won over, not the newspapers. Although the atmosphere of crisis dragged on for several weeks as the governors procrastinated, Birt survived and so did Bell. But Pamela Taylor left the BBC later that year and the Lowe Bell contract never was fully renegotiated.

In April 1996, Tim Bell resigned the BBC account. Officially, the contract was not renewed because of a 'potential conflict of interests' between Lowe Bell's BBC consultancy and its work for BSkyB. This was a curious reason: although the BBC have an interest in digital and satellite broadcasting, it is long-term and far from committed. What's more, Lowe Bell have acted for BSkyB since September 1994. Even more pertinent is that Bell has faced almost permanent conflicts of interests: BBC producers at *Panorama* and *Newsnight* have been constantly working on stories about Lowe Bell clients such as Terry Venables (1994), the lottery company GTech (1995) and British Airways (1996). The programme-makers were often unaware that Bell also represented the BBC when they received hostile and abusive calls from Lowe Bell account executives enquiring about the stories.

On the other hand, Bell has made little secret of the fact that he never lets his personal views interfere with his work for clients. He often argues that, like a barrister, he can be objective about a particular case in hand and ignore other determining factors. Conflicts of interests can be resolved therefore by compartmentalising and 'Chinese walls'. The BBC consultancy was a classic example, given his past hostility to the Corporation.

OUT OF GAS

Some businessmen are brilliant at understanding their industry, but inept at marketing and promoting it. For six months, beginning in November 1994, Cedric Brown, the former chief executive of British Gas plc, was a case in point. When he was awarded a massive 75 per cent pay rise to take his salary to £475,000 a year plus substantial benefits, he faced a media and public onslaught of almost unprecedented intensity. His increase was announced at the same time as salary cuts for British Gas showroom staff, 25,000 redundancies, and a little later news came of the reduction of the pipeline safety budget. Brown was under seige and, despite his recent mixed record on crisis management, he turned to Tim Bell.

Nobody knows more about the gas industry than Cedric Brown. He started as a pupil distribution engineer in 1953 aged eighteen and worked his way up to chief executive in 1992. But he was a simpleton when it came to the PR and media responsibilities of his job. He was captivated by Bell's star status as one of Mrs Thatcher's Praetorian Guard and his flamboyant persona. Brown, from a modest background was a model and product of Thatcherism, and viewed his new adviser as a kindred spirit. Bell acted more as a confidant than a PR consultant: he coached and prepared Brown for his televised appearance before the Commons select committee on employment on executive pay. 'Cedric was impressed by Bell,' said a senior British Gas source, 'because he has that capacity to have the common touch at the highest levels. He has a real bedside-manner voice that is soothing in a crisis. Cedric lacked confidence and needed to be told by Bell that everything would be OK and he was doing fine. Like a lot of these guys, Cedric was also prone to flattery.' It was a set of circumstances that suited Bell perfectly.

On 21 December 1994, six weeks after the furore erupted, Bell gave a private presentation to most of the British Gas executive directors and some consultants. He addressed what he saw as a series of 'difficult events' and 'possible controversies' due in the first six months of 1995. Among the potentially explosive items on the agenda was more large pay increases for a select group of top executives, which would attract media and public criticism because more junior managers were to be forced to take fixed-term contracts, thereby losing job security. Then there was the proposal to contract out meter reading to Securicor and Group 4, the private security firms. Another controversial issue was the unannounced increase in service charges, due in April. Finally, British Gas was considering a 'possible withdrawal from demand servicing' of domestic appliances, forcing customers to look elsewhere except in an emergency.[47]

Bell argued that the company's problems were exacerbated by a hostile political environment: the public were uneasy about privatisation, 'corporate greed' and 'sleaze' in general. 'As little as four weeks ago', he said, 'British Gas was seen as a highly successful privatised industry, one of Britain's most admired companies, highly regarded for its services, prices and customer care.' But the pay scandal now meant it was perceived as 'greedy, uncaring, badly managed and incompetent. Today, British Gas is seen as not in control but out of control. And it's not going to go away.'

A key part of Bell's solution was 'to cut off the flow of further bad news' and 'seize the high ground'. This could be achieved by enlisting sympathetic 'right-wing journalists' to write articles about how 'British Gas champions privatisation and the free market against the politics of envy'. He also put forward what he called 'Project Turnaround', which would be run by a special news management unit called the No. 12 Committee.

Bell warned that the company's reputation was on the line. 'You must address it urgently with focus, commitment and resources,' he concluded.[48]

His analysis was greeted with a muted response from the board, who were still shell-shocked by media criticism. But Brown was enthusiastic and endorsed Bell's recommendations. Two weeks later in January 1995, his company's retainer was substantially increased to at least £30,000 a month. This was negotiated on a 'special project' basis, which meant dealing with the media and political fall-out of Brown's pay rise.

Of Bell's twenty initiatives and ideas only the No. 12 Committee – named after the whips' office at 12 Downing Street – was implemented. It was essentially a crisis forum, designed to anticipate, and devise contingencies for troublesome issues and avoid 'media elephant traps' before they went public. The committee met once a week. Bell rarely attended, usually sending his two senior consultants, Stephen Sherbourne and Jonathan Hill. When he did appear, he would indicate which editors he was close to and could speak to. He also referred to the latest comments by cabinet ministers, mentioning Michael Heseltine and Tim Eggar, the ministers responsible for the gas industry at that time. 'He impresses people with high-level political gossip from the top table,' said a committee member. 'Some of it is anecdotal, some of it indicates he's on good terms with ministers and editors.'

Bell had a dual function for British Gas. First he was a political middleman, an intermediary between his client and the government. Lowe Bell had originally been hired in early 1992 on a relatively small retainer – to broker regulatory agreements between British Gas and the energy department, whose secretary of state at the time was John Wakeham, and this political lobbying resulted in a closer, more co-operative relationship with government in a highly regulated industry. Second, Bell tried to create a more favourable media climate for his client, which proved less successful.

One problem was Bell's basic PR strategy, which was similar to his advice to Lord Hanson: don't talk to the media unless they're friends or 'one of us' or known to be trustworthy. The attacks on British Gas executive gluttony were often published and broadcast without a response from Brown, which made matters worse. The company stumbled from one crisis to another. For example, BBC's *Newsnight* invited Brown to appear, with various critics, to be interviewed by Jeremy Paxman. At first he agreed and was still keen during a dinner that evening. But then, for reasons that left his PR advisers mystified, he abruptly changed his mind. The inevitable result was that British Gas were slaughtered throughout the programme with no one there to defend them.

Despite the unrelenting media attacks, Bell's attitude was uncompromising and obstinate. 'His basic view was to carry on regardless, tell the critics, "You're all wrong"', and ride out the storm,' said a former British Gas executive. 'He was not good at listening or adjusting to the circumstances. There was not much lateral thinking going on. It was just, "Tell it to them straight." In the long-term, that did not help Cedric. It just gave the media a target to shoot at.'

Publicly, Bell adamantly defended the massive salary increases. He described the widespread criticism as 'a black cloud hanging over the business world' and tantamount to a 'public lynching'. 'The announcement of some of the recent pay rises for senior executives could have been handled better', he told a Coopers and Lybrands Awards meeting on 9 March 1995, 'but this is quite distinct from the issue of the actual amount of the pay rises and share options. On the whole, these were richly deserved, but the point is that it is nobody else's business – and most certainly not the government's. These are companies in the private sector and remuneration is a matter for the directors and share-holders . . . It should be the rate for the job, have real performance-related incentives and be transparent. Any government interference beyond this is a restriction on the free market. Restrictions on the market are socialism and should therefore be resisted tooth and nail. Socialism does not work . . . We are not having a serious debate. All we are hearing is a one-sided tirade from the Labour Party, and instead of counter-attacking, business leaders are presenting a landscape of pinstriped corporate bottoms, pointing towards the sky.'[49]

After the PR débâcle of Brown's pay rise, Rudolph Giordano, the equally well-remunerated chairman, was increasingly dissatisfied with Lowe Bell's work. But he was advised that Bell would be more dangerous outside British Gas. 'Don't kick him out of the tent,' he was told, 'he'll just piss back in'. However, their £30,000-a-month 'special project' contract was ended at the time of Brown's retirement in early 1996, and reduced to a small retainer for Lowe Bell Political. 'The work is no longer necessary,' said Bell.[50]

One of the advantages of being in crisis management and PR is that success or failure is generally unquantifiable and unidentifiable. If a client resigns or is sacked, the consultant may be blamed and if he or she succeeds then praise is often apportioned. But it is the perception of achievement that is most significant: the image-maker's reputation rests as much on myths and received wisdoms about the switches of fortune for which he is responsible as any verifiable triumphs.

So it was with Tim Bell. The publicity his activities generated created as many opportunities to secure new clients as any private hustling or orthodox pitching. Despite the demonstrable disasters like Hanson v. ICI and the David Mellor affair, and to a lesser extent British Airways and John Birt, Bell continued to be seen as 'Superflak' – the man who has seen and survived more disasters than any ambulance. But a dispassionate analysis of his record in crisis management indicates that his judgement was not astute. He was too prone to tell the patient that everything would be all right and to downplay the seriousness of the illness when the diagnosis stated otherwise. After all, he would say, you can trust me, I'm a spin-doctor.

Chapter Ten

A Remarkable Reunion

'I can fall into the sewer and come up smelling of roses'

Tim Bell

Helping beleaguered cabinet ministers, prominent industrialists and the BBC director-general enhanced Bell's reputation as a power-broker and spin-doctor. Whether he was successful and effective is, in one sense, irrelevant. The publicity about his role encouraged the perception that he was the man to hire if you were in a fix. Bell has often claimed that he does not welcome such press coverage, but he has never rejected or discouraged it.

For most of his career he was referred to as 'Mrs Thatcher's favourite adman' or 'the Prime Minister's media adviser', which infuriated the Saatchis but delighted Bell. 'I love being her PR guru,' he said.[1] The benefit of such an image was the acquisition of new clients, such as foreign governments, presidential candidates and international businessmen.

Lowe Bell, like most PR firms, have been hired for specific projects rather than to promote a country's image. It ranges from organising state visits, handling media relations and promoting inward investment to direct lobbying on trade issues and parliamentary intelligence work. 'From my experience and that of others, it is a growing market,' said Stephen Sherbourne, managing director of Lowe Bell Political. 'Appointments often come via the Prime Minister or foreign minister who has seen a slick operation and recognise that their embassy cannot provide the necessary service.'[2] This is tantamount to the privatisation of diplomacy. Such work has also involved raising the profile of a 'new' country: the fragmentation of the Eastern and Balkan blocs have resulted in Lowe Bell being hired by the ex-Soviet Republic of Kazakhstan to promote overseas trade, but also to raise the profile of Crown Prince Alexander, who in 1992 staked a claim to the throne of Yugoslavia.

Lobbying for foreign governments is highly lucrative and some agencies charge up to £500,000 for a six-month project. There are no figures to demonstrate the value of the market because, unlike the USA where political consultants are obliged to register any foreign government clients, there is no requirement to disclose such information. But the financial benefits are countered by the sensitivity and controversial nature of the work. Regimes that seek PR advice to gain political or diplomatic recognition are often those with unpopular and unsavoury reputations and poor human-rights records.

Bell's overseas clients are spread indiscriminately far and wide. European governments have included Romania and Norway. The Gulf and Middle East has been a particularly fruitful region, where the Abu Dhabi regime has been a long-standing client. In 1991, Lowe Bell Financial represented their ruling family after Bank of Credit and Commerce International (BCCI) was closed down for unprecedented fraud and embezzlement. Full-page advertisements in *The Times* and the *Daily Telegraph* attacked the Bank of England for removing the bank's licence without consulting the Abu Dhabi government, which owned 77 per cent of the shares. Other Arab clients have been Wafic Said, the Syrian-born financier who was a broker on the AI-Yamamah arms deal, and Dr Nasser Khalili, an Iranian Jew, who is a prominent and wealthy art dealer.

In the Far East Bell has been retained by the Sultan of Brunei and the Malaysian government. On 20 February 1994, he was right in the crossfire when the *Sunday Times* revealed that Dr Mahathir Mohamed, the Malaysian Prime Minister, and other politicians had been offered bribes by the British construction firm, Wimpey, through well-placed middlemen. The article did not state that any payments had been made or accepted but the disclosure infuriated Mahathir and his cabinet immediately declared a ban on any new contracts with UK companies, particularly involving government aid.

Bell had several commercial stakes in both camps. His company was the PR consultant for the Malaysian government in the UK and for Tan Sri Arumugam, who owned 70 per cent of GEC Malaysia and was a private adviser to Mahathir. He also represented GEC, P & O and Cable and Wireless, whose contracts with Malaysia were under threat from the embargo.

On the Sunday that the bribes story appeared, Bell telephoned Mahathir's private office to inform him about it and soon learned of the Prime Minister's fury. The next day he was again on the phone to Kuala Lumpur. In a classic Bell manoeuvre he suggested that the negative publicity could be offset by an advertising campaign in the British national newspapers. This was agreed and five days later, on 26 February, the full-page advertisements appeared under the headline 'We Are Proud To Work In Malaysia'. The text listed major British companies working in the country – several of whom were Lowe Bell clients – and declared that this had been done 'in order to put some perspective into the current debate'.[3] This tactic not only pleased both the Malaysians and the UK firms but also provided lucrative advertising business to News International whose newspaper, the *Sunday Times*, had first created the row. In a delicious ironic twist, News International's PR consultants were . . . Lowe Bell Communications. According to one of Bell's loyal lieutenants, Donna Cullen, the Malaysian affair sums up his job in microcosm. 'It shows how extraordinarily powerful the press is,' she said, 'but it also shows how Sir Tim turns that power around to help get his clients out of trouble.'[4]

* * *

In Europe, Turkey was one of Lowe Bell's most lucrative, and for some people, controversial clients. For several years Turkey had been keen to win membership of the European Community (EC) but had little idea of how PR works. Their approach was to hire the biggest name and throw money at the account. In 1989 Saatchi and Saatchi was known as the prestigious agency and so were recruited. Saatchi's conducted an energetic but not very fruitful campaign, and when their standing diminished, Turkey looked elsewhere.

In September 1992, after Bell and Peter Luff, a Tory MP and then a consultant to Good Relations, visited Turkey during the election, Lowe Bell was hired on a contract worth an estimated £250,000 a year to continue the lobbying campaign for EC membership, promoting Turkish culture and developing Anglo-Turkish relations.

However, the account seemed more advisory than promotional – lunches and introductions rather than actual PR. 'The great thing about these people is that they can introduce me to people like Mark Thatcher,' said Candemir Onhon, the laid-back Turkish ambassador to the UK. Bell delivered and Onhon and Mark Thatcher had lunch together in January 1993. The ambassador seemed pleased by this meeting.

Another service Lowe Bell provided for clients hoping to do business in Turkey was to compile 'contract reports', which amounted to thick documents proposing all kinds of events, notably business lunches and seminars. But in business terms little happened. One project in which Lowe Bell had a role was the production of a brochure in summer 1993 called *Turkey: Europe's Rising Star*. Yet even this was instigated in Istanbul, written by a journalist, David Tonge, and funded by private companies to the tune of £80,000.

After three years Turkey had made little progress towards EC membership and the contract was not renewed.

PROMOTING THE PRESIDENT

Advising Mrs Thatcher through three general elections has made Bell the equivalent of a political export: he has been a consultant to right-wing presidential candidates on four continents, in Malta, Ghana, Venezuela, Colombia, the United States (for Ronald Reagan in 1980), France (for Jacques Chirac in 1988) and Russia (for Boris Yeltsin in 1996). In 1995 Lowe Bell was also active in Sweden during the referendum about whether to join the European Community.

One of Bell's happier elections was advising F.W. De Klerk, leader of the South African National Party, in his bid to be president in 1994. It was a poignant moment for Bell as his father had been such a celebrity in the Republic and he himself had visited the country many times, to advise tycoons like Anton Rupert, owner of Rembrandt Tobacco. Now, though, he was at centre stage in the most important even of the country's troubled history. Sitting on the National Party platform at its annual conference, Bell and De Klerk received a standing ovation from the delegates.

However, it was a tricky assignment. De Klerk was an intelligent and respected figure who had had the courage to dismantle apartheid. But he had also served for many years in National Party governments, which had enslaved and disenfranchised the black people whose vote he was now seeking. Also he was a reserved personality outside his familiar surroundings and had a rather stilted manner. Lowe Bell primed him to be more informal on the campaign trail. This worked well and De Klerk became increasingly less the reformed Afrikaaner and more the born-again South African. 'All we are really urging the president to do is to reach out to the people,' said Michael Taylor, the Lowe Bell director in charge of the account. 'It's all about reaching the hearts and minds of the people.'[7]

Despite a promising start, the National Party media advisers tended to exaggerate the significance of their work. 'Bill Clinton's spin-doctors were doing Mandela, and Thatcher's lot were doing F.W. De Klerk,' said a source working on the campaign. 'They [Mandela's team] saw themselves as hard ball-players, but we put the wind up them. For instance, when the two men met on TV, Clinton's lot had primed Mandela to stick out his hand. They hoped De Klerk would hesitate and keep his hand by his side a fraction too long and there would be a picture taken of Mandela offering a hand that was refused. But we'd primed De Klerk, so he swiftly stuck his hand in Mandela's. The picture was an excellent image for our guy and was printed everywhere.'[8]

Whether such tactics made a significant difference is unclear but the National Party did better than expected, increasing their share of the vote from an estimated 16 per cent at the beginning of the campaign to 22 per cent, and De Klerk became deputy president. It reduced the ANC share of the vote, which had been a major aim of their strategy. Lowe Bell had promised that 'the NP is poised to spring a real surprise'.[9] It did not turn out that way, but Bell had reason to be cheerful about his South African venture.

Encouraged by this relative success, in 1995 Lowe Bell Africa opened in Cape Town, specialising in political lobbying and corporate and financial PR. One of their first clients was the government, who needed advice on their privatisation programme, and others included Gold Fields and South African Breweries.

*   *   *

By far Bell's most controversial foreign client was Hernan Buchi, who ran for President of Chile in December 1989. For four years Buchi had been finance minister for General Pinochet, the military dictator whose brutal, repressive regime had been widely reviled, and had worked in his administration for fifteen years. He was the chosen candidate of Pinochet's supporters in Chile's first election for almost twenty years.

As Mrs Thatcher had been revered by right-wing Chilean politicians and Pinochet, Bell was warmly welcomed into their camp. The account was handled by Bertie Way, the six-foot-seven Old Etonian director of new business at Lowe Bell and a former army officer. Despite having no political experience, he was despatched to Santiago to work in Buchi's HQ.

In many ways, Buchi was an unlikely heir to Pinochet. A forty-year-old technocrat, he preferred the bleak back-room to the limelight and adopted an informal style designed to attract the huge youth vote. However, as the campaign got under way, the polls showed that his support was derived from older voters, especially women, who feared change.[5]

Under Lowe Bell's advice, his campaign slogan was 'Buchi is different', but he always languished behind the favourite, Patricio Aylwin, head of a coalition that opposed the Pinochet regime. On polling day Buchi secured only 28 per cent of the vote, lagging behind Aylwin who became president with 54 per cent.

Bell was always sensitive about the Chile account. When asked by the *Observer*'s John Sweeney whether Buchi was effectively 'an accomplice to torture' because of his service in Pinochet's government, he replied, 'You've got to have a very twisted mind to want to smear somebody in that way.'

In fact, he had supported Pinochet's reluctant decision to hold a referendum on whether he should remain President. In late 1988 he had been at a dinner party at the house of Lady St Just, his next-door neighbour in Gerald Road, Belgravia. The other guests included the playwright Harold Pinter, the historian Lady Antonia Fraser and the author Gore Vidal. 'I made some harmless remark about how General Pinochet was introducing a bit more democracy now,' recalled Bell. 'Harold Pinter exploded. "Pinochet is a murderer." Gore Vidal rapped,' You know *nothing* about Chile. I know *everything* about Chile.' At which point I did a very wicked thing. I invented a person who I called "Jack Robinson" [the same fictitious character used at Saatchi's to plant misinformation in *Campaign*], the head of an American bank in Chile, and I made up lots of facts that this guy had told me about how the country really is. That really shut Gore Vidal up, I imagine because he doesn't actually know all that much about Chile. But after a while I decided to come clean and admitted I had invented "Jack Robinson", which sent Harold Pinter out of control. He was furious, really mad at me, and demanded I stand up at the dinner table and apologise to everyone, which I did. At this juncture Antonia Fraser went home saying she couldn't take me any more.'[6]

Bell had agonised privately over whether to take on the Chile account. Late one night he debated the issue with an old friend who had worked for him at both Saatchi's and Lowe Howard-Spink. His former colleague argued that it was morally indefensible to help to elect someone so closely associated with a regime that had indisputably tortured political opponents. Bell countered, as usual, that in a democracy everyone deserved to be represented and allowed to hire PR consultants – regardless of their background.

AUSTRALIA

Tim Bell's most unusual and least well-known overseas assignment was the development work he put in for Sydney's bid to stage the Olympic Games in 2000. This was a labour of love for Bell as he has had a lifelong passion for the country and its people. In London he was involved with 'Australians In The Media', which met for lunch in a private room at the White Tower restaurant in Percy Street three times a year. Other members included Christine Barker, former editor of *Campaign*, Bill Muirhead of Saatchi's, Amanda Platell, an executive at Mirror Group newspapers, and Bruce Gyngell, former chief executive of TV-am. After two years the Lowe Bell chairman lost his invitation because he 'talked too much'.

In Sydney, Bell was something of a celebrity in media circles, where his exploits for Mrs Thatcher were well publicised. In early 1992 he was hired to advise the Clemenger advertising agency on all their submissions to secure privatisation contracts. 'We'll send him the brief for his thoughts,' said Greg Daniel, its managing director, who had acted for the right-wing Liberal Party in Australian general election. 'If we're short-listed, we'll bring him out to Australia for the presentation. If we win a privatisation account, Tim will have a watching brief on how the programme is developed.'[10]

Ambitious Australian politicians visited him in London for advice, the most noticeable being John Hewson, the former Liberal Party leader, and Senator Bronwyn Bishop, who had aspirations for the leadership. After meeting Bell in mid-1992, Bishop adopted a distinctly Thatcherite style in both style and substance. For a time she was viewed as a strong contender, but 'her star then waned when she proved unable to either hold her tongue or a brief, but for quite a while she was taken very seriously,' said a Sydney-based PR consultant.

It was shortly after this that Bell was drawn into the controversial PR project that caused consternation among the higher echelons of the Australian Olympic movement. The director of the Sydney bid, the dynamic lawyer Rod McGeoch, decided that merely promoting the city was not sufficient to secure victory: he wanted to attack his chief rival, Beijing. But he was restrained by the rules. 'Bidding for an Olympic Games is a very discreet affair with all sorts of long-standing conventions,' recalled McGeoch. 'One of the strongest was that you did not publicly criticise your opponents. One had to subtly point out one's own strengths and leave it to others to conclude how well you shaped up compared to your rivals. Comparative advertising, in any of its forms, was just not on.'[11]

McGeoch wanted to expose China's human-rights record, its true political situation and Beijing's inadequacies as a venue. He and his communications consultant, Gabrielle Melville, devised a plan whereby an overseas-based PR firm would be hired to run a covert campaign against the Beijing bid: 'It was a sensitive issue of handling,' said McGeoch. 'We had to create a strategy which looked like it came from somewhere else and had nothing to do with us.'[12]

The plotters focused on a London-based firm because regard for the Chinese had been low in the UK since the Tiananmen Square massacre three years earlier. 'We needed PR experts to enhance our case in Europe and disrupt the Chinese bid,' McGeoch told me, from his office in Sydney.

The Sydney Olympic chief was introduced to Tim Bell by

Kim Santow, a former Australian Supreme Court judge who was the London partner of an Australian law firm called Freehill Hollingdale and Page. In late 1992 McGeoch flew to London for a meeting with Bell at the Dorchester Hotel and proposed the strategy. The Australian noticed that his prospective consultant had some background knowledge about the Olympics, particularly the Manchester bid, and expressed great interest. It was a friendly introductory meeting and McGeoch asked Bell not to inform Shandwick, the PR agency that handled the pro-Sydney account, about their discreet arrangement. Bell, or 'my private weapon' as McGeoch described him, agreed.

For the clandestine campaign to proceed, Lowe Bell needed to be briefed for McGeoch's requirements, and propose a budget and specific ideas. Gabrielle Melville then flew to London and worked in some secrecy at Lowe Bell's offices for a week. 'Covert was the operative word when I arrived in London,' Melville told me from Sydney. After two meetings, she and Bell had agreed a strategy. A human-rights group based in London would be funded to speak out about China issues. This would arrange a speakers' circuit, which would hold public meetings and generate its own publicity. The campaign would culminate in a book about China, to be entitled *The So-Called Suitable Candidate*, which would be published about a month before the final decision was made in Monte Carlo.

Ostensibly the book would be produced by the human-rights group, but the writing, publishing, media launch and distribution were to be arranged by Lowe Bell Communications. 'It was Tim's idea to publish the book', recalled Melville. 'I was amazed how easy he found it to pull together. In no time he was able to call on two publishers and a ghost-writer. The book was going to be an attack on China and the Beijing bid, but we could not appear to be racist so it had to be about the politics and economics of the country and needed to be written by someone who was British and of impeccable credibility. Tim was going to provide the introductions, and facilitate everything.'

Allied to this, there would be an international PR campaign. 'This was not discussed in great detail,' said Melville. 'I assumed he [Bell] meant the usual type of stuff – advertisements run by minority groups no one has ever heard of which carry outrageous messages designed to elicit media comment and public outcry, media stories of atrocities and stories on the politics of China.' The priority was subtlety and secrecy. 'If people felt there was a force out there trying to kick heads,' said McGeoch, 'it would be assumed that it was another bid city doing it and could have rebounded on us.'[18]

After Melville's week in London, she compiled a report and Bell remained committed to the project. In January 1993 he met McGeoch in Sydney and fees ranging between A$50,000 and A$500,000 were discussed for the total budget. At first, McGeoch tried to keep his proposed 'quiet campaign' hidden from the Sydney Olympic board as they 'might not want to know about it'. But then the committee pressurised him to develop a strategy against the China bid. He replied that a document had been prepared and that everything was in hand. Half an hour later a senior official telephoned on behalf of the Prime Minister of New South Wales. 'What is this paper all about?' he asked. 'Have you got a paper that's going to destroy the entire Australia–China relationship?'

'If you people don't want to know, don't ask,' replied McGeoch.[14]

The Australian Olympic Committee was nervous about using Lowe Bell in this way. 'Too risky,' one said. 'If it ever came out it would destroy the Sydney bid.' At a meeting to resolve the dispute, McGeoch argued that they had received A$15 million in corporate sponsorship, which was riding on their performance. 'If the companies knew about the plan, they would say: "Go on. Give it everything you've got. We want to win,"' he told them and added: 'Look out if we lose, because if there's one or two votes in it we'll all have to bear the responsibility of not doing everything we could.' But the board was unmoved and passed a resolution that prevented McGeoch hiring Lowe Bell and implementing the covert PR campaign. 'They argued we didn't need to do it because we were ahead in the polls and were going to win anyway,' recalled McGeoch. 'I was annoyed and angry because you have to play to win. I personally don't think we were doing anything unethical. We were just using all the weapons in our armoury. It is perfectly legitimate in commercial marketing to ensure the truth about everything is out there.'

As it happened, American human-rights groups and politicians then started to campaign actively against the Beijing bid, because of the atrocious Chinese human-rights record. This had a telling impact on the International Olympic Committee. In October 1993, after some heavy lobbying by Shandwick, Sydney was awarded the honour of hosting the Olympics in 2000. In a dramatic night in Monte Carlo, they won by just one vote.

COMMEMORATION NOT CELEBRATION

Six months later Tim Bell was embroiled in an event that was equally prestigious but caused more damage to his reputation than perhaps any other campaign. It concerned the arrangements to commemorate the fiftieth anniversary of D-Day, the allied invasion of Western Europe on 6 June 1944. During a two-month onslaught, some 37,000 British servicemen had died as wave after wave of troops landed on the beaches of Normandy to begin the liberation of Europe from the Nazis. Most veterans wanted a series of solemn, respectful events to honour their old comrades who had been gunned down in the service of their country.

However, when Iain Sproat, the ambitious heritage minister responsible for the D-Day anniversary, studied the Ministry of Defence (MoD) plans for the commemoration he had other ideas. A former PR adviser and consultant to the advertising agency D'Arcy Masius Benton and Bowles, he felt that more should be done to mobilise a civilian operation that would involve the whole country. Why not turn the events involving old soldiers into a series of parties and rallies that would draw the nation together in a euphoric mood of celebration?

The minister felt his own civil servants did not have the expertise to achieve this so, in January 1994, he welcomed bids from PR firms. Five applied and were, unusually, scrutinised by Sproat himself. On 24 January, Lowe Bell secured the account, because their quote of £62,500 (£50,000 fee plus £12,500 expenses) was lower than the others and they promised to deliver private corporate sponsorship to save the government further funding.

Two months later Lowe Bell delivered their proposals. Under the heading 'The Nation Gives Thanks', a circular was distributed to all local authorities listing fourteen initiatives to be undertaken by voluntary organisations, chambers of commerce, charities, the police, fire and ambulance services. They included Second World

War craft fairs or dances with 1940s-style music and dress; D-Day sandcastle competitions at seaside towns; sewing Second World War quilts or tapestries for display in local museums; encouraging school choirs to sing 1940s hit songs at old people's homes and hospitals; collecting wartime artefacts for veterans' descendants to open fifty years on; and encouraging schools to develop wartime themes for fairs and sports days.[15]

When John Major announced these ideas as a 'stunning' national programme of events, which also included street parties as suggested by the *Sun* and a 'fun day' at Hyde Park, there was uproar. The Royal British Legion, which represents 750,000 former servicemen but which had not been fully consulted, strongly objected to the 'light entertainment tone'. The Normandy Veterans Association denounced the proposals as 'trivial', and other former soldiers said that dignified silence, not raucous music, was the appropriate way to mark the occasion. Bell was not diplomatic in his response: 'Of course you're going to be able to find disaffected people and of course you're going to find people who think they should have been consulted,' he said. 'This is a commemoration of something extraordinary that resulted in a free world for the last fifty years. If somebody wants to go and mess the party up by moaning and groaning, that's their problem not mine.'[16]

His insensitive remarks made matters worse and the reference to 'party' seemed to emphasise that his strategy was about celebration rather than commemoration. And when Major referred to the D-Day 'celebrations' four times during his press launch, it was obvious that the government and Lowe Bell had misjudged the mood of the nation. Suddenly they were under fire from all sides – Tory and Labour MPs, the veterans' organisations and the press. Ministers hurriedly arranged meetings with the servicemen's groups to try to repair the damage, but it was too late: by the third week of April 1994, the public were expressing their fury. An NOP poll showed that 62 per cent of voters preferred 'solemn national ceremonies' to fireworks and entertainment on D-Day.

Perhaps for the first time Tim Bell was a household name, but for the wrong reasons. And he handled the flak remarkably badly. When told that the British Legion was unhappy, he replied brusquely: 'They have probably not been given enough tickets or something.'[17] That fanned the flames and servicemen wrote letters to newspapers attacking Bell for misreading the public attitude. Another new experience was that he received an almost universally critical press. Even in restaurants strangers were heard to comment, 'How's D-Day?' as he was led to his table.[18] Outside his office he was door-stepped by *Daily Mirror* journalists, asking if he was going to pay back the £62,500 fee. It was all rather embarrassing and undignified.

As D-Day approached even Dame Vera Lynn, the forces' sweetheart, threatened to boycott the event as the government was accused of turning D-Day into a circus. War widows expressed their distress: they did not want 'a dazzling day of entertainment' but a dignified remembrance. Eventually the message got through and the events for the momentous day were rearranged to accommodate the wishes of the veterans.

Later Bell said that his firm had been hired 'to interface with all the organisations involved and come up with ideas for "commemorating and celebrating"'.[19] But this was demonstrably not the case as the British Legion and others had not been properly and fully consulted.

D-Day was a disaster for Bell. Until then he had seemed to be the original Teflon Man – nothing sticks – despite his crisis-management failures. But this time the criticism stung. Although he kept cool under the pressure, it was a real blow to his reputation as the man who could judge and interpret the public mood. Interestingly, after the storm had blown over he gave his first-ever full-length newspaper interview. He must have thought he needed some decent PR.

Despite the D-Day débâcle, Lowe Bell Communications continued to prosper. Its holding company, the Chime Group, retained its position as the UK's second largest PR consultancy behind Shandwick, and between 1992 and 1994 its operating income grew by 13 per cent. In June 1993, Lord Carrington, the former foreign secretary and defence minister, joined the board of Chime, a month after serving for five years as chairman of Christie's International plc. He was also a director of the Telegraph plc. Other notable directors include Sir Ronald Grierson, vice-chairman of GEC between 1968 and 1991, Sir David Hannay, former head of the Foreign Office Energy Department and UK Permanent Representative at the United Nations from 1990 until 1994, and Julian Seymour, fomer director of corporate finance of Lowe Group plc and director of Margaret Thatcher's private office and her UK Foundation since 1991.

The heavyweight appointment of Carrington was seen by media analysts as preparation for the company to be floated on the Stock Exchange. This was a risky undertaking as the flotation of PR firms has not always been successful: the market views them as volatile commercial entities. But in June 1994 Chime went public, through the reverse takeover of Chartwell, a tiny portable lavatories and carpet tiles company based in Kent. The flotation went well and left Chime with a capitalisation of nearly £20 million and profits of £1.1 million. By early 1995 the company declared retaining 457 clients. Close to 50 per cent of its income comes from thirty-five clients that generates annual fees of more than £100,000 from each.

This left Bell a millionaire, although he had sold 45 per cent of his shares to repay debts dating back to the management buy-out of Lowe Bell Communications in 1989. Apart from his annual salary of £357,000, his 30 per cent shareholding netted him £1.6 million in cash. Financially, the 53-year-old PR doyen was set up for life, but even he could not have foreseen the next ironic and dramatic twist in his life.

AN UNLIKELY REUNION AND ELECTION '97

When Bell walked out of Charlotte Street in January 1985, his colleagues knew that he would be ostracised by the Brothers and during the 1987 general election campaign the rift between the Saatchis and Bell grew wider. Maurice, in particular, was furious with his former managing director and blamed him for the break-up of Saatchi's relationship with the Conservative Party. Feelings ran so high that by the end of the campaign a mutual hatred had been established. 'There was a period when we didn't speak to each other,' Bell later confirmed.[20]

It was not until 5 September 1989 that a form of reunion took place, when Bell and Charles Saatchi had breakfast together at the Mayfair Hotel just off Berkeley Square. It is unclear why and how this meeting came about. One account states that Charles felt uneasy about the way he had treated Bell at Saatchi's and that he had only realised the depth of Bell's resentment when he read Ivan Fallon's book on the agency.[21] This is highly unlikely, given Charles's unforgiving personality, but in any case the book was published a year before the reunion. A more feasible explanation is that the meeting took place when Saatchi's were in commercial trouble: they had just made 700 staff redundant and their share price only rallied because a US investment fund, Southeastern Asset Management, bought nearly 10 per cent of the agency's stock. From that moment the Brothers began to court Bell. Even Maurice swallowed his pride and twice asked his former colleague to rejoin the company as chief executive. The two rarely met socially but they saw each other at the Tory Party Conference in 1991. The early 1990s were a bleak period for the Saatchis, who were gradually losing control of the company. A group of shareholders, led by the American fund manager David Herro, were increasingly unhappy at what they saw as gross financial mismanagement, and watched with horror as the share price plunged. By late 1994 they wanted an executive purge – and that meant the departure of Maurice as chairman.

On 3 January 1995, Maurice resigned amid an atmosphere of acrimony and recrimination, and there were bitter exchanges between those loyal to the company and to the agency's co-founder. Bell immediately called Maurice and offered his help. He found him in angry mood. 'The level of rage is extraordinary,' said Bell at the time.[22] But the two suddenly became effusively complimentary about each other. 'First he built our business,' said Maurice. 'Then he built his own. Quite simply, nobody does it better.'[23] Bell repaid the tribute: 'This is a tragic and foolish move by the Saatchi board,' he said. 'The agency has now lost its key inspiration.'[24]

Bell was hired by the Brothers as their PR consultant to represent them in the fall-out and the setting up of their new agency. The advertising world was shocked. Even some former colleagues were amazed. 'Deep down perhaps Tim loved to have the Brothers needing him and wanting him,' said Paul Bainsfair, a former account executive from the old days. 'Perhaps coming to the rescue like that met some unfulfilled need he had.'[25] But to others it was not so surprising. 'Maurice was vulnerable,' said another colleague. 'He needed Tim and he certainly couldn't afford him to be an enemy.' It was business survival, no sentiment involved.

Bell threw himself into the account, firing on all cylinders. On 11 January 1995, Maurice announced the establishment of his new agency, M. and C. Saatchi. British Airways terminated their multi-million account with Saatchi and Saatchi and Mars and Dixons declared that they, too, were reviewing their business. It was now a major international story and Bell was receiving up to 120 calls a day from journalists all over the world. He proceeded to orchestrate a barrage of carefully timed disclosures about Saatchi and Saatchi, of clients defecting, key staff resigning and lawsuits brewing – both threatened and pursued.

Bell, amazingly, had become the voice of Maurice, co-ordinating all his public statements and updating him on the latest press calls. He even arranged for Maurice to be filmed by a TV camera, strolling through airports with his Louis Vuitton luggage. 'Once you've got something working, you've got to feed it,' he said, 'or journalists get bored and move on to something else. Given that Maurice was setting up a company, it wasn't that difficult.'[26]

Bell was always on hand to brief editors about the 'real story', how the noble Maurice had been usurped by the 'colourless beancounter', as he described Charles Scott, Saatchi's acting chairman.[27] This generated tremendous sympathy for his client, particularly in the advertising creative community. The inconvenient fact that, under Maurice Saatchi's stewardship, his company's share value had plunged by 94 per cent was rarely mentioned.

The old Saatchi and Saatchi, renamed Cordiant plc in March 1995, was stunned by Bell's media broadside. They tried to hit back, claiming that a co-ordinated campaign was being waged to destabilise their company, its employees and clients, but they were outmanoeuvred. By the end of that week their shares had dropped by 25 per cent.

Meanwhile, despite legal battles over the Saatchi name, M. and C. Saatchi was up and running. When asked on BBC Radio 4 if Maurice could repeat the success of his earlier agency, Bell replied: 'I think not only can you duplicate the success, I think you can improve on it because he's now twenty-five years older and wiser, got all that experience, plenty of money, probably the best network of contacts that anybody can think of and he probably won't make the mistakes, whatever they were, that he made in running the old Saatchi agency.'

The blanket media coverage generated by Bell contributed to the most successful start-up in the history of British advertising. In April 1995, the new agency secured the treasured British Airways account and within a year had billings of just over £100 million. Bell was retained as the new agency's PR consultant on an *ad hoc* basis. During its first birthday party on 19 June 1996, at the Saatchi art gallery in St John's Wood and later at Icenis, a nightclub in Shepherd's Market, he was there to gladhand the cabinet ministers present, notably John Major and Michael Howard, the home secretary.

Friends and former colleagues from the old days at Charlotte Street could hardly believe their ears when they heard Bell praising and promoting Maurice Saatchi. They recalled the bitter times of the early 1980s when Bell had been frozen out by the Brothers, his acrimonious departure, the declaration of war after the 1987 election, and how for several years they had sullenly refused to speak to each other. The events of early 1995 were a remarkable reunion. But as another general election approached, another old relationship would be revived.

Tim Bell's relationship with John Major's government in its early years was cool and semi-detached: he was too closely associated and identified with Mrs Thatcher's regime. However, after the 1992 general election victory, enough time had elapsed since Heseltine's bid for Bell's ideas to be received more readily. He also retained a direct line into 10 Downing Street, which he had cultivated for some time: since 1983 three of the five political secretaries to the Prime Minister have been directly connected to Bell or his company. Stephen Sherbourne, who held the position from 1983 until 1988, joined him as managing director of Lowe Bell Consultants. Jonathan Hill, Major's political secretary from 1992 until 1994, had spent two years with Bell from 1989 until 1991. When he left 10 Downing Street he returned to Lowe Bell as a senior consultant. His successor was Howell James, one of Bell's closest friends, who had worked at Lowe Howard-Spink in the mid-1980s. Working for the Prime Minister resulted in a massive pay cut for James: his previous job had been at Cable and Wireless on £160,000 a year but in 1996 he is only being paid £45,000.

Privately, Bell remained critical of Major's premiership. He complained to a colleague that the Conservative Party was not marketing itself to the public in mid-term and was spending too much time complaining about the media. But he remained anxious to be part of the Prime Minister's inner circle. In May 1993, after some disastrous local elections, Bell and Sherbourne wrote a rare article, headlined 'Thatcher's Men On How Major Can Succeed'. Published in the *Daily Express*, it complimented the Prime Minister as 'a good and decent man' with 'considerable charm . . . Above all, he understands the dangers of the arrogance of power.' They attacked Sir Bernard Ingham: 'He [Major] is right to ignore previous press secretaries and over-ambitious or discontented MPs who have their own hidden agendas.'[28] But Major's Tory Party was praised for having the 'right principles and philosophy and first-class policies'. They concluded by brazenly plugging their own clients: 'Without Conservative governments, there would be no great British companies like British Airways, P&O, GEC, Hanson, NFC, Cable and Wireless.'

Despite Lady Thatcher's repeated criticism of her successor's government, Bell gradually worked his way into John Major's favour. Bell would never be as close to him as he had been to Mrs Thatcher, but he could not bear to be outside the political loop. In late June 1995, John Redwood challenged Major for the Conservative Party leadership. It was a delicate situation for Bell: Lady Thatcher praised Redwood's candidature, without fully endorsing it, but her former media adviser offered his services to the Primer Minister. And when Howell James was absent during the weeks of the leadership campaign, Lowe Bell executive Jonathan Hill returned to 10 Downing Street. Bell immersed himself in the campaign. 'This whole [political] debate is taking place in the media and none of you have any votes,' he berated one political journalist.[29]

After Major's re-election as leader, the Tories set their minds to the 1997 general election. As Tony Blair has moved Labour so far to the right, there is now very little difference between the two major parties. The campaign will concentrate on which sets of politicians can better manage the economy and government. In these circumstances, perception is everything: presentation and marketing will be a crucial factor in determining which side wins. This was recognised in December 1995 when M. and C. Saatchi were hired as the Conservatives' advertising agency. The commission was agreed only after a debt of £600,000 owed to the old Saatchi and Saatchi by Central Office and arising from the 1992 election, had been settled. 'Tory supporters', including Maurice Saatchi, were reported to have paid it off.[30] The remarkable reunion between Bell, Central Office and Maurice Saatchi was complete soon afterwards. 'He [Bell] had been talking to people in the party,' a former senior Tory official told me. 'He was desperately keen to get involved in the arrangements for the election campaign and persuade the Party that he was just what they needed.' Informal meetings took place between Michael Trend, the party's deputy chairman, and Hugh Colver, then director of communications, to discuss a role for Bell.

Eventually, he was installed as a member of a communications troika comprising himself, Maurice Saatchi and Peter Gummer, chairman of Shandwick. Dubbed 'Faith, Hope and Charity' by Party officials, the three had regular meetings at Central Office with the party chairman, Brian Mawhinney, and Bell and Gummer also met for monthly breakfast meetings at the Connaught Hotel in Mayfair. They agreed that the attacks on Blair as the smiling face of old Labour and portraying him as a hidden radical had backfired badly. Also there was little point in referring back to the last Labour government and the Winter of Discontent of 1978–9 when many of the first-time voters for the 1997 election had not even been born, let alone remembered it. Instead, Tory fire needed to be redirected on the threat posed by 'New Labour', and on promoting the government's achievements. This strategy was written up by Maurice Saatchi and, in January 1996, presented by the troika to Mawhinney. It signalled that they will effectively be running the party's overall communications strategy in the next general election.

It was a poignant return to the old days: Bell was now responsible for selling M. and C. Saatchi's advertisements to the party, media and public. The old gang was back in town.

Despite the party's overdraft of £11 million in 1995, nearly £10 million was suddenly available for the pre-election campaign in 1996–7. Their first broadside was fired on 14 May 1996, when Bell promoted a series of nationwide posters under the slogan of 'Yes It Hurt. Yes It Worked', at a cost of between £500,000 and £750,000. It was a veiled revival of the Thatcherite 'no pain, no gain' theme, combined with positive messages about the economy. The smaller print on the posters claimed that 26 million people have had income tax reductions and that Britain has the lowest unemployment of any major European country. But it was a risky strategy and tended to remind people that Conservative policies had been painful and unpopular. 'I think it is a bit apologist,' said Alfredo Marcantonio, vice-chairman of Abbot Mead Vickers, who had worked closely with Bell at Lowe Howard-Spink. 'It is rather like saying at least Mussolini got the trains to run on time.'[31]

Bell's advocacy of positive advertising was well received by John Major, who liked to bounce his own ideas off the veteran PR guru usually on the telephone. But the next instalment was a full-frontal negative attack on Labour. At 6 p.m. on 25 June 1996, Bell, Maurice Saatchi and Peter Gummer had a meeting with the Prime Minister at 10 Downing Street to show him the proposed new advertisements. Saatchi unveiled the slogan, 'New Labour, New Danger', above a pair of sinister dark eyes staring out between parted red curtains. It had been devised after private research showed that voters recognised that Labour had changed under Tony Blair's leadership. Bell was closely involved in deciding what became the Tory election theme, and a few days later gave a joint presentation with Maurice Saatchi to the full cabinet. Major approved the new strategy.

A week later the advertisements were launched, and on 10 July 1996, Bell was in Central Office to view the party political broadcast using the same catchphrase. The following month, the theme was intensified and personalised with an M. and C. Saatchi advertisement featuring a pair of red, demonic, almost satanic eyes superimposed on a photograph of Tony Blair, under the same slogan. This caused controversy and condemnation across the political spectrum. Within days of its release the Advertising Standards Authority ruled that it depicted Blair as 'sinister and dishonest', and asked for the advertisement to be withdrawn.

INSIDE THE ESTABLISHMENT TENT

Tim Bell's public reputation rests almost entirely on his record as the man who sold Mrs Thatcher to the nation and helped to keep her in office. He has argued that Saatchi's advertising played a crucial role and has made grand statements in defence of his profession. 'People in advertising are the bastions of democracy,' he said in 1986. 'We want to give people more information, not starve them of it. We are the ones who want an open society where issues are debated publicly, not one where secret deals are done behind closed doors. It is quite bizarre that we are the ones who are thought, by a vociferous minority, to be in the business of peddling lies when, in fact, advertising offers less distortion than newspaper articles, TV programmes or any other form of communication.'[32]

It can be troublesome to evaluate objectively the impact of political advertising on voting behaviour. Its critics, like Sir Bernard Ingham, argue that its power has been exaggerated. 'The influence of Saatchi's advertising was marginal at best,' Sir Bernard told me. 'What is important at election times are the mood of the times, policies and personalities. The presentation of those policies can help but it has been greatly exaggerated. I can understand why she took political communications seriously because she was in the business of winning elections, but I could never detect what influence her outside advisers ever had. I sometimes think their own PR was better than the PR advice they administered.' Lord Lawson, chancellor of the exchequer from 1983 to 1989, goes further. He has argued that the electorate have already made up their minds by the time a campaign starts.[33] It follows, therefore, that advertising is a colossal waste of time, effort and money.

My analysis is that advertising's effect has been exaggerated but cannot be discounted. It can, and has, set the media agenda simply by the way in which politicians have reacted to specific posters and broadcasts. Advertising can help to rally the party faithful by reminding them why they are supporting a particular political party. Finally, specific ads have focused and exposed opposition weaknesses. There is little doubt that 'Labour Isn't Working' had real impact in the run-up to the 1979 election. This was not due to the power of the slogan, but because at that time the electorate were susceptible to short-term influences. They were less committed to traditional allegiances and more likely to switch their vote.

In 1979 Bell was convinced that advertising shifted voting patterns. 'The cinema advertising we did was aimed directly at young people who were first-time voters,' he said, seven months after the campaign. 'I think that was the first time a political party had made a direct communication to first-time voters, and it appears from the numbers published in the newspapers that the young vote for the Conservatives was higher than it had been in previous elections.'[34] Sir Larry Lamb, editor of the *Sun* during that campaign, cautiously agreed that media coverage had a decisive impact. 'I think it is too easy for those of us in the newspaper business to exaggerate our effect upon the way people are thinking,' he said. 'Having said that, we all know that general elections are decided upon swings of 1.5 per cent and in 1979 the 1.5 per cent who mattered most were probably *Sun* readers. We had to shift a big chunk of working-class voters . . . and we perhaps moved some of the people who were capable of being moved.'[35]

Bell now takes a more sanguine view, arguing that advertising does not make the difference between success and failure but is a contributory factor. It can enhance, enforce and emphasise a party's position on a particular issue. 'As I look back on the campaign ads I have worked on,' he reflected, 'I do not think we changed anything. All we could do was reinforce a mood.'[36] Instead, he believes that television has the real power to change people's minds.

What is exaggerated is the visual detail of image-making – the stunts, symbols, physical appearance, voices and photo opportunities. Practitioners of this art and politicians take it seriously. Sir Edward Heath, for instance, believed that Harold Macmillan's spinning of the globe during a party political broadcast swung the election in 1959. Peter Mandelson, the closest Labour has to a left-wing Tim Bell, claims that the red rose was one of the most influential factors in the party's 1987 election strategy. 'Without overstating the case,' he said, 'it created a unique harmony and cohesion.'[37]

After Labour lost the election by 101 seats, Norman Tebbit reacted characteristically: 'The voters can smell a dead rat, even if it's wrapped in red roses.'[38]

Sir Larry Lamb, editor of the *Sun* from 1969 until 1981 and the *Daily Express* from 1983 until 1986, was equally dismissive. 'I think it was all absolutely splendid advice,' he said of the work by his friend Sir Gordon Reece for Mrs Thatcher. 'I am sure the Prime Minister benefited as a result. But I don't think in the end it mattered a damn.'[39]

As far as Mrs Thatcher was concerned, Bell was as much a friend as an adviser and that was why he secured such access to her and wielded such influence. He understood that, deep down, behind the stern demeanour, she was as insecure and vulnerable as the rest of humanity. Once he had reassured her, it was easier to persuade her about the importance of selling her message. For Mrs Thatcher was always a true believer in specialist political communications. For her it really was like selling cornflakes or soap. If you have a product, you need to ensure that the customers know about it, she would often say. That means marketing. If she was the chief executive of Thatcherism plc, then Bell was her sales director.

Unlike many advertising executives, PR consultants and prime ministerial aides, Bell lived and breathed the political message he was trying to sell. He was never detached. He was a believer, and part of that faith was in what Mrs Thatcher called 'Victorian values'. To Bell that meant charity and voluntary work, which did not necessarily exclude the self-interest feature so integral to Thatcherism. 'We live in a capitalist society,' said Bell. 'Capitalism is founded in the pursuit of self-interest. The Victorian philanthropist gave to charity because he made a lot of money, and he felt he ought to put something back. The modern philanthropist does it because it makes it easier for him to earn more.'[40]

Inspired by his wife Virginia, Bell has been actively involved in a number of charities, notably as a director and fund-raiser for Comic Relief and chairman of Charity Projects, an umbrella group for many voluntary groups. He has also donated large sums to Charity Projects. 'They needed £50,000 and I had it, so I gave it,' he told *Harpers and Queen*.[41] For Bell, charity is good for business and a crucial ingredient of Thatcherism. 'It is no good standing around wringing our hands saying that the government, the council or somebody else should do something,' he told a conference on voluntary work in 1994. 'If we care about something then it is up to us to do something about it . . . I firmly believe that if the government were to take funds it spends away from its own agencies and give it to the small voluntary sector, then that money would be better and more imaginatively spent.'[42]

Sir Tim Bell has come a long way from the comfortable if nondescript blandness of Barnet suburbia in the late 1950s. His life is not a romantic rags-to-riches story but he has achieved his reputation through his own efforts.

Bell's life has been about an outsider always with something to prove, and with a constant desire for recognition, respect, love and status. That has been his motivation. He sought to gain membership of the Club by building his own new Establishment from the outside. Instead of trying to infiltrate the grandees, he set up his own iconoclastic and convention-breaking clubs. In advertising it was Saatchi and Saatchi, in politics it was Margaret Thatcher and in public relations it was Lowe Bell Communications. All three played by different rules and introduced new ways of doing things. And Bell, who has always been a very clubbable person, was in the right place at the right time to take advantage of such phenomena.

However, he was not always the founder or head of the Club: his focus instead has been to please the leader, whether Charles Saatchi or Margaret Thatcher. Many of his friends have argued that when Bell was working for Saatchi and Saatchi and the Prime Minister he was at his best. He preferred to serve a mentor and be directed, acting as a broker, mediating between warring parties. He was happiest in a room in a semi-informal setting with a small number of people, selling a Charles Saatchi advertisement or an idea to the Prime Minister. That was when he was most successful. Being one of life's eternal optimists, he was so much more adept at selling a positive product or message than dealing with a negative crisis. After leaving Saatchi's and Mrs Thatcher's departure from Downing Street, he has done less well. As his own boss Bell's strategic judgement has been shown to be defective – witness David Mellor, D-Day and many of the disaster zone accounts.

Tim Bell will be remembered as the salesman of Thatcherism and a great advertising account man. The first fifty-five years of his life have been lived as if every day was his last. For most people, having a knighthood, being a millionaire, chairman of their own company, confidant to prime ministers, celebrities and tycoons, and a secure, happy family life would be enough. Somehow I think Tim Bell will be looking for more. He never could resist picking up that telephone.

Appendix

CLIENTS OF LOWE
BELL COMMUNICATIONS:

In 1995 Lowe Bell Communications declared a total of 457 clients, either on a retainer or *ad hoc* basis. The company has never published its full client list, only a selected version. The following 180 accounts are based on published sources:

Energy and Privatised Utilities

Atomic Energy Authority (AEA) Technology
British Gas plc
East Midlands Electricity
National Power
Railtrack
Thames Water
United Utilities
Water Services Association

Finance, Banking and Insurance

Bank of Ireland
Bank of Scotland
BP Investments
Bradford and Bingley Building Society
Brewin Dolphin Holdings
CAPITA

Cater Allen Holdings plc
Citicorp
Coopers and Lybrand
CVC Capital Partners
The Exchange
Fairbairn Investment Trust
Fidelity
Robert Fleming
Framlington Unit Management
Friends Provident
General Accident
Henderson Administration
Henry Ansbacher
HSBC Holdings
IMRO
Investcorp
KPMG
Mercury Asset Management
Merrill Lynch
Morgan Grenfell
Mortgage Operation
Murray Johnstone
NPI Ltd
Pinsent Curtis
Provident Financial
Prudential
Record Treasury Management
Royal Life International
Salomon Brothers
Scottish Investment Trust
Standard Chartered Bank
Standard Life
Sun Life
SBC Warburg
Threadneedle Asset Management

Food and Drink

Asda
Bulmer (H.P.) Holdings
Burn Stewart Distillers
Coca Cola
Grand Metropolitan
Highland Distilleries
Nutrasweet
Pet City Holdings plc

Remy Cointreau
Schweppes
Scottish and Newcastle
Seagram UK
Searle Consumer Products
Tate and Lyle
Tesco
Whitbread
Wrigleys

Foreign Governments

Abu Dhabi
Malaysia
Norway
Sultan of Brunei
Turkey (1993–5)
Zimbabwe

Industrial and Marketing

ADT
Allied Colloids
Alusuisse-Lonza
Alvis plc
British Aggregate Construction Materials Industries
BPB Industries
BSG International
Braun UK
Cable and Wireless
Caledonian Paper
Caradon-Everest
Cookson Group
Daimler Benz
Deutsche Aerospace
English China Clays
Finlay (James) plc
GEC
GTE Corporation
Gold Mines of Sardinia
Gradus Group plc
Hanson
Honda
IBM
International Business Communications
Linx Printing Technologies

Lynton Group
Michelin
Millennium Chemicals
NFC (until 1995)
Newman Tonks
Pace Micro Technology
Pentland
Philips Electronics
Richemont
Robert Bosch
Securicor
Simon Engineering
Sinclair (William) Holdings plc
Smiths Industries
Stoves plc
Vardy (Reg) plc
Volkswagon
Westland

Law Firms and Professional and Trade Bodies

Chamber of Shipping
Freshfields
Linklaters and Paines
National Union of Teachers
Newspapers Publishers Association
Union of Communication Workers

Luxury Goods

Asprey
Baume and Mercier
Cartier
Dunhill
Harrods
Karl Largerfeld
Pittards plc
Scholl
Theo Fennel
Vendome

Media and Publishing

Bell Cablemedia
BBC (until 1996)

British Sky Broadcasting
Carlton Communications
Classic FM
Clinton Cards plc
Copyright Promotions
The European
Golden Rose Communications
HarperCollins
M. and C. Saatchi
John Menzies
News International
Scottish Television
West Country Television

Property

British Land
Canary Wharf
Chelsfield
DTZ Debenham Thorpe
Healey and Baker
Primary Health Properties
Sharpe and Fisher plc

Public Sector

British Rail
Department of Energy
Department of Health
Department of National Heritage
London Docklands Development Corporation
Milk Marketing Board
Royal Mint
Welsh Development Agency (until 1995)

South Africa

BOE NatWest
Gold Fields
South African Breweries
South African Ministry for Public Enterprises
Thyssen Rheinstahl

Travel and Leisure

All England Lawn Tennis Club
British Airports Authority plc
British Airways
Docklands Light Railway
GTech Corporation
Hilton International
Ladbroke
London Clubs International
Northern Leisure
P & O
The Player Club
Rank Organisation
Really Useful Group
Savoy Hotel
Science Museum
SEGA
South Bank Centre
Stagecoach
Wilmington Group

Charities

Queen Elizabeth Foundation
Salvation Army
Save the Children

PRIMARY SOURCES

Public Relations Consultants Association Yearbook, Lowe Bell Communications brochures, and *The Hambro Company Guide* for 1996

Notes and References

Full publishing or programming details of books and television documentaries are given at the first reference only. Subsequent references include, as appropriate, short titles, broadcasting authority and page number.

CHAPTER ONE

1 *Class Rule*, BBC1, interview with Michael Cockerell, 17 December 1991.
2 *Financial Times*, 16 July 1988. Quoted in Judy Bevan and John Jay, *The New Tycoons* (London: Simon and Schuster, 1988), pp. 11–12.
3 *George* magazine, Washington D.C., February / March 1996.
4 *The New Tycoons*, pp. 11–12.
5 *Sydney Morning Herald*, weekend supplement, 20 July 1985.
6 'Voices on the Radio', article from the South African Broadcasting Corporation archives, 1951.
7 *Independent*, 24 May 1994.
8 *Milady*, South African magazine, December 1954.
9 Ibid.
10 *Harpers and Queen*, April 1989.
11 *Independent*, 24 May 1994.
12 *Harpers and Queen*, April 1989.
13 *Marylebone Record*, 31 March 1961.
14 *Harpers and Queen*, April 1989.
15 *Marylebone Mercury*, 2 June 1961.
16 *Marylebone Mercury*, 13 April 1962.
17 Ernest Jenkins, *Elizabethan Headmaster, 1930–61* (London: The Old Elizabethans Association, 1972), p. 170.

18 Ibid., p. 170 and p. 186.
19 Ibid., p. 180.
20 *The Elizabethan*, school magazine, December 1958.
21 Ibid., December 1959.
22 *Sunday Express*, 8 September 1991.
23 *Harpers and Queen*, April 1989.
24 *Sydney Morning Herald*, 20 July 1985.
25 *Harpers and Queen*, April 1989.
26 *Sydney Morning Herald*, 20 July 1985.
27 Jeremy Paxman, *Friends in High Places – Who Runs Britain?* (London: Michael Joseph, 1990), p. 183.
28 Ivan Fallon, *The Brothers – The Rise and Rise of Saatchi and Saatchi* (London: Hutchinson, 1988), p. 125.
29 Ibid.
30 *Class Rule*, BBC1.
31 *Independent*, 24 May 1994.
32 *Barnet Free Press*, 8 June 1965.

CHAPTER TWO

1 Fallon, *The Brothers*, p. 17.
2 Ibid., pp. 24–25.
3 Ibid., p. 38.
4 Ibid., p. 54.
5 Ibid., p. 55.
6 Ibid., p. 57.
7 Ibid., p. 61.
8 Ibid., p. 61.
9 Ibid., p. 72.
10 Ibid., p. 76.
11 Ibid., p. 78.
12 *Campaign*, 5 January 1996.
13 *The Pushers*, interview with Peter York, BBC2, 20 January 1996.
14 *Independent*, 24 May 1994.
15 *Harpers and Queen*, April 1989.
16 *Vogue*, June 1996.
17 Fallon, *The Brothers*, p. 110.
18 Alison Fendley, *Commercial Break – The Inside Story of Saatchi and Saatchi* (London: Hamish Hamilton, 1995), pp. 67–8.
19 Ibid., p. 37.
20 *Sunday Express*, 8 September 1991.
21 Fallon, *The Brothers*, p. 162.
22 *Vogue*, June 1996.

23 Fendley, *Commercial Break, p. 119.*
24 *The Pushers.*
25 *Sunday Express,* 8 September 1991.
26 Fallon, *The Brothers,* p. 131.
27 Winston Fletcher, *Creative People – How to Manage Them and Maximise Their Creativity* (London: Hutchinson Business Books, 1989), pp. 32 and 126.
28 *Campaign,* 28 April 1979.
29 Ibid.
30 *Independent,* 24 May 1994.
31 Interview with Virginia Bell, *New Idea,* Australian magazine, 29 November 1989.

CHAPTER THREE

1 Margaret Scammell, *Designer Politics – How Elections Are Won* (London: Macmillan, 1995), p. 68.
2 *Observer,* 12 June 1983.
3 *Daily Mirror,* 20 April 1979.
4 *Observer,* 12 June 1983.
5 Margaret Thatcher, *The Path To Power,* (London: HarperCollins, 1995), p. 294.
6 *Daily Telegraph,* 3 October 1975.
7 Ibid.
8 Michael Cockerell, *Live From No.10* (London: Faber and Faber, 1988), p. 213.
9 Ibid., p. 220.
10 Ibid., p. 220.
11 'The Image Makers', interview with Angela Rippon, BBC2. Quoted in the *Live From No.10,* p. 222.
12 Thatcher, *The Path to Power',* p. 295.
13 Ibid., p. 295.
14 Penny Junor, *Margaret Thatcher – Wife, Mother, Politician* (London: Sidgwick and Jackson, 1983), p. 118.
15 Brendan Bruce, *Images of Power – How the Image-Makers Shape Our Leaders* (London: Kogan Page, 1992), p. 153. Also *Designer Politics,* p. 79.
16 Cockerell, *Live At No.10,* p. 233.
17 *Tatler,* March 1995.
18 *Observer,* 12 June 1983.
19 Fallon, *The Brothers,* p. 187.
20 *Observer,* 5 January 1986. *The Brothers,* p. 187.
21 Fallon, *The Brothers,* p. 188.
22 *The Manipulators,* BBC Radio 4, 5 February 1980.
23 Ibid.
24 Fallon, *The Brothers,* p. 109.

25 Ibid., p. 189.
26 Thatcher, *The Path to Power*, p. 411.
27 *The Pushers*, BBC2; Christopher Ogden, *Maggie – An Intimate Portrait of a Woman In Power* (New York: Simon and Schuster, 1990), pp. 144–5
28 Scammell, *Designer Politics*, p. 68.
29 *Esquire*, June 1983.
30 Rodney Tyler, *Campaign – The Selling of the Prime Minister* (London: Grafton Books, 1987), p. 7.
31 *Class Rule*, BBC1.
32 Dennis Kavanagh, *Election Campaigning – The New Marketing of Politics* (Oxford: Blackwell, 1995), p. 56.
33 Robert Worcester and Martin Harrop (eds), *Political Communications – The General Election of 1979* (London: Allen and Unwin, 1982), p. 12.
34 Ibid.
35 Ibid.
36 Fendley, *Commercial Break*, pp. 61–2.
37 Speech by Maurice Saatchi in 1994 to Mid-Norfolk Conservative Association, represented by Richard Ryder, Tory Chief Whip, 1990–95. Extracted in London *Evening Standard*, 12 October 1994.
38 Fallon, *The Brothers*, p. 195.
39 Nicholas Wapshott and George Brock, *Thatcher* (London: Macdonald, 1983), p. 171.
40 Fallon, *The Brothers*, p. 196.
41 Worcester and Harrop, *Political Communications*, p. 12.
42 Thatcher, *the Path to Power*, p. 413.
43 *Sunday Telegraph*, 15 September 1985.
44 *The Thatcher Factor*, Brook Productions for Channel 4, 20 February 1989.
45 Ronald Millar, *A View From the Wings – West End, West Coast, Westminster* (London: Weidenfeld and Nicolson, 1993), p. 247.
46 Ibid., p. 248.
47 Worcester and Harrop, *Political Communications*, p. 12.
48 *Class Rule*, BBC1.
49 Kavanagh, *Election Campaigning*, p. 57.
50 Peter Chippindale and Chris Horrie, *Stick It Up Your Punter* (London: Heinemann, 1990), p. 60.
51 *The Thatcher Factor*, Brook Productions for Channel 4.
52 Ibid.
53 Ibid.
54 *Class Rule*, BBC1.
55 *The Thatcher Factor*, Brook Productions for Channel 4.
56 *Class Rule*, BBC1.
57 Ogden, *Maggie*, p. 148.
58 Maurice Saatchi speech. See note 37.
59 Fallon, *The Brothers*, p. 201.
60 Millar, *A View From the Wings*, p. 271.
61 *Maggie's Minister*, interview with Kenneth Baker, BBC2, 11 September 1993.

62 Thatcher, *The Path to Power*, p. 411.
63 *The Pushers*, BBC1.
64 *Maggie's Minister*, BBC2.
65 Ibid.
66 Ogden, *Maggie*, p. 203.
67 *Harpers and Queen*, April 1989.
68 Ibid.
69 Ibid.
70 *The Star*, South African newspaper, 9 May 1994.
71 Bernard Ingham, *Kill the Messenger* (London: HarperCollins, 1991), p. 352.
72 *Advertising Age*, 27 November 1995.
73 Carol Thatcher, *Below the Parapet – The Biography of Denis Thatcher* (London: HarperCollins, 1996) p. 147.
74 Ibid., p. 148.
75 *Event*, 16 October 1981.
76 *Sunday Telegraph*, 7 May 1995.

CHAPTER FOUR

1 Fendley, *Commercial Break*, p. 63.
2 Fallon, *The Brothers*, p. 426.
3 Ogden, *Maggie*, p. 301.
4 Cecil Parkinson, *Right From the Centre* (London: Weidenfeld and Nicolson, 1991) p. 218.
5 Margaret Thatcher, *The Downing Street Years* (London: HarperCollins, 1993), p. 287.
6 Kavanagh, *Election Campaigning*, p. 165.
7 Thatcher, *The Downing Street Years*, p. 288.
8 Fallon, *The Brothers*, p. 217.
9 Mark Hollingsworth, *The Press and Political Dissent* (London: Pluto Press, 1986), p. 215.
10 Michael Cockerell, Peter Hennessy, David Walker, *Sources Close to the Prime Minister* (London: Macmillan, 1984), p. 214.
11 *The Times*, 25 March 1995.
12 Fendley, *Commercial Break*, p. 66.
13 Parkinson, *Right From the Centre*, p. 232.
14 *Campaign*, 20 March 1981.
15 Fallon, *The Brothers*, p. 197.
16 *Independent*, 24 October 1987.
17 *Sydney Morning Herald*, 20 July 1985.
18 *The Pushers*, BBC2.
19 Fallon, *The Brothers*, p. 211.

20 Ibid., p. 211.
21 Ibid., p. 219.

CHAPTER FIVE

1 Fallon, *The Brothers*, p. 220.
2 *Sunday Times*, 12 February 1984.
3 *Mail on Sunday*, 1 April 1984.
4 *Event*, 16 October 1981.
5 *Harpers and Queen*, April 1991, and *Guardian*, 30 November 1992.
6 Paul Halloran and Mark Hollingsworth, *Thatcher's Gold* (London: Simon and Schuster, 1995), p. 108.
7 *Sunday Times*, 26 January 1992.
8 *Observer*, 12 July 1987.
9 Hollingsworth, *The Press and Political Dissent*, p. 258.
10 Halloran and Hollingsworth, *Thatcher's Gold*, p. 109.
11 Ibid., p. 111.
12 *Daily Mirror*, 30 January 1986.
13 *Sunday Times*, 26 January 1992.
14 Nigel Lawson, *A View from No. 11* (London: Bantam Press, 1992), p. 142.
15 Ian MacGregor, *The Enemies Within* (London: Collins, 1986), p. 256.
16 Lord Young, *The Enterprise Years – Businessman In the Cabinet* (London: Macmillan, 1990), p. 99.
17 MacGregor, *The Enemies Within*, p. 303.
18 *Sydney Morning Herald*, 20 July 1985.
19 *The Thatcher Factor*, Brook Productions for Channel 4.
20 Hollingsworth, *The Press and Political Dissent*, p. 256.
21 Peter Wilsher, Don MacIntyre, Michael Jones, *Strike: Thatcher, Scargill and the Miners* (London: Andre Deutsch, 1985), p. 183.
22 *A Strike Out of Time*, Brook Productions, drama-documentary on the 1984–5 miners' strike, Channel 4, 25 February 1990. Also *The Thatcher Factor*, Brook Productions for Channel 4.
23 *A Strike Out of Time*, Brook Productions for Channel 4.
24 Ibid.
25 *The Thatcher Factor*, Brook Productions for Channel 4.
26 *The Times*, 11 October 1986.
27 MacGregor, *The Enemies Within*, p. 255.
28 Martin Adeney and John Lloyd, *Loss Without Limit – The 1984–85 Miners' Strike* (London: Routledge and Kegan Paul, 1986), p. 190–91.
29 Nicholas Jones, *Strikes and the Media* (Oxford: Basil Blackwell, 1986), p. 103.
30 MacGregor, *The Enemies Within*, p. 304.
31 Ibid., p. 305.
32 *A Strike Out of Time*, Brook Productions for Channel 4.
33 MacGregor, *The Enemies Within*, p. 301.

34 Adeney and Lloyd, *Loss Without Limit*, p. 197.
35 *The Thatcher Factor*, Brook Productions for Channel 4.
36 Adeney and Lloyd, *Loss Without Limit*, p. 197.
37 *The Thatcher Factor*, Brook Productions for Channel 4.
38 *Daily Mirror*, 15 January 1985.
39 *Guardian*, 7 November 1984.
40 MacGregor, *The Enemies Within*, p. 306.
41 *Guardian*, 6 October 1986.
42 Peter Walker, *Staying Power* (London: Bloomsbury, 1991), p. 178–9.
43 *A Strike Out of Time*, Brook Productions for Channel 4.
44 *Class Rule*, BBC1.
45 Fallon, *The Brothers*, p. 221.
46 Ibid., p. 222.
47 Fendley, *Commercial Break*, p. 69.
48 Fallon, *The Brothers*, p. 221.
49 *Sunday Telegraph*, 29 January 1985.
50 Fallon, *The Brothers*, p. 206.

CHAPTER SIX

1 *Sunday Telegraph*, 29 January 1985.
2 *Campaign*, 25 January 1985.
3 Ibid.
4 *Sunday Times*, 23 October 1988.
5 Speech to Marketing Society, 8 November 1995. Quoted in *Campaign*, 5 January 1996.
6 *Observer*, 27 August 1989.
7 Michael Regester, *Crisis Management* (London: Business Books, 1989), pp. 89–90.
8 James Saunders, *Nightmare – The Ernest Saunders Story* (London: Hutchinson, 1989), p. 141.
9 *Daily Express*, 8 January 1987.
10 Saunders, *Nightmare*, p. 158.
11 *Daily Mirror*, 28 September 1990.
12 *Observer*, 27 August 1989.
13 Peter Pugh, *Is Guinness Good For You?* (London: Financial Training Publications, 1987), p. 97.
14 *Sunday Times*, 13 July 1986.
15 Pugh, *Is Guinness Good For You?*, p. 115.
16 *Observer*, 27 August 1989.
17 Saunders, *Nightmare*, p. 276.
18 *PR Week*, 13 October 1995.
19 *PR Week*, 18 September 1986.
20 *The Pushers*, BBC2.

21 *Independent*, 1 April 1990.
22 *PR Week*, 13 October 1995.
23 *The Times*, 14 September 1994.
24 *Sunday Times*, 20 October 1991.
25 *Guardian*, 10 July 1993.
26 *Campaign*, 5 January 1996.
27 *Harpers and Queen*, April 1989.
28 *Independent*, 1 April 1990.
29 *Harpers and Queen*, April 1989.
30 Ibid.
31 Ibid.
32 *Illustrated London News*, June 1988.
33 *Harpers and Queen*, April 1989.
34 *The Pushers*, BBC1.
35 *Independent*, 1 April 1990.

CHAPTER SEVEN

1 *Advertising Age*, 27 November 1995.
2 Fendley, *Commercial Break*, p. 71.
3 Thatcher, *The Downing Street Years*, p. 570.
4 *Maggie's Minister*, BBC2, 11 September 1993.
5 Tyler, *Campaign*, pp. 16–17.
6 *Evening Standard*, 6 August 1986.
7 Norman Tebbit, *Upwardly Mobile* (London: Weidenfeld and Nicolson, 1988), p. 250.
8 Ivor Crewe and Martin Harrop (eds), *Political Communications – The General Election of 1987* (Cambridge: Cambridge University Press 1989), p. 64.
9 Fallon, *The Brothers*, p. 336.
10 Tyler, *Campaign*, p. 63–4.
11 Lawson, *A View from No. 11*, p. 698.
12 Tyler, *Campaign*, p. 89.
13 *Independent*, 24 October 1987.
14 *The Enterprise Years*, p. 143.
15 *The Times*, 12 June 1985.
16 Tyler, *Campaign*, p. 131.
17 Ibid., p. 131.
18 Ogden, *Maggie*, pp. 294–5.
19 Tyler, p. 133.
20 Tebbit, *Upwardly Mobile*, pp. 263–4.
21 Crewe and Harrop, *Political Communications*, p. 47.
22 Tyler, *Campaign*, p. 175.
23 Ibid., p. 171.
24 Ibid., p. 177.

25 Young, *The Enterprise Years*, p. 210.
26 Tyler, *Campaign*, p. 183.
27 Ibid., p. 193.
28 Ibid., pp. 197–8.
29 Thatcher, *Below the Parapet*, p. 244.
30 Tyler, *Campaign*, p. 216.
31 Thatcher, *The Downing Street Years*, p. 585.
32 Tyler, *Campaign*, p. 216.
33 Thatcher, *The Downing Street Years*, p. 585.
34 Fallon, *The Brothers*, p. 345.
35 Young, *The Enterprise Years*, p. 221.
36 Ibid.
37 Ibid.
38 Ibid. p. 222.
39 Ibid. p. 223.
40 Crewe and Harrop, *Political Communications*, p. 70.
41 *The Thatcher Factor*, Brook Productions for Channel 4.
42 Kavanagh, *Election Campaigning*, p. 65.
43 Cockerell, *Live from No. 10*, p. 327.
44 Lawson, *A View from No. 11*, p. 699–700.
45 Fendley, *Commercial Break*, p. 72.
46 Young, *The Enterprise Years*, p. 234.
47 *Daily Telegraph*, 17 June 1987.
48 Fallon, *The Brothers*, p. 355–6.
49 Ibid.
50 Ibid.
51 Ibid.
52 *Observer*, 12 July 1987.

CHAPTER EIGHT

1 *Tatler*, June 1994.
2 *House and Garden*, August 1994.
3 *Independent*, 24 May 1994.
4 *Harpers and Queen*, April 1989.
5 *The Pushers*, BBC2.
6 *Daily Express*, 10 April 1985.
7 *New Idea*, Australian magazine, 29 November 1989.
8 *Harpers and Queen*, April 1989.
9 *Sunday Express*, 27 November 1988.
10 *New Idea*, 29 November 1989.
11 *Daily Express*, 23 April 1991.

12 *Harpers and Queen*, April 1989.
13 *New Idea*, 29 November 1989.
14 *Independent*, 24 May 1994.
15 *Financial Times*, 7 September 1989.
16 *Observer*, 12 January 1992.
17 *Independent*, 8 January 1992.
18 *Campaign*, 8 September 1989.
19 *PR Week*, 28 May 1992.
20 Ibid.
21 *Campaign*, 24 November 1988.
22 House of Commons, Hansard, written question 92, 12 February 1990.
23 Ibid., WQ 91.
24 Ibid., WQ 618, 6 June 1990.
25 Ibid., WQ 31, 25 June 1990.
26 *Harpers and Queen*, April 1989.
27 *PR Week*, 28 May 1992.
28 Evidence to public inquiry into Designated Sales at Westminster City Council,
    4 November 1992, p. 35.
29 *Evening Standard*, 20 February 1989.
30 *Private Eye*, 1 June 1996.
31 *Maggie's Minister*, BBC2.
32 Ibid.
33 Kenneth Baker, *The Turbulent Years* (London: Faber and Faber, 1993),
    p. 274.
34 Thatcher, *Below the Parapet*, p. 253.
35 Lawson, *A View from No. 11*, p. 922.
36 *The Times*, 20 June 1989.
37 Bruce, *Images of Power*, p. 106.
38 *Campaign*, 30 June 1989.
39 *Evening Standard*, 19 June 1989.
40 Ibid.
41 *Independent*, 24 June 1989.
42 *Maggie's Minister*, BBC2.
43 Lawson, *A View from No. 11*, p. 953.
44 Baker, *The Turbulent Years*, p. 323.
45 Ibid. p. 325.
46 Thatcher, *The Downing Street Years*, p. 658.
47 *Maggie's Minister*, BBC2.
48 Baker, *The Turbulent Years*, p. 135.
49 Thatcher, *The Downing Street Years*, p. 659.
50 Bruce, *Images of Power*, p. 140.
51 Malcolm Balen, *Kenneth Clarke* (London: Fourth Estate, 1994), p. 181.
52 *Independent on Sunday*, 29 April 1990.
53 Balen, *Kenneth Clarke*, p. 181.
54 Ibid.
55 *Mail on Sunday*, 6 May 1990.
56 *Maggie's Minister*, BBC2.

57 Penny Junor, *The Major Enigma* (London: Michael Joseph, 1993), p. 192, and *Maggie's Minister*, op. cit.
58 Baker, *The Turbulent Years*, p. 373.
59 Thatcher, *The Downing Street Years*, p. 840.
60 *Maggie's Minister*, BBC2.
61 *Thatcher: the Final Days*, drama-documentary, made by Granada Television for ITV, 11 September 1991.
62 Ibid.
63 Thatcher, *Below the Parapet*, p. 262.
64 Thatcher, *The Downing Street Years*, p. 841.
65 Baker, *The Turbulent Years*, p. 392.
66 *Maggie's Minister*, BBC2.
67 Ibid.
68 Junor, *The Major Enigma*, p. 197.
69 Ibid.
70 *Maggie's Minister*, BBC2.
71 *Daily Mail*, 6 March 1991.
72 *Advertising Age*, 27 November 1995.

CHAPTER NINE

1 Halloran and Hollingsworth, *Thatcher's Gold*, p. 245.
2 *Guardian*, 2 October 1993.
3 Scammell, *Designer Politics*, p. 241.
4 Nicholas Jones, *Spin Doctors and Soundbites: How Politicians Manipulate the Media and Vice-Versa* (London: Cassell, 1995), p. 100.
5 Ibid., p. 101.
6 *Mail on Sunday*, 19 January 1992.
7 *Observer*, 5 April 1992.
8 Kavanagh, *Election Campaigning*, p. 167.
9 *Daily Telegraph*, 9 March 1992.
10 *Guardian*, 11 April 1992.
11 *Independent*, 24 May 1994.
12 *The Pushers*, BBC2.
13 Ibid.
14 *Independent*, 24 May 1994.
15 Ibid.
16 *The Mistresses*, BBC1, September Films, 14 March 1996.
17 *Harpers and Queen*, April 1989.
18 Alex Brummer and Roger Cowe, *Hanson: A Biography* (London: Fourth Estate, 1994), p. 153.
19 Ibid.
20 *Observer*, 13 October 1991.
21 *PR Week*, 17 October 1991.

22 *Sunday Times*, 20 October 1991.
23 *Guardian*, 2 November 1992.
24 Matthew Parris, *Great Parliamentary Scandals* (London: Robson Books, 1995), p. 286.
25 Jones, *Spin Doctors and Soundbites*, p. 62.
26 *Daily Mail*, 25 September 1992.
27 *Daily Telegraph*, 11 September 1992.
28 *Sunday Telegraph*, 27 September 1992.
29 Martyn Gregory, *Dirty Tricks − BA's Secret War Against Virgin Atlantic* (London: Little, Brown, 1994), p. 29.
30 *PR Week*, 28 January 1993.
31 *Sunday Times*, 28 February 1993.
32 *Esquire*, June 1993.
33 Gregory, *Dirty Tricks*, p. 366.
34 Gregory, *Dirty Tricks*, p. 369.
35 *Independent*, 24 May 1994.
36 Mihir Bose, *Screening the Image − A Biography of Michael Grade* (London: Virgin, 1992), p. 288.
37 *Guardian*, 2 November 1992.
38 Chris Horrie and Steve Clarke, *Fuzzy Monsters − Fear and Loathing at the BBC* (London: Heinemann, 1994), p. 269.
39 *Media Week*, 26 July 1985.
40 Horrie and Clarke, *Fuzzy Monsters*, p. 81.
41 Ibid., p. 82.
42 *Broadcast* magazine, 31 March 1988.
43 Horrie and Clarke, *Fuzzy Monsters*, p. 269.
44 Ibid., p. 270.
45 Ibid., p. 270–71.
46 *Today*, 18 March 1993.
47 *Observer*, 2 January 1995.
48 Ibid.
49 *The Times*, 11 March 1995.
50 *PR Week*, 8 March 1996.

CHAPTER TEN

1 *The Pushers*, BBC2.
2 *PR Week*, 8 October 1992.
3 *Sunday Times*, 27 February 1994.
4 *Tatler*, June 1994.
5 *Daily Telegraph*, 7 December 1989.
6 *Harpers and Queen*, April 1989.
7 *Sunday Times*, 23 January 1994.
8 *Tatler*, March 1995.

9 *Financial Times*, 25 April 1994.
10 *Australian Financial Review*, 21 January 1992.
11 Rod McGeoch, *The Bid: How Australia Won the 2000 Games* (Melbourne: William Heinemann, 1994), p.220.
12 Ibid., p.227.
13 Ibid., p.228.
14 Ibid., p.233.
15 *Guardian*, 20 April 1994.
16 *Sunday Times*, 17 April 1994.
17 *Sunday Times*, 24 April 1994.
18 *Independent*, 24 May 1994.
19 Ibid.
20 *Advertising Age*, 27 November 1995.
21 *Business* magazine, October 1989.
22 Fendley, *Commercial Break*, p.148.
23 *Sunday Times*, 14 April 1996.
24 *Sunday Times*, 18 December 1994.
25 Fendley, *Commercial Break*, p.170.
26 *Advertising Age*, 27 November 1995.
27 Fendley, *Commercial Break*, p.176.
28 *Daily Express*, 12 May 1993.
29 *Advertising Age*, 27 November 1995.
30 *PR Week*, 19 December 1995.
31 *Guardian*, 15 May 1996.
32 *Guardian*, 6 October 1986.
33 Lawson, *A View from No. 11*, p.699.
34 *The Manipulators*, BBC Radio 4, 8 February 1980.
35 Kavanagh, *Election Campaigning*, p.150.
36 Scammell, *Designer Politics*, p.283.
37 Ibid.
38 London *Evening Standard*, 1 May 1990.
39 *The Thatcher Factor*, Brook Productions for Channel 4.
40 Paxman, *Friends in High Places*, p.258.
41 *Harpers and Queen*, April 1989.
42 Speech to a national conference on Effective Voluntary and Community Action, 22/23 September 1994.

Bibliography

Adeney, Martin, and Lloyd, John, *Loss Without Limit – The 1984–85 Miners Strike* (London: Routledge and Kegan Paul, 1986)

Anderson, Bruce, *John Major: The Making of the Prime Minister* (London: Fourth Estate, 1991)

Baker, Kenneth, *The Turbulent Years* (London: Faber and Faber, 1993)

Balen, Malcolm, *Kenneth Clarke* (London: Fourth Estate, 1994)

Bevan, Judy, and Jay, John, *The New Tycoons* (London: Simon and Schuster 1989)

Black, Conrad, *A Life In Progress* (Toronto: Canada, Key Porter Books, 1993)

Bose, Mihir, *Screening The Image – A Biography of Michael Grade* (London: Virgin, 1992)

Bruce, Brendan, *Images of Power: How the Image-makers Shape Our Leaders* (London: Kogan Page, 1992)

Brummer, Alex, and Cowe, Roger, *Hanson: A Biography* (London: Fourth Estate, 1994)

Chippindale, Peter, and Horrie, Chris, *Stick It Up Your Punter* (London: Heinemann, 1990)

Cockerell, Michael, Hennessy, Peter, and Walker, David, *Sources Close to the Prime Minister* (London: Macmillan, 1984)

Cockerell, Michael, *Live from No. 10* (London: Faber and Faber, 1988)

Crewe, Ivor, and Harrap, Martin, *Political Communications – The General Election of 1983* (Cambridge: Cambridge University Press, 1986)

Crewe, Ivor, and Harrap, Martin, *Political Communications – The General Election of 1987* (Cambridge: Cambridge University Press, 1989)

Fallon, Ivan, *The Brothers – The Rise and Rise of Saatchi and Saatchi* (London: Hutchinson, 1988)

Fendley, Alison, *Commercial Break – The Inside Story of Saatchi and Saatchi* (London: Hamish Hamilton, 1995)

Fletcher, Winston, *Creative People – How To Manage Them and Maximise Their Creativity* (London: Hutchinson Business Books, 1989)

Franklin, Bob, *Packaging Politics – Political Communications in Britain's Media Democracy* (London: Edward Arnold, 1994)

Gregory, Martyn, *Dirty Tricks – BA's Secret War Against Virgin Atlantic* (London: Little, Brown, 1994)

Halloran, Paul, and Hollingsworth, Mark, *Thatcher's Gold: The Life and Times of Mark Thatcher* (London: Simon and Schuster, 1995)

Harris, Robert, *Good and Faithful Servant* (London: Faber and Faber, 1990)

Hollingsworth, Mark, *The Press and Political Dissent* (London: Pluto Press, 1986)

Horrie, Chris, and Clarke, Steve, *Fuzzy Monsters – Fear and Loathing at the BBC* (London: Heinemann, 1994)

Ingham, Bernard, *Kill The Messenger* (London: HarperCollins, 1991)

Jones, Nicholas, *Strikes and the Media* (Oxford: Basil Blackwell, 1986)

Jones, Nicholas, *Spin Doctors and Soundbites: How Politicians Manipulate the Media – and Vice-Versa* (London: Cassell, 1995)

Junor, Penny, *Margaret Thatcher – Wife, Mother, Politician* (London: Sidgwick and Jackson, 1983)

Junor, Penny, *The Major Enigma* (London: Michael Joseph, 1993)

Kavanagh, Dennis, *Election Campaigning – The New Marketing of Politics* (Oxford: Blackwell, 1995)

Kleinman, Philip, *The Saatchi and Saatchi Story* (London: Weidenfeld and Nicolson, 1987)

Lawson, Nigel, *A View from No. 11* (London: Bantam Press, 1992)

Maggregor, Ian (with Rodney Tyler), *The Enemies Within* (London: Collins, 1986)

McGeoch, Rod, *The Bid: How Australia Won the 2000 Games* (Melbourne: William Heinemann, 1994)

Millar, Ronald, *A View from the Wings – West End, West Coast, Westminster* (London: Weidenfeld and Nicolson, 1993)

Ogden, Christopher, *Maggie – An Intimate Portrait of a Woman in Power* (New York: Simon and Schuster, 1990)

Parkinson, Cecil, *Right at the Centre* (London: Weidenfeld and Nicolson, 1991)

Parris, Matthew, *Great Parliamentary Scandals – Four Centuries of Calumny, Smear and Innuendo* (London: Robson Books, 1995)

Paxman, Jeremy, *Friends In High Places – Who Runs Britain?* (London: Michael Joseph, 1990)

Pugh, Peter, *Is Guinness Good For You – The Inside Story of the Bid for Distillers* (London: Financial Training Publications, 1987)

Ranelagh, John, *Thatcher's People – An Insider's Account of the Politics, the Power and the Personalities* (London: HarperCollins, 1991)

Regester, Michael, *Crisis Management: How To Turn a Crisis Into an Opportunity* (London: Business Books, 1989)

Saunders, James, *Nightmare – The Ernest Saunders Story* (London: Hutchinson, 1989)

Scammell, Margaret, *Designer Politics – How Elections Are Won* (London: Macmillan, 1995)

Tebbit, Norman, *Upwardly Mobile* (London: Weidenfeld and Nicolson, 1988)

Thatcher, Carol, *Diary of an Election* (London: Sidgwick and Jackson, 1983)

Thatcher, Carol, *Below The Parapet – The Biography of Denis Thatcher* (London: HarperCollins, 1996)

Thatcher, Margaret, *The Downing Street Years* (London: HarperCollins, 1993)

Thatcher, Margaret, *The Path to Power* (London: HarperCollins, 1995)

Tyler, Rodney, *Campaign – The Selling of the Prime Minister* (London: Grafton Books, 1987)

Walker, Peter, *Staying Power* (London: Bloomsbury, 1991)

Wapshott, Nicholas, and Brock, George, *Thatcher* (London: Macdonald, 1983)

Wilsher, Peter, Macintyre, Don, and Jones, Michael, *Strike: Thatcher, Scargill and the Miners* (London: André Deutsch, 1985)

Worcester, Robert, and Harrap, Martin, (eds), *Political Communications – The General Election of 1979* (London: Allen and Unwin, 1982)

Young, Hugo, *One of Us* (London: Macmillan, 1990)

Young, Lord, *The Enterprise Years – A Businessman In the Cabinet* (London: Headline, 1990)

Index

The following abbreviations have been used: PR = public relations; TB = Tim Bell